Alice Walker's Metaphysics

Alice Walker's Metaphysics

Literature of Spirit

Nagueyalti Warren

ROWMAN & LITTLEFIELD
Lanham • Boulder • New York • London

Published by Rowman & Littlefield
An imprint of The Rowman & Littlefield Publishing Group, Inc.
4501 Forbes Boulevard, Suite 200, Lanham, Maryland 20706
www.rowman.com

Unit A, Whitacre Mews, 26-34 Stannary Street, London SE11 4AB

Copyright © 2019 by The Rowman & Littlefield Publishing Group, Inc.

All rights reserved. No part of this book may be reproduced in any form or by any electronic or mechanical means, including information storage and retrieval systems, without written permission from the publisher, except by a reviewer who may quote passages in a review.

British Library Cataloguing in Publication Information Available

Library of Congress Cataloging-in-Publication Data

Names: Warren, Nagueyalti.
Title: Alice Walker's metaphysics : literature of spirit / Nagueyalti Warren.
Description: Lanham : Rowman & Littlefield, [2019] | Includes bibliographical references and index.
Identifiers: LCCN 2018039278 (print) | LCCN 2018039292 (ebook) | ISBN 9781538123980 (Electronic) | ISBN 9781538123973 (cloth) | ISBN 9781538158470 (pbk) Subjects: LCSH: Walker, Alice, 1944—Criticism and interpretation. | Metaphysics in literature. | Spirituality in literature.
Classification: LCC PS3573.A425 (ebook) | LCC PS3573.A425 Z895 2019 (print) | DDC 813/.54—dc23
LC record available at https://lccn.loc.gov/2018039278

To Rueben C. Warren
and for our progeny,
Alkamessa, Asha, and Ali

Contents

Acknowledgments ix

Introduction xi

1 Dark Beginnings 1
2 Spirit in the Dark: The Metaphysics of Poverty 21
3 What We Love, We Save 41
4 Amazing Grace 63
5 Dear God 81
6 Entering the Temple 101
7 Sexual Healing 121
8 Opening to Spirit 145
9 When the Other Dancer Is the Self 161
10 Mystic Walker 175

Selected References 191

Index 195

About the Author 205

Acknowledgments

I am deeply appreciative of the help received in the completion of this book. I sincerely thank my friend and colleague Sally Wolff-King for her sharp eye and helpful suggestions. The Stuart A. Rose Manuscript, Archives, and Rare Book Library's archivist, Gabrielle Dudley, was tremendously supportive. I am thankful for the efforts of my late friend and colleague, Rudolph P. Byrd, along with the wizardry of curator Randall K. Burkett, for successfully bringing the complete Alice Walker archive to Emory University Libraries in 2009.

In my circle of sustainers, special thanks to Rev. Mary Louise Ruffner for spiritual wisdom, and to Delores P. Aldridge and Vera Rorie for our breakout days for having fun. For your friendship and support, I will always be grateful.

Introduction

In 1982, Alice Walker published *The Color Purple*. Within weeks, the novel made the *New York Times'* best-seller list and catapulted her to fame. The book was Walker's third novel. My first encounter with her work occurred that same year, when I lived in Jackson, Mississippi. In a bookshop off I-55, I purchased a copy of *The Color Purple* to take along on a trip to the beach. The store clerk asked if I knew Alice Walker, and informed me that Walker had once lived in Jackson; I had not known that fact. I had intended to read the book on the ride down to the Gulf Coast, but out of curiosity, I decided to read a few pages the night before. I finished the book that night and read it again at the beach. Thus, began my long journey in reading Alice Walker.

By the time the movie, *The Color Purple*, was released, I had read all of Walker's books; we had moved away from Mississippi, and in the firestorm of criticism that followed the release of Spielberg's movie, I began offering a seminar on Walker's novels. My course at Fisk University was the first to examine the works of a single female author, and my 1992 course, titled "Reading Alice Walker," was the first at Emory University to concentrate on a single black woman author. This book is the culmination of thirty years of reading, studying, and teaching Alice Walker's work.

I believe that Walker's oeuvre, from its beginning, presents a metaphysical interpretation of life. The blindness in her right eye that resulted from a childhood injury surely helped to produce the insight that emerges in her works. From the time she was eight years old and disfigured by what she calls a patriarchal wound inflicted by her older brother Curtis, by her own admission she has felt like an outsider. Once outgoing and vivacious, Walker became shy and withdrawn; yet her solitude provided the space for developing what became her piercing perceptiveness about herself and others. Readers often dismiss Walker's nonlinear approach to history, and the luminal dimensions of reality that her writings expose, and focus instead on the clearly political content. Nonetheless, even her politics and activism reveal a metaphysical and deeply spiritual essence.

Walker's poetry is the chthonic root of her emergence as a writer. Many of her poems are reflective of her experiences, and some provide the cast for her fictional characters. Her collective works of fiction, nonfiction, poetry, and children's books shift the paradigm from a dualistic perception of life as good and evil to a forward-looking and optimistic view for those readers brave enough to remain open to the infinite possibilities that she presents. The message from her work is that we live in a spiritual universe. Everything is Spirit. We are all connected. Walker's works push the boundaries to insist that *we* includes humans, plants, animals, the earth, water, the air. Her concept of God, a word with Christian connotations, is more often referred to as Great Spirit, situating it closer to Native American and other traditional beliefs.

In Walker's works, Spirit is love, pure and unadulterated. This loving Spirit is alive, omnipresent, and awaits our recognition. No judgmental God in heaven waits for us to die, kills us, or condemns us to an everlasting hell. Walker does not embrace Christology, such as the womanist theologians discuss. Jesus is both human and Divine, as is everything. Life is everlasting. It changes form; therefore, people and all things appear to die only to transition into another form, in what some may see as reincarnation, although Walker herself does not use the term. Walker's character Lissie Lyles is the fictional representation of eternal life. She does not privilege the Bible as holy, but respects books in general.

Walker dramatizes life through a comic rather than a tragic lens. Defining tragedy and comedy, ecocritic Stephen O'Leary states: "Tragedy conceives of evil in terms of guilt; its mechanism of redemption is victimage, its plot moves inexorably toward sacrifice and the 'cult of the kill.' Comedy conceives of evil not as guilt, but as error; its mechanism of redemption is recognition rather than victimage, and its plot moves not toward sacrifice but to exposure of fallibility."[1] Walker exposes evil as erroneous thoughts and actions. Human agency as choice dominates her works. The agency that some people want to ascribe to God or to the devil belongs entirely to human beings. Within the comic paradigm, a moral ambiguity exists, whereas in tragedy a schism emerges between good and evil with no room for ambiguity. No open-ended possibilities are available.

Classified as a feminist, womanist, bohemian, white liberal's lackey, and practically called, according to her, "everything but a child of God,"[2] Walker, as novelist, essayist, poet, and storyteller, is above all a spiritual seeker. The search for truth and wholeness dominates her texts. A primary example is in *Living by the Word*, where Walker declares the unity of all, stating, "We are the African and the trader. We are the Indian and the settler. We are the slaver and the enslaved. We are the oppressor and the oppressed. We are the women and we are the men."[3] Alice Walker is a present-day mystic. If, as Margaret Furse[4] claims, the mystic experiences Spirit as immediate and present in all things, then mysticism is a worldview that aligns with Walker's writings.

Gerda Lerner has written that what the mystic knows appears in a variety of ways. She states: "Some mystics' visions amount to a coherent theological system, others are fragmentary and unsystematic. Some build upon biblical and traditional ritual imagery; others are astonishingly original in concept and symbolism. Mystics used whatever materials their own lives could provide."[5] Alice Walker writes from her lived experiences.

Following in the tradition established by Sojourner Truth, Walker illuminates issues of both race and gender and draws heavily from her lived experience as a black girl growing up in the segregated South. Like nineteenth-century black women mystics Jarena Lee, Amanda Berry, and Rebecca Jackson, Walker has stunned organized religion with her independence. Her eclectic theology and claim to be pagan embrace Spirit wherever she finds it.

NOTES

1. Stephen O'Leary, *Arguing the Apocalypse: A Theory of Millennial Rhetoric* (Oxford: Oxford University Press, 1984), 68.
2. For further discussion, see Greg Garrard, *Ecocriticism* (London: Routledge, 2004).
3. Alice Walker, "In the Closet of the Soul," *Living by the Word* (New York: Harcourt Brace, 1988), 89.
4. Margaret Furse, *Mysticism: Windows on a Worldview* (Nashville: Abingdon Press, 1977).
5. Gerda Lerner, *Feminist Consciousness: From the Middle Ages to Eighteen Seventy* (New York: Oxford University Press, 1993), 106.

Chapter One

Dark Beginnings

Born in Eatonton, Georgia, in 1944, Alice Walker entered a world at war, a region in which apartheid was the law of the land, and a family with seven siblings that lived on a Georgia plantation as sharecroppers. As an African American infant, her chances of survival were small. The infant mortality rate for "Negroes" was more than twice that of whites in Georgia, and the influenza epidemic of 1943–1944 further increased the death rate. African Americans were forced to drink from separate water fountains, enter through back doors, and attend segregated schools, even one that was formerly a prison.[1] Walker, who wanted to become a painter but whose family could not afford paints, grew up to become a poet, a novelist, and the first African American woman to win a Pulitzer Prize for fiction. Always fighting against injustice, she was active in the civil rights movement in her home state and in the state of Mississippi. Today Walker continues her activism through her essays, blogs, and speeches, as she travels around the globe and still participates in mass demonstrations.

As a young child growing up in rural Georgia, Walker often played with her older brothers. One day while she was playing cowboys and Indians with the boys, her brother Curtis shot her in the eye with a pellet gun. Walker did not believe that the shooting was an accident. She called her injury a patriarchal wound, because she was a girl and did not have a gun. The injury to her right eye resulted in blindness. More devastating to Walker, however, was the fact that her brothers coerced her into lying about what happened. Poverty prevented the family from taking her to see a physician right away, and when they finally had the means to go, the doctor examined the eye and told the parents in front of the child that eyes were sympathetic, and she would most likely lose the sight in her other eye as well. Frightened of becoming completely blind, angered by her brother's lie and her complicity in it, and called names at school ("one-eyed bitch"), Walker metamorphosed from a vivacious young scholar to a dispirited and low-achieving student. Fortunately, by the time she turned fourteen, her older brother Bill, who had moved to Boston, arranged for her to have eye surgery to remove the unsightly scar tissue.

At the age of fifteen, Walker created a scrapbook that clearly demonstrates her intention to become a writer. Her book opens with the following declaration:

> I, ALICE MALSENIOR WALKER, ON THIS DAY, MY 15th BIRTHDAY, FEBRUARY 9, 1959, DO DEDICATE THIS COLLECTION OF MY WORKS TO MY [sic] SELF, AND TO THOSE WHOM [the M is scratched out with a pencil] HAVE INSPIRED ME MOST: MOTHER, FATHER, RUTH, UNCLE FRANK, MR. ROBINSON. MR. HORTON, MR RICE, AND MR NELSON. THIS BOOK CONTAINS THE: "POEMS OF A CHILDHOOD POETRESS" [the r is crossed out with a pencil].[2]

The writing contained in the scrapbook demonstrates her early inclination toward mysticism. She writes: "Reality is created by wishes."[3] As an adult, she might have used a word stronger than wishes, but at fifteen, she was already on the path to understanding that intentions and desires can create reality. Her attitude toward activism also develops early. She says that she will die for a cause but not for "nothing."[4] Following her eye surgeries, Walker emerged from the depression and, while her vision was not restored, her self-confidence was.

Little consensus exists about how mystics develop; however, some aspects of their lived experiences are similar. One commonality among many mystics is an early trauma that often seems to lead to a lonely pathway.[5] Walker seems to have experienced three traumatic episodes; the first was the traumatic injury to her eye when she was eight years old. She gained introspection by her withdrawal from family and friends, wrote often of death and dying, and signed her name with the closing "Yours in death," but amended by writing "—not literally."[6] The other traumatic episodes were an unwanted pregnancy and abortion, and the long illness that she claimed was Lyme disease but was never diagnosed. These life-altering events represented gateways to self-knowledge.

Ernest Holmes, founder of the Science of Mind philosophy, defines another characteristic of mystics. He says, "A mystic is one who intuitively perceived Truth and who without conscious mental process arrives at Spiritual Realization."[7] Paul Davies, a cosmologist, suggests that mysticism could be a way of direct knowing, a comprehension of the unity that physics acknowledges but cannot completely describe. Walker seems intuitively to have perceived the truth about organized religion. At fifteen, she addressed her African Methodist Episcopal (AME) church with a speech titled "The

Part Education Plays in the AME Church." She told the parishioners that times had changed, that even the smallest child "takes nothing without an explanation."[8] She said it was time for people to think for themselves, and that the word of the preacher should not depend solely on the fact that he was the minister. Walker made a strong case for education—not for credentials, but for the ability of people to be informed and to think critically. Walker's views became unorthodox when she was a teen. The early works examined in this chapter represent the beginnings of Walker's mystical orientation.

In *Once*, her first published collection of poetry, Walker as a young college student took mental snapshots and recorded them as poems about East Africa, where she had studied and worked among the Kikuyu. Twenty-five years later, in the preface to *Her Blue Body: Everything We Know*, which includes *Once*, she writes of oneness with herself and the world.[9]

This unity is apparent in the stark simplicity of the poems, as well as in the civil rights poems in the second part of *Once*. The title poem introduces the topic of her return to America and the violence that bombarded the nonviolent movement in which she participated. The poems chronicle not just the injustice toward African Americans demanding their rights; Walker turns a critical eye on the abuse white supporters endured for daring to be human and supporting justice and equal rights.

Walker's depiction of the civil rights movement in her poems is balanced and unified. Sadness is evident in the poem that begins, "One day in Georgia," that describes a white mother who accuses her daughter of wanting to have sex with the "niggers" in the movement. Some poems are humorous, like the one about the charming half-wit who wanted to walk naked after his bath to show off his pretty black skin. During a time of black rage, however, there are no angry poems, only poems that show the utter absurdity of racism and hatred, poems that startle in their portrayal of human cruelty. In the middle of the Black Power movement and its cultural arm, the Black Arts movement, Walker stands apart and, with a clear-eyed detachment, chronicles the actions and emotions of the times without screaming her rage toward whites or valorizing blackness. She affirms Spirit in all. The final section of *Once* clearly demonstrates her awakening theology. In the poem "South: The Name of Home," she prays for eyes to see beyond the violent racist person, and she asks God for trees for people to nurture and love.

While her peers were plotting revolution (the violent kind), Walker chose a spiritual path. As a young person, she did not just recognize God in herself, and love her, she recognized Divinity in everything, the red earth, the bent trees that wept, the ravished land, and she deplored how people abuse the earth. Walker's attention to nature in the early poems is significant because it grows into her theology. In the early poems of *Once*, Walker began to question openly the religion of her childhood. In "Hymn," she recalls a time when "Amazing Grace" was a popular black hymn, but in this poem, she also takes to task the uneducated pontificating preachers[10] who refused to take a stand against oppression and preached submissiveness to black women. Walker challenges the Beatitudes' injunction that the meek will inherit the earth. She calls into question those pews where abused, weary women weep, and remembers the gospel rhythm produced by the music. Indeed, a part of the Southern, black, poverty-plagued tradition of religion, Walker is careful not to lose what she deems most valuable in this black Christian tradition: the music. The poem ends with bearing witness to Mahalia Jackson, Clara Ward, and the sacred singers, but also includes Fats Waller and Ray Charles. Early on Walker conflated the sacred and the secular. She continued to do so in the corpus of her works. Undoubtedly many thinkers influenced Walker. She quotes French philosopher Albert Camus' statement about poverty at the beginning of *Once*: "Poverty was not a calamity for me. It was always balanced by richness of light." Existential questions began for Walker within the context of the black church, Ward's Chapel AME, and continued to grow as her education and reading became more expansive.

The second traumatic event that occurred in Walker's life was a pregnancy. When she returned to the United States from a 1965 study abroad trip to East Africa and Eastern Europe, to complete her senior year at Sarah Lawrence College, she discovered that she was pregnant. The pregnancy was unplanned and unwanted. Her limited choices[11] as to what to do about it caused her to become suicidal. "Ballad of the Brown Girl" is most reflective of her anguish and poses the poignant question: How to face her black father with a mixed-race baby?[12] Followed by the poem titled "Suicide," these poems foreshadow the dilemma in which she would place herself in 1967 when married to a white man, Mel Leventhal; she became the brown daughter to take her white baby to her black father. This time, however, hers was a conscious choice, not an accident. She was married to Mr. Civil Rights, an enthusiastic civil rights attorney. For friends and family, both hers and his, the fact that he fought for civil rights made little difference. It mattered only that he was white. In the now famous 1973 interview with John O'Brien, Walker says that "Ballad of the Brown Girl" fails to work in the way that she most wanted. In her self-critique, she says the poem does not produce a new way of seeing.[13] Whether this critique is accurate depends entirely on the audience/reader.

Walker's friends arranged for her to have an illegal abortion. Locked in her dorm room, she wrote the poems that would appear in *Once*, and although her condition caused panic, her poems show total control—snapshots with rhythm like raindrops on a hot tin roof. Syllabic three, four, three, three, four beats, the poems mark the spiritual path Walker chooses to walk. "African Images: Glimpses from a Tiger's Back," the first section of poems, moves from the physical fact of no tigers in Africa, to the metaphysical tiger—symbol of mindfulness and singleness of purpose, solitary and silent, sensual and deeply psychic. The image of the giant cat in native lore (African and Native American) represents the unity of the physical and spiritual worlds. Walker, like the mystical poet William Blake, calls forth the symmetry of the sun, most apparent in the Bengal tiger's orange color. The sun somehow deliberately or inadvertently became the "son" in Christianity that led to an issue addressed in many of Walker's works, for the sun of God has a far different meaning than the Son of God. Walker was only twenty-one years old when she recognized the sun inside herself.

Poems in the final section of *Once* are personal, confessional and apolitical, if such a thing is possible. When the book appeared in 1968, the so-called revolutionaries considered it mundane. The final poems speak of love, sensual and heartbreaking; a subject unpopular in the revolutionary sixties. Walker recognized that subjects dealing with romantic love and black family life are deemed unimportant, even by black critics.[14] One poem in the final section, "Suicide," addresses the stereotypes surrounding suicide, particularly during the revolutionary sixties. Suicide was considered counterrevolutionary for black people.[15] There also was the belief that black people did not take their own lives. Walker's choice to write about love or of her father sleeping in church and of her grandmother as the medicine that heals her sick grandfather defies the strictures of pseudo–black correctness. Her choice to have an abortion and speak about it, and to then marry a white man, further cast her as an outsider, a role that she accepts gladly, evidenced by her poem "Be Nobody's Darling."[16] In this poem she embraces her outcast status.

The poems in *Once* also reveal Walker's experiences in Africa, in distress when she returned to campus, and in the civil rights movement. In the poem "South the Name of Home," Walker introduces the friend and civil rights worker mentioned earlier, whose mother writes to say she must be having sex with all the black men.[17] The friend closely resembles Lynn in Walker's novel *Meridian*. Walker distills the memories and images of the movement in her poetry. In addition to her trip to East Africa and her unwanted pregnancy and abortion, *Once* centers on once-upon-a-time in the American South, a story that exposes the insanity of race prejudice. The final poem in the section on home is dedicated to the martyrs. "They Who Feel Death" recognizes the threat of death to all who dared resist the customs and laws of Jim Crow. The poem ends with the word "Crucified," and suggests Christian symbolism while simultaneously referring to black people daily nailed to crosses of hatred, suffering humiliations, crucified in cotton fields and/or actually left hanging from trees. The poem speaks of these circumstances in all of eleven lines.

Walker exhibits concern for the environment in these early poems. She writes of bent and weeping trees, the red earth, and how people abuse and rape the lands.[18] The environment holds a significant place in Walker's writing from the very beginning, evident in her passion for trees. Simon James, writing in *The Presence of Nature,* uses Walker as an example of one who cares deeply for nature by citing her grief over the death of an old tree. He attempts to decipher how morals, aesthetics, and spirituality contribute to values, and admits that while some readers might be prone to dismiss Walker's claims as melodramatic or disingenuous, he insists that her statement of grief gives voice "to a familiar kind of moral response to the natural world."[19] As a pagan, Walker sees the natural world as sacred.

TO HELL WITH DYING

Metaphysical Bible Dictionary defines hell as a state of mind; in Greek, hell was thought to be a region of lamentations, a place of purifying fires, a place of defilement. The Hebrew language defines it as a hollow, empty place; a place of unquenchable consuming desires.[20] In *To Hell with Dying,* Walker's short story—sometimes categorized as a children's book—the narrator informs the reader about the hell that Mr. Sweet is suffering: disillusionment with his unfulfilled dreams of becoming a doctor or lawyer, the frustration of losing the woman that he loved, and pressure to marry someone else. His hell is the purifying fire of alcohol and the unquenchable consuming desires for his true love and for a different life. When this hell brings him to the brink of destruction, the unconditional love of his neighbor's children saves him. The voice of the narrator's father saying: "to hell with dying, these children want Mr. Sweet,"[21] reminds him that he is not forsaken, and he is not judged. The father commands Mr. Sweet to send his frustration, desires, and depression to hell, a fitting place for those negative emotions, and return to the love that will sustain him.

Walker introduces here a theme that she will develop with Grange in *The Third Life,* and even more fully with Mister in *The Color Purple*. Grange's family forced him to marry Margaret instead of Josie because of Josie's reputation as a prostitute. The same is true for Mister, who wanted to marry Shug Avery. Not only does Walker show how love can save, she demonstrates through these male characters what happens when love is frustrated. Critics have written about Walker's didacticism. They assume that she is writing in the Anglo-American tradition instead of the African American. Indeed, much of her work is didactic, as are most sermons and spiritual texts. *To Hell with Dying* is multilayered. For Christians, this work represents the promise of overcoming death through resurrection. Mr. Sweet rises from the metaphorical grave many times. The spiritual significance is the importance of love without judgment. The yellow roses that the neighboring family planted long before Mr. Sweet finally dies at the age of ninety represent, in Eastern traditions, the color of the sun and suggest joy, wisdom, and power as well as friendship. On another level, the biblical meaning of the rose represents true love and, in Catholicism, the rose is a symbol for the Virgin Mary and for Christ as well. Rose also is a verb meaning "to rise," and doubles back on resurrection. The feast of *rosalia* in ancient Rome was the feast of the dead. The multiple layers of meaning in this work earn it a place in classic juvenile literature.

In addition to being frustrated with his life, Mr. Sweet is an artist, another character type that continues to emerge in Walker's work. The guitar-playing Mr. Sweet finds full expression as Truman in the novel *Meridian*, Hal and Arveyda as well as Ola in *The Temple of My Familiar*, and the artist Yolo in *Now Is the Time to Open Your Heart*. Whether through music, painting, singing, or writing, art looms large in Walker's work for the simple reason that creative expression is as necessary as breath. Nevertheless, art is not enough to change the lives of black people in the United States. Walker makes this point in the essay, "Recording the Seasons," in which she voices her fear that her art will not be the change agent she strives for and wonders if it will produce any difference in the lives of black people, or any people.[22] The rhetoric of the Black Arts movement proclaimed that revolutionary art must be functional, collective, and committed; that it must be useful. An example might be using a poem to incite a revolution, collectively coming from the people and giving back to the people; and being committed to black people.[23] This straitjacket political approach clearly curtailed the artists' quest for truth. For if the truth was a sharp critique of the people, it would be condemned, although not so much by the people themselves but by the self-appointed Black Arts critics. Walker's own experience as an artist deepens her awareness about the risks that being an artist imposes on a person who, like Mr. Sweet, must experience his own suffering to bring forth words and music.[24] Detailing her last year in Mississippi and the burden of remaining nonviolent in the face of violence, Walker proposes a way of seeing beyond material reality.[25] Her creative work seeks to unveil that which is unseen.

Walker's 1983 collection of essays, *In Search of Our Mothers' Gardens: Womanist Prose* clarifies her spiritual rendering of life. The garden is metaphor for the soul. Walker invites the reader to find our mothers' gardens so that we can find our own souls buried deep in mother earth, sprouting new roots along fallow fields, cotton bare or sometimes flowering unexpectedly. When we search, we find our mothers' hands, dark and quick, working with sun and rain, creating a photosynthesis of love and a symbiotic bridge between yesterday and tomorrow.

A quotation from the Gnostic Gospels introduces part 2 of the essays. Jesus warns that failure to bring forth what is within oneself is destructive. This idea connects with another prominent motif in Walker's works: choice. The choice to remain in the South, Walker acknowledges, risks losing the love for it, and what she loves about the South is the natural landscape and environment, woods, and sky. The choice to live free is a central theme in the essay "Choosing to Stay Home." At the 1963 March on Washington, Dr. King encouraged people to claim the land of their birth, to go back to Mississippi, Alabama, and Georgia. Walker does choose to return to the South, and in this early essay she writes of the hurtful memories of past injustices that taint the progress that the South has made. Memory is a challenge to forgiveness.[26] This essay introduces a basic premise for understanding Walker the writer, and her works. The dichotomy of forgiveness and un-forgiveness is apparent throughout her works. "Choosing to Stay Home" is written in a style as eloquent as any Sunday morning sermon, and summarizes the progress that has taken place in the South. Her words echo the cadence in Dr. King's "I Have a Dream" speech. She says although the mountain of despair is not what it used to be, black people have become complacent and enamored of capitalist materialism, acquiring material wealth instead of focusing on ever-elusive freedom and keeping the eye on the prize.[27]

Walker concludes the essay with two words, like a preacher returning to the text after having meandered through the metaphors of life. Those words about whether she will leave Mississippi are her choice.[28] Discussing freedom, forgiveness, love, and choice, this essay also reveals the challenge to peace and nonviolence. Walker says insulting people's dignity invites retaliatory violence, which is dangerous to everyone.

Claiming that spirituality is the basis of art, and Spirit is the source of creativity, Walker believes all are endowed with the breath of Spirit and, by their very nature, are creative. In her signature essay, "In Search of Our Mother's Gardens," Walker focuses on the cruel and deliberate efforts to stifle the creative impulse in black women through overwork, violence, and sexual abuse. Her rhetorical devices in this essay rival the sermons in James Weldon Johnson's 1927 book, *God's Trombones*. For instance, she describes the mothers and grandmothers moving to music unheard by others, inspired by an unnamed muse,[29] and her description would produce an "Amen" or "Can I get a Witness!" Or listen to the cadence in the line that calls the women saints insane and wild or subdued and suicidal. Their god like a rock is mute.[30] From focusing on the barriers to creativity, Walker turns to the question of how individuals kept such creativity alive. She discovers that ritual and memory function as twin guardians of the creative process. Stories from the oral tradition, bequeathed from memory, kept alive a narrative tradition.

Writing about Walker's essays, Maria Lauret comments on how they feed her fiction and how her fiction and nonfiction contain a unity. For Lauret, Walker's "essayistic autobiographical voice"[31] is problematic because it leaves the critic with little to discover. She complains that Walker's authorial voice is increasingly loud and intrusive. Lauret states that "as a commentator on her own work in *In Search of Our Mothers' Gardens* and *Living by the Word*, and . . . in *Anything We Love Can Be Saved* and *The Same River*

Twice . . .[Walker] seeks to be, in an important sense, her own first critic."[32] Walker's texts may be sermons as much as essays, because sermons are inherently didactic and effective in the black homiletic tradition. Literary texts indeed have a life of their own, as both Roland Barthes[33] and Lauret assert. Information about this very-much-alive author, however, need not delimit as they suggest, but rather enrich the interpretation. The black homiletic tradition recognizes that language is performative and anchored in narrative.[34] Walker's essays offer a way of entering her work and being transformed by the experience. In narrating her story, she invites the reader to make similar connections and comparisons.

An example of the didactic- and sermonic-styled essay that irritates Lauret is "My Father's Country Is the Poor," in which Walker presents the narrative of Black Panther Huey Newton in exile, and a homosexual Cuban writer rejected by the Revolution, who commits suicide in Rome. The narrative launches a discussion about homophobia. Readers can either side with the essayist and condemn the prejudice, or identify with the well-articulated argument advanced by the revolutionary Cubans against condoning homosexuality because it weakens the traditional family. Or, the reader might identify with the homosexual, so hurt and depressed by the rejection of the revolutionaries, that he no longer desires to live. The essay exposes the flaws in revolution and makes clear that revolution takes years, maybe even generations, to change injustice. In this essay Walker recognizes her own prejudice regarding skin color; the reader, too, if born and reared in the United States, will recognize Walker's dilemma when she faced the multicolored Cubans who identified themselves as Cuban and appeared not to know what racism was all about.

Walker begins the essay with a long quotation from Angela Davis's autobiography that anchors what follows. The third part of the narrative relates her dead father's presence in her dreams. Like a preacher who enacts a metaphorical switch, Walker's father, who died in 1973, metamorphosed into Pablo Diaz, a poor man like her dad, and who physically resembled him as well. But Diaz was able to join a revolution. In this one sermon we have heard from Angela Davis, Huey Newton, Castro, and a Cuban peasant turned historian, and have learned of Walker's father enmeshed in capitalist poverty that eventually alienated him from his upwardly mobile daughter. The essay also makes clear Walker's intention in writing the letter to former president Bill Clinton that appears in the book; this is one of the texts that Lauret questions. Walker ends the letter by asking Clinton to think of her when considering the Cuban boycott. Lauret asks why thinking of her would or should make a difference. Walker suggest that if President Clinton thinks of her, he will remember that Cuba consists of individual people like her and like Hillary and Chelsea.

Walker's second collection of nonfiction, *Living by the Word* (1988), mirrors Jesus' declaration: "Man shall not live by bread alone, but by every word."[35] Although Walker is not a Bible-quoting Christian, neither was Jesus. Walker recognizes Jesus as a political radical and activist. Some might argue that Walker did not have in mind the biblical passage when she named the book, but rather was referring to the two-headed woman in her dream of April 17, 1984. In the dream, the two-headed woman says to Walker: "Live by the Word and keep walking."[36] Whether or not the connection is intentional is of little consequence. The point is that Walker's work engages the spiritual and metaphysical. The narrative about Blue, the horse in Walker's neighborhood, is one example of her spiritual context and the unfortunate misreading of her works. The narrative was banned, and was Walker accused by the meat industry of advocating for vegetarianism, when in fact the narrative proclaims the unity of all life.

The question that her title: "Am I Blue?" poses is answered in "We Are One Lesson," and that lesson is about much more than eating or not eating meat; it concerns the spirit inherent in all living things, a consciousness of oneness, and the relationship between slavery/racial oppression and the abuse of nature and the environment. The story mirrors Walker's statements that Earth has been denigrated, as have black and native peoples.[37]

Living by the Word received a cool literary reception. Karla Simcikova argues that critics could not fairly assess Walker's new collection of essays because of their failure to see beyond the womanist context of *In Search of Our Mothers' Gardens*. She refers to Jill Nelson, who described the essays in *Living by the Word* as "banal and pedestrian."[38] Nelson further stated that the essays do not break new ground. That the essays do not break new ground is incorrect, for they do so in terms of Walker's spiritual content; however, several of the essays in the collection do seem self-indulgent and of little consequence. The journal entries primarily tend to irritate, and seem misplaced and irrelevant. The essay on food, "Not Only Will Your Teachers Appear, They Will Cook New Foods for You," probably prompted Cronan Rose's remark about Mendocino values[39] and lifestyle politics in her 1989 review of *Living by the Word*, however, those most critical of the collection failed to grasp its spiritual significance. One of the most profound spiritual texts in the collection is "Am I Blue?"

A major theological question that has concerned humans, and continues to do so, is the issue of suffering. For the most part, theologians and philosophers have thought only of human suffering. Greg Garrard has written that relations between animals and humans in the humanities is divided between the philosophical and the cultural.[40] That there is any focus on animals at all is due in large part to the 1975 publication of Peter Singer's *Animal Liberation*. Jeremy Bentham, writing as long ago as the 1800s, states:

> [T]he day may come when the rest of the animal creation may acquire those rights which never could have been withholden [*sic*] from them but by the hand of tyranny. The French have already discovered that the blackness of the skin is no reason why a human being should be abandoned without redress to the caprice of a tormentor. It may one day come to be recognised that the number of the legs, the villosity of the skin, or the termination of the sacrum, are reasons equally insufficient for abandoning a sensitive being to the same fate.[41]

The central issue for Bentham is whether beings can suffer. For Walker, suffering also is a pertinent issue in the essay, "Am I Blue?" Utilitarian philosopher Bentham (1748–1832) suggested that cruelty to animals was not significantly different from slavery. Walker makes the same point. Racism, sexism, and "speciesism" (Bentham's term) are triple evils, with the latter going mostly unnoticed in the Christian west. In Christian culture, theologians specifically have represented not humans, but man as ruler of the earth, with a God-ordained charge to have dominion and use scripture to reinforce the idea. In other traditions, no such charge is followed. Swami Vivekananda summarizes precisely the Hindi philosophy when he says: "All differences in this world are of degree, and not of kind, because oneness is the secret of everything."[42]

Peter Singer explains the attitudes and historical genesis of mainstream Christianity regarding animals when he writes:

> There are a few laws indicating some awareness of animal welfare in the Old Testament, but nothing at all in the New, nor in mainstream Christianity for its first eighteen hundred years. Paul scornfully rejected the thought that God might care about the welfare of oxen, and the incident of the Gadarene swine, in which Jesus is described as sending devils into a herd of pigs and making them drown themselves in the sea, is explained by Augustine as intended to teach us that we have no duties toward animals.[43]

The Catholic Church accepted this philosophy, and Pope Pius IX even refused to allow the establishment of a Society for the Prevention of Cruelty to Animals in Rome.

Living by the Word opens with a journal entry dated April 17, 1984. In this entry Walker recalls a vivid dream of a two-headed woman. This woman establishes the tone for the essay "Am I Blue?" that follows. The woman's instructions expand on the biblical context and embrace the African American tradition in which the word is particularly significant. Black vernacular language reveals the importance of *word* in such phrases as *word up*, *what's the word?* In agreement with someone's statement, the listener often replies, *word*. In the essay "Am I Blue?" the horse in Walker's backyard reminds her of the connection between humans and what she calls human animals. Just as during slavery, when whites tended to forget their connection to Mammy once they were older, she has forgotten her own connection to the animals of her youth. Her analogy is accurate, from the forgetting of relationships to the traumatic selling away of mates of the enslaved women once the man used as a stud accomplished his mission. Blue is a lonely horse who is given a companion, and Walker observes how happy he is to have company. Suddenly one day she sees that he is alone again. She finds out that his only role was to impregnate his companion. She recognizes the parallels between the treatment of enslaved Africans and the mistreatment of the horse. The message in the essay is a spiritual one, although some see it as political. The spiritual *is* political, just as the personal is political. Whatever stands in opposition to the generally accepted beliefs becomes a political issue. Walker's reason for calling attention to the treatment of animals is the unjustified mistreatment of them.

"Am I Blue?" first appeared in *Ms.* magazine, November 1986. Once in print, however, the essay, which was also included as a short story in the California Learning Assessment System (CLAS) test for California schools, caused some citizens to complain that "Am I Blue?" was anti-meat-eating; the California State Board of Education then removed it from the test. It became a political brouhaha. The problem with the banning of "Am I Blue?," "Roselily," and *The Color Purple*, which were all banned from the California test, is censorship. When the "Am I Blue?" controversy erupted, Patricia Holt, editor of the *San Francisco Chronicle Book Review*, had the foresight to publish the banned work in the newspaper and invite readers to write the editor and express their opinions. More than six hundred letters arrived; most were against the ban. Eventually the California State Board of Education reversed its decision. According to Holt, Walker is one of the most censored writers in American literature.[44]

The religious right led the movement to ban Walker's works. "Am I Blue?" proclaims the unity of all life. Fundamentalists who read the Bible literally focus on the chapter, verse, and line in Genesis 2:28: "Be fruitful and multiply, and replenish the earth, and subdue it: and have dominion over the fish of the sea, and over the fowl of the air, and over every living thing that moveth upon the earth." *Subdue* and *dominion* are the key words that have been used to oppress women, children, blacks, and other minorities with what some perceive as holy justification. Walker's essay about the sad-eyed white horse reveals the insensitivity of two-legged humans. If young students read and think seriously about what she has written, they might become more sensitive humans. Fear motivates the attacks on Walker's works.

"Why Did the Balinese Chicken Cross the Road?" addresses many of the same issues. In that essay, Walker sees the humanity of the chicken or, put another, more spiritually correct way, she beholds Divinity in the chicken. Her writing pen, she says, "is a microphone held up to the mouths of ancestors,"[45] and these include horses, dogs, chickens, and rivers. This essay proclaims meat-eating is cannibalistic.[46] Ironically, or perhaps humanly, the next lines reveal that Walker herself is eating chicken satay. Her self-confessional style is reminiscent of a preacher making a moral conclusion and then revealing her own clay feet. Stories of backsliding seem to offer encouragement to the faint of heart.

Unity of Spirit as a core value in Walker's belief and evolving worldview is mistaken as Native American in origin. Simcikova writes: "Walker's thought cannot be explained outside of Native American spirituality."[47] But of course it can. Belief in the unity of all life is part of many native cultures, as well as the theological basis of the New Thought movement in the United States. Walker herself has attended the Science of Mind Church in Oakland, where she would have been exposed to teachings like those of Native Americans. New Thought teaches that Spirit is all, that matter is Spirit in form, and that all is connected. Simcikova's claim denies influences other than Native American. New Thought philosophy expresses the belief that all truth is one. Truth intuitively can be absorbed wherever one finds it. Hybridity is irrelevant. Walker has traveled Africa and many parts of the world absorbing indigenous spirituality. In *The Healing Wisdom of Africa: Finding Life Purpose through Nature, Ritual, and Community*, Malidoma Patrice Somè writes: "It is only through a massive investment in denial of indigenous spirituality that many Westerners have arrived at the relatively comfortable thinking that 'modern' means that which has overcome primitivism, that which is superior to the indigenous."[48] The concepts are not limited to one particular group of people. Embedded in American poetry are aspects of the same truth; Whitman's "Song of Myself" proclaims unity when he says, "For every atom belonging to me/as good as belongs to you."[49]

While Native Americans figure large in Walker's works, they do not just appear, as Donna Haisty Winchell suggests, during a time in the late 1990s when Walker appeared to be changing her creative focus. Their presence is in her early work as well. *Meridian*, for example, highlights a Native American ancestor, Feather Mae, as well as the destruction of the Native burial grounds. Walker's comments about the Native Americans being compared to animals and the comparison being derogatory are discussed at length by Greg Garrard in *Ecocriticism*. Garrard says the theriomorphic use of animals (the opposite of anthropomorphic) often includes racial stereotyping; the example he offers is that Nazis described Jews as rats. Comparing Native Americans to animals implied they had no souls, that they were less than human. Erica Fudge in *Perceiving Animals* talks about the "insuperable line"[50] between human and nonhuman, and concludes that such a line may be nonexistent despite the rhetoric surrounding immortal soul, human language, dexterity of the human hand, and tool making.

Walker summarizes the central message in "Am I Blue?" near the end. Whether to eat steak (which comes at the end) is not the main question, but rather the acknowledgement of oneness—a belief in karmic justice is the issue, for she writes that the animals are our teachers and that what happens to them will happen to us.[51] Whereas "Am I Blue?" sets the tone for the critical issues broached in *Living by the Word*, the essay merely is a warm-up for the pieces that follow.

Steeped as it is in the tradition of the black preacher, "In the Closet of the Soul" could have been delivered as a Sunday sermon. In this essay, Walker is passionate in her response to a question about black people's reaction to *The Color Purple*. She addresses black men's negative responses to her works, beginning with *The Third Life of Grange Copeland* and *Meridian*. She charges that those critical of the works are unable to recognize how sexism oppresses black women.[52] In their often heated and sometimes hateful responses to *The Color Purple*, the men turned the focus from the story and movie about black women to themselves. Walker's argument builds in momentum with her comparison to the black freedom struggle. She points out that all struggled for freedom, and a double standard favoring men was not mentioned. Further, she states that she was shocked to realize that anyone assumed that black women would not fight injustice except when the foe was white.[53] In *The Color Purple*, Walker demonstrates that both Mister and Celie change, and transformation is another key element in her writing. This conversion takes place on a spiritual level. Walker has stated her surprise that a novel beginning with "Dear God" could be so misinterpreted.

In the poem "Family Of," included in the essay "In the Closet of the Soul" and published in *Horses Make the Landscape Look More Beautiful*, Walker emphasizes the notion of unity. Clearly both literal and spiritual in significance, the idea of unity angered some critics. On a literal level, when she says that African Americans are not only descendants of slaves but also the offspring of the slave owners, she is stating a fact that perhaps is more widely known now than when she wrote the poem. In an attempt at authenticity, Walker claims all her known ethnic lines including Native American, Caucasian, and African. In the now infamous review of Walker's essay that attempted to integrate her disparate selves, K. T. H. Cheatwood criticizes her for pointing out her rapist great-grandfather, and calls her efforts twisted and pathological.[54] Unfortunately Cheatwood could not see beyond the racial politics of the times. Coming on the heels of the Black Power/Black Pride movement of the late 1960s and 1970s, Walker's attempt at integrating all her selves was challenged. Identifying only with her black ancestry was de rigueur. Denial is likely to be as detrimental as embracing parts of the self that might seem to be better forgotten. An integrated personality cannot remain in denial about a shadow self or white ancestor, evil as he might have been, and Walker states that hers was indeed despicable. What is to be gained by sharing this information is the question. In opening herself up, in becoming vulnerable to her readers, perhaps they too can see the unity in life.

Walker moved past the ego of the individual into mystical consciousness. From that vantage point, she was able to see the suffering of both blacks and whites. Her compassion was healing. Embracing the oneness in all, she insists: "We are the oppressor and oppressed."[55] She goes on naming and enumerating as if God's trombones were driving home the message, one that some are too resistant to receive.

"Everything Is a Human Being" brings Walker's spirituality into even sharper focus. Critics of Walker's position tend to embrace only duality— they see good versus bad, black versus white, right versus wrong, instead of the wholeness Walker's works uncover. The conclusion of Walker's essay focuses on a unity that indicts all. We are all guilty, because we are all one. In her conversation with the trees, they indict all people who believe that they are exonerated as individuals. According to Walker, nature judges us by our worst collective behavior, and no one escapes responsibility for what happens to the earth. Our individual choice yields a collective result. It rains on both the just and the unjust. The answer in terms of what to do is simple but difficult, clearly, for we have not mastered it. Love the self, love each other, love the earth, and love all that is on it is Walker's message, ancient as the hills and still rejected as New Age baloney. Critic Richard Bernstein wrote that Walker "seems to have substituted the heartfelt concerns that motivated *The Color Purple* for a mediocre sort of spiritualist philosophizing that is both cloying and predictable."[56] Critics have compared Walker's effort, especially in her novels published since *The Color Purple*, as the rhetoric of hippies and flower children.[57] While it may be cliché to say that all we need is love, what is more predictable is the response to the idea of love, which is often cynical. In her 1956 book *Love or Perish*, psychiatrist Smiley Blanton, a Cornell-trained doctor, lest she be considered a crackpot, wrote that full growth is not possible without love.[58]

Walker announced early on that she is most concerned with people's complete survival and wholeness. According to the late Leo Buscaglia, infants do not enter the world knowing how to love. They must be taught and ultimately learn from adults who might or might not know themselves. Walker employs a variety of methods and literary genres to teach. Nevertheless, some psychiatrists believe the major opponent of love is fear. Gerald Jampolsky, a Stanford University–trained psychiatrist, argues that love is eternal in *Love Is Letting Go of Fear*.[59] Fear is transitory. The message to love, at times an urgent directive, is delivered from all parts of society from the pulpit to the physician's office. The message is as old as the man from Galilee, the Indian Vedas, and the African shrines. Few have perfected the practice of love.

Walker quotes Black Elk, who declared: "It is the story of all life that is holy and is good to tell, and of us two-leggeds sharing in it with the four-leggeds and the wings of the air and all green things; for these are children of one mother and their father is one Spirit."[60] Here Walker uses the Native American worldview to ground her essay, but she performs what Matthew Fike describes as a swerving from the original quotation, for she writes, "Are not the 'fathers,' rather, those Native Americans, those 'wild Indians' like Black Elk?"[61] While her point to refute the denigration of Indians is well taken, the spiritual content of the quotation is undermined. Perhaps Black Elk was not talking about his compatriots as father but rather Spirit as mother/father, as he so clearly stated. Fike points out that Walker, in the essay "In Search of Our Mothers' Gardens," performs a swerve, that is, she shifts the original meaning of a quotation to make her point, in both the epigraph from Jean Toomer and the paraphrase of Okot p'Bitek's poem. Fike identifies her paraphrase as an enallage, using one grammatical form to replace another. Further, Fike claims that Walker "[s]ees wholeness and unity where others see binary opposition or misreading."[62] While this point seems to be true in most cases, it does not hold regarding the Black Elk quotation.

To what extent Walker is converted, as it were, to Native American philosophy is unclear. Simcikova misreads Walker when she claims that Walker's Native American consciousness is so deep as to detract from her "established persona *as a black woman writer.*"[63] Walker uses the example of Native Americans because it is readily available and, indeed, part of her heritage. She broaches a womanist inclusiveness, and her tendency is to view all truth as one where ever she finds it. When she finds truth, if it rings true she uses it; if it needs tweaking to support her point, she does that as well.

Walker might easily have chosen to use some other primal spirituality (which she does in *The Temple of My Familiar*) to make her point. What is disturbing about both Simcikova's and Donna Winchell's claims about Walker is their assumption, first, that womanism is limited to black women only, ergo it is narrow; and second, that what critics saw as a change in her writing was due to some crisis of identity that Walker solved when she found her Native American and white ancestors. Womanism is universal. Nowhere in her definition does she state that womanism is exclusively black; however, it is culturally black—as purple to lavender, it deepens feminism and contributes the culture and lived experiences of black women. Walker's interest in Native American culture reaches back to the writing of *Meridian*, if not further. She was not searching for her identity, which by the age of twenty seemed quite fully formed. Walker, like her character Fanny in *The Temple of My Familiar*, was trying to come to terms with the idea of the unity. To accomplish this, she was forced to start with herself. She recognized, like St. Augustine, that self-knowledge is not only the path to happiness but finally to salvation. She did not want to hate the Wasichus that had oppressed both Africans and Native peoples. The way around or through the anger and hatred is to recognize that even the most detestable person is, in fact, part of the whole. She recognizes, like Mr. Miyagi in *The Karate Kid II,* that living without forgiveness is worse than death. Hers was a spiritual working through just as Fanny's is, and Winchell's comments about Walker as an "aging flower child of the 1980s"[64] may demonstrate Winchell's inability to see beyond the surface.

Of the twenty-seven essays in *Living by the Word*, three discuss Native American issues and ideas. Furthermore, two significant statements frame the piece: one a long quotation from Ayi Kwei Armah's *Two Thousand Seasons*, and the other an epigram by Daniel Ortega: "The victory belongs to love." The African statement foreshadows the reception of *Living by the Word* and establishes the thematic underpinnings of the spiritual essays that follow. Armah writes: "No fundi (teacher) could work effectively when torn away from power . . . the life of a fundi whose people have lost their way is pain . . . a fundi's craft is turned to trash . . . easy as slipping on a riverstone to see his craftsmanship actually turned like a weapon against his people. . . . Our way . . . is not a random path. It . . . aims at preserving knowledge of who we are . . . our way is reciprocity. The way is wholeness."[65] The Ghanaian and Nicaraguan presidents' statements clearly influence Walker's ideas, along with Native American thought. To grant any one more weight than any other is to risk misreading Walker.

A historian of world religions, Huston Smith has long documented the similarities in what he calls primal religions, stating that they exist today in "Africa, Australia, Southeast Asia, the Pacific Islands, Siberia, and among the Indians of North and South America."[66] Smith observes that as societies develop and advance in technology, they become more divided, and hierarchy develops between clergy and laity, as well as the lines that are drawn between the sacred and the secular. In a 1981 interview with Kay Bonetti, Walker commented that to suppose the ancients were ignorant is unwise.[67] Smith concurs that it is prejudiced to believe that later means better. He states that primal religions are all similar in their muted focus on worship and central focus on identification with and acting out of archetypal paradigms.[68] What attracts Walker to the earth-based religions is their honoring of the natural environment. Her statement that "Earth itself has become the nigger of the world,"[69] concretizes pollution and abuse in no uncertain terms. The essay sermonizes and postulates our future destruction if we fail to heed the warnings. Walker, in the John O'Brien interview, announced that she does not believe there is a God, at least not one apart from nature.[70] She was in her early twenties. The metaphysical context of these early works leads directly to her more fully developed philosophy today.

NOTES

1. See Evelyn White, *Alice Walker: A Life* (New York: Norton, 2004).
2. Periods are missing in the original and the text is in all caps.

3. Scrapbook, Alice Walker Archive, Stuart A. Rose Manuscript, Archives, and Rare Book Library, Emory University.

4. Ibid.

5. Mystics Sojourner Truth and Amanda Berry Smith experienced the enslavement as the first trauma. Rebecca Cox Jackson was severely traumatized by thunderstorms, and Berry Smith suffered a life-threatening illness at sea. *Africans in America: Part 3*, www.pbs.org; see also Amanda Smith, *An Autobiography: The Story of the Lord's Dealings with Mrs. Amanda Smith, the Colored Evangelist* (UNC Chapel Hill, 1893/1999). Retrieved from https://docsouth.unc.edu/neh/smitham/smith.html.

6. Alice Walker Archive, Stuart A. Rose Manuscript, Archives, and Rare Book Library, Emory University.

7. Ernest Holmes, *The Science of Mind* (New York: Putnam [1938], 1998), 419.

8. Scrapbook, Alice Walker Archive, Stuart A. Rose Manuscript, Archives, and Rare Book Library, Emory University.

9. Walker, *Her Blue Body: Everything We Know*, preface.

10. Walker, *Once*, reprinted in *Her Blue Body*, 103.

11. Abortion was illegal in 1965.

12. Walker, *Once*, in *Her Blue Body*, 135.

13. Walker, *In Search of Our Mothers' Gardens*, 271.

14. Ibid., 261.

15. Walker, *Once*, in *Her Blue Body*, 137.

16. Walker, "Be Nobody's Darling," *Revolutionary Petunias*, reprinted in *Her Blue Body*.

17. *Her Blue Body*, 76.

18. Walker, "South the Name of Home," *Her Blue Body*, 101.

19. Simon James, *The Presence of Nature* (New York: Palgrave Macmillan, 2009), 82.

20. Charles Fillmore, *Metaphysical Bible Dictionary* ([1931] 2007), 271.

21. Walker, *To Hell with Dying*, 1.

22. Walker, *In Search of Our Mothers' Gardens*, 226.

23. See Ron Karenga, "Black Cultural Nationalism," in *The Black Aesthetic*, ed. Addison Gayle (New York: Anchor Books, 1971), 31–37.

24. Walker, *To Hell with Dying*, 38.

25. Walker, *In Search of Our Mothers' Gardens*, 228.

26. Ibid., 166.

27. Ibid., 168.

28. Ibid., 170.

29. Ibid., 232.

30. Ibid., 168.

31. Maria Lauret, *Alice Walker* (New York: Palgrave MacMillan, 2011), 14.

32. Ibid., 221.

33. Roland Barthes, "The Death of the Author," in *Image Music Text*, trans. Stephen Heath (New York: Hill and Wang, 1977), 142–48.

34. See Edmund Steimle, *Preaching the Story* (Eugene, OR: Wipf & Stock, 2003).

35. Luke 4:4. All biblical quotes in the text are King James Version.

36. Walker, *Living by the Word*, 2.

37. Ibid., 147.

38. Jill Nelson, "The World According to Alice Walker," *Washington Post Magazine* (May 29, 1988).

39. See Cronan Rose's review of *Living by the Word* in *Journal of Modern Literature* 16, no. 2–3 (Fall 1989), 429.

40. Greg Garrard, *Ecocriticism* (New York: Routledge, 2012).

41. Jeremy Bentham, quoted in Peter Singer, *The Animal Liberation Movement: Its Philosophy, Its Achievements and Its Future* (New York: Old Hammond Press, 2000), xliii.

42. Swami Vivekananda, *Practical Vedanta* (Kolkata: Advaita Ashrama, 2004), Part 1, no. 32.

43. Singer, *Animal Liberation Movement*, 177.

44. See Alice Walker and Patricia Holt, *Alice Walker Banned* (San Francisco: Aunt Lute Books, 1996).
45. Walker, *Living by the Word*, 170.
46. Ibid., 172.
47. Karla Simcikova, *To Live Fully in the Here and Now* (New York: Lexington Books, 2007), 9.
48. Malidoma Somè, *The Healing Wisdom of Africa: Finding Life Purpose through Nature, Ritual, and Community* (New York: Tarcher, 1999), 13.
49. Walt Whitman, "Song of Myself," in *Leaves of Grass*, 1892. www.Googlebooks.com.
50. Erica Fudge, *Perceiving Animals* (New York: St. Martin's, 2000), 143.
51. Walker, *Living by the Word*, 7.
52. Ibid., 79.
53. Walker, "In the Closet of the Soul," *Living by the Word*. 79.
54. Ibid., 89. Walker refers to Cheatwood's review of *Horses Make the Landscape More Beautiful*, which appeared in the *Richmond News Leader*, 1984.
55. Ibid.
56. Richard Bernstein, "*By the Light of My Father's Smile:* Limp New-Age Nonsense in Mexico," *New York Times Book Review* (October 7, 1998), n.p. https://archive.nytimes.com/www.nytimes.com/books/98/10/04/daily/walker-book-review.html.
57. See J. O. Tate's review, "Smiley Face with Dreadlocks," *National Review* 41, no. 12 (June 30, 1989), n.p.
58. Smiley Blanton, *Love or Perish* (New York: Simon and Schuster, 1956).
59. Gerald Jampolsky, *Love Is Letting Go of Fear* (New York: Celestial Arts, 2004).
60. Walker, "Everything Is a Human Being," *Living by the Word*, 145.
61. Matthew Fike, "Jean Toomer and Okot p'Bitek in Alice Walker's 'In Search of Our Mothers' Gardens,'" *MELUS* 25, no. 3–4 (Fall/Winter 2000), 149. http://doi.org/10.2307/468240.
62. Ibid.
63. Simcikova, *To Live Fully in the Here and Now*, 17 (italics in the original).
64. Donna Haisty Winchell, *Alice Walker* (New York: Twayne, 1992), 113.
65. Walker, *Living by the Word*, frontispiece.
66. Huston Smith, *The World's Religions* (New York: HarperCollins [1958] 1991), 365.
67. Kay Bonetti, *Alice Walker* (Columbia, MO: American Prose Library, 1981).
68. Ibid.
69. Walker, "Everything Is a Human Being," *Living by the Word,* 147.
70. Walker, "Interview with John O'Brien," in Rudolph Byrd (ed.), *The World Has Changed* (New York: New Press, 2010), 35.

Chapter Two

Spirit in the Dark

The Metaphysics of Poverty

Walker's first novel, *The Third Life of Grange Copeland*, published in 1970, is a meditation on choice. Free will, fate, and destiny are core issues. Racism, sexism, classism, and poverty are intersecting symptoms of these core issues. Maria Lauret characterizes the novel as patriarchal and the plot, feminist.[1] Other critics have commented on the polemics of the novel but seem to miss the central homiletic. Three quotations, Walker's grounding texts, provide the context for the metaphysical meaning of her message, which is threefold. The first text is from *The Children of Sanchez* by Oscar Lewis[2] and shows that the result of poverty can be cynicism.

This text points to the culture of poverty that Lewis's anthropological study posits. The idea that poor people have a different value system, however, is not Walker's point. The reason that poverty persists is that the poor adapt to lack and limitation in many instances and within the context of Walker's novel. The metaphysics of poverty is enmeshed in the way penury can diminish the spirit. Even more limiting is the sense of separation that exists among the poor in Lewis's account. The poor feel marginalized and helpless. Walker has said that she wants her writing to help people "see their connectedness to other people who had survived."[3] The situation, she says, "may seem permanent because it's always happening, but it's not always happening to the same people."[4]

Both Grange and Brownfield, central characters in *The Third Life of Grange Copeland*, are paragons of victim mentality. The feelings of powerlessness and inferiority deepen their sense of unworthiness. They recognize no Divinity within themselves. Additionally, the impoverished often have little sense of history and believe they are the only ones who are suffering.

Brownfield exemplifies this lack of historical connection when orphaned by his mother's suicide and his father's abandonment. He does not even know how to follow the North Star to escape the South, facts his ancestors knew because of their historical connection to African wisdom passed on through the oral tradition, the Underground Railroad, and spirituals that taught them to read the night sky. Brownfield, instead of reading the right signs, follows the sun. The failure to make connections with others in similar conditions leads to passivity. Not all people who are poor are part of a culture of poverty; clearly, Walker and her family were not. Nonetheless, the characters in *The Third Life of Grange Copeland* are perfect examples of a culture of poverty. Winchell writes that "Fate leads Brownfield not only down the same road but into the same juke joint earlier frequented by his father."[5] Choice, not fate, is the point Walker makes. Brownfield's journey begins as the hero's, but he is the antihero. The first person that he meets on the road is Mamie Lou Banks, who assumes that he is fleeing from white people.[6] Even with the clue that she gives Brownfield in saying that she cannot understand why he would run backward,[7] he still fails to recognize that he is going the wrong direction.

The second grounding text is from *Song of Lawino: A Lament* by Okot p'Bitek, which Walker quoted (in modified form) in her essay "In Search of Our Mothers' Gardens." The lament mourns the death of a husband, prince, and the destruction of all the young men. The destruction caused by masculine violence is presented here as a parable. Unless the violent nature of the masculine is consumed "By a great Fire!"[8] all will be lost. Male critics have commented on what they see as Walker's effort to feminize her male characters, but how the elimination of violence becomes feminine is unclear.

Walker's third quotation is a statement Richard Wright made to Jean-Paul Sartre questioning what it means to be a human being.[9] What it means to be human is a question that exists in the novel. Humans have choices. The novel opens with an example. Uncle Silas and Aunt Marilyn arrive in the Georgia backwoods in a new 1920 Buick. They have chosen to live in the North. They display what seems to be wealth, especially in the eyes of Brownfield, Grange's only son. While the new automobile represents a different choice from the economic condition of rural sharecropping, Walker presents it as a capitalist materialist alternative that does not lead to self-discovery, but rather to material entrapment and destruction. Silas becomes a drug addict, and the police kill him in an attempted store robbery. Property ownership, protected by laws that sanction killing, make clear Walker's point that the choice Silas and his wife make is not a paradigm to follow. Grange and his wife Margaret, on the contrary, do nothing, which also is a choice. Seeing his parents paralyzed and trapped in the cycle of poverty, Brownfield wonders why they do not leave their present circumstances and, at ten years old, he does not fail to notice that his mother takes every opportunity to placate his father. When Brownfield wishes they had an automobile like his uncle's, Grange snaps, "Well, we don't." Brownfield's mother echoes: "No, we don't."[10] Her response causes Brownfield to wonder about her behavior. He notices that his mother is subservient to his father, and characterizes her behavior to that of their dog.[11] From the beginning of the novel, Walker engages Wright's question of what it means to be human. The poverty and violence introduced by the previous quotations frame her answers.

Self-possession is a key part of humanity. Naming and enumerating one's nomenclature is an African cultural practice that may in fact be universal. Names help to compose an identity. During American enslavement, depriving the African of her or his true name was more than just a convenience for enslavers who might have difficulty pronouncing it, but rather was a deliberate stripping away of African identity. Ironically, Grange and Margaret select for their son a name that predicts his future in the uncanny way of their African ancestors. Brownfield receives his name when Grange looks outside and sees a brown field. The name makes a significant point. A brownfield is a toxic waste site. Clearly, Brownfield's childhood is indeed such a site, contaminated with crushing poverty and violence. The word also means a place from which contamination is removed, however, and is available for reuse. Humans may recycle experiences. Walker seems to argue for this possibility and necessity. The term *brownfields* did not come into existence until 1992, and Walker's choice for this character's name is serendipitous.

Grange's name is also meaningful. Gerri Bates writes that Grange refers to a farmer or to farming, which of course is what Grange does without much success.[12] Grange also includes (G)range and enables the reader to see beyond the limits of his frustrating first life, when he farms for someone else, to his success when he works for himself. The range of choices available to Grange is a central focus of the novel/homily. There is always choice. An issue that some wrestle with is whether humans have choice if they are unaware of their choices. Holmes says: "The mind is the fashioning factor, and according to its range, vision, and positiveness, will be the circumstance or experience."[13] One response that invariably irritates and rarely satisfies is that being human carries with it the responsibility of self-knowledge and the necessity of investigating what choices are available. Some may see this responsibility as shifting blame to the victim. Walker suggests that victimizers are not exempt from responsibility or blame, and that people can also choose not to remain victims.

Even though Brownfield is badly affected by a childhood of oppressive circumstances, nonetheless the possibility exists for him to transcend these experiences. He learns to fear white men from his father's example, because in front of Mr. Shipley, Grange wore a mask that froze him into an automaton.[14] Brownfield can escape. When the white landowner Shipley tries to coax him into assuming his father's debt, Brownfield flees. What could be the beginning of a better life for Brownfield never materializes because of his ignorance. Walker has said that "the foundation of suffering is ignorance."[15] Brownfield suffers, but moreover he allows his suffering to infect others.

Bates characterizes the novel as an *Erziehungsroman,* a novel of education.[16] The successful characters, Grange and his granddaughter, Ruth, both learn from their experiences. The least successful characters, with Brownfield the least successful of all, apparently learn little, at least nothing that will save them. Even while in prison for his wife's murder, Brownfield complains that she got on his nerves because of her physical appearance. Brownfield's irrational thinking blames his wife for her murder because she was skinny.[17] While one might easily conclude that he is a fool, the narrator follows Brownfield's asinine reasoning, by saying that he is no fool. He knew enough to protect himself from his own guilt. His actions bring up the issue of evil and how the manifestation of evil can exist in a philosophical worldview that embraces Spirit as all. Walker has said, "Everything is God."[18] Furthermore, she claims that "evil, like good, is an energy."[19] Apparently, one characteristic of the human condition is freedom to demonstrate negative energy.

In *Women Who Run with the Wolves*, Clarissa Pinkola Estes addresses "irredeemable evil."[20] Paraphrasing Carl Jung, Estes writes: "Jung once said that God became more conscious as humans became more conscious. He postulated that humans cause the dark side of God to become struck with light when they rout their personal demons out into the light of day."[21] Still another way of understanding evil is to see that God or Spirit has no dark side, that it is only the human experience that introduces what appears to be evil or the absence of light, and that is the result of slipping out of alignment with Spirit, or having a consciousness that denies the Divine. Put another way, philosopher and founder of the Science of Mind teachings Ernest Holmes is emphatic that God knows no evil. He writes: "Why should it disturb anyone to be told that God knows nothing of his sin, nothing of his want, nothing of his lack of any kind? *The tragedy would be if God did know.*"[22] Holmes insists that "Evil is *man created,* while God—the Eternal Goodness—knows nothing about it. . . . Evil is the direct and suppositional opposite to good, and has no reality behind it, or actual law to come to its support."[23] Psychiatrist M. Scott Peck attempts a psychology of evil in *People of the Lie*. A medical doctor, Peck begins by offering a medical model to understand humans. His method is dualistic and views people as having disease or health. Concerning evil, however, he admits that no body of scientific knowledge about evil exists that can be called "a psychology."[24] Peck suggests that while the concept of evil has been central to religious thought, science has resisted because religious models are immiscible and mutually incompatible. Evil is a mystery and, according to Peck, too large for science to tackle comfortably. He claims that science likes small mystery. Theologians, on the contrary, and mystics as well, find mystery compelling. Walker has said on many occasions how mystery intrigues. Peck could well be describing Walker when he writes that "while some seek in religion an escape from mystery, for others religion is a way to approach mystery . . . they . . . use more integrative 'right brain' means of exploration: meditation, intuition, feeling, faith, and revelation. For them the bigger the mystery, the better."[25]

Walker is among those for whom mystery works. Brownfield displays several characteristics of evil, but those who look for a neat answer do not find one. Peck believes that goodness is an even greater mystery than evil, but that evil and good are inextricable. The issues of good and evil ultimately, he concludes, are beyond our comprehension. Regarding the issues of good or evil, Peck writes: "Whether we know it or not, we are literally treading upon holy ground."[26] Walker treads with awareness and determination where others fear to go; this novel is just the beginning. Walker's own answer about evil reveals itself in the 2004 television interview with Bill Moyers. She declines to call anyone evil, including Idi Amin, the former dictator of Uganda, whom she claims "was profoundly ignorant."[27] Her position on evil comes from the childhood teachings of her parents. As a child growing up in the South, where lynching and other acts of terror directed toward African Americans could inspire hatred, her parents told her that white people who behaved in hateful ways did not know any better. In what Walker calls a spiritual lesson, she said they told her if the whites knew better, they would do better. She internalized her parent's teachings, and her work illustrates her position that profound ignorance of our connection to each other and to the earth is the cause of the -isms that plague humanity.

Critics approach Walker's novel from a variety of angles. A sociohistorical reading focuses on the external events that affect the Copelands. This category of analysis includes feminism, Marxist theories of dialectical materialism, and economic determinism. The history of slavery, racism, and economic deprivation factor into the reading and analysis of *The Third Life* from a sociohistorical viewpoint. Much has been written from this context. The deleterious effects that poverty and racism have wreaked upon black people in the United States are undeniable, and the novel presents a clear example. Walker would not deny, as some of her mostly male critics accused, that black men did not suffer the evils of oppression. What she will not concede, however, is that oppression is an excuse for cruelty and evil toward the self or toward women and children. In the face of evil, Walker suggests that resistance is the secret. People must resist the inclination to blame even when people appear blameworthy. The tendency to place blame appears to make it easier not to accept responsibility for one's own life, enabling one to focus instead on that over which he/she has no control, instead of a focus on that which is controllable. Victim mentality allows a person to plead innocent when, in fact, she or he is not. Oppressor and the oppressed occupy a tangled web, as Walker makes clear in *The Third Life*. Grange sees clearly his mistake in not taking responsibility for his life. He tells Brownfield it is dangerous to place the blame for his own mistakes on someone else. That even when racism and poverty seem overwhelming, to think that whites are all-powerful corrupts the soul. He tries to make his son understand that he has power within his soul. He asks Brownfield if people do not own their souls. Grange poses the crucial question—what it means to be human. Brownfield says his father is an apologist for whites, deliberately, it appears, missing the point. Brownfield retorts: "you sure done turned into a cracker lover!"[28] Refusing to face the truth, Brownfield is always searching for the scapegoat. Ironically, his projection onto whites is not unwarranted, just unwise, for while one person may not single-handedly change the facts of racism and oppression, a person can change his responses to the experiences.

Shipley, the white landowner, represents the individual oppressor, the villain in the lives of the Copeland family. He in turn is part of a system that promotes the idea of limited resources (capitalist competition); therefore, his rationale for cruelty is to get what he needs. He uses Brownfield and black people generally as scapegoats. Peck defines evil as that which "seeks to kill life or liveliness. And goodness is its opposite. Goodness is that which promotes life and liveliness."[29] Thus Shipley, the sharecrop system, and the Jim Crow South are evil for the black people they exploit. Those who perpetrate the evil, according to Walker, do so from ignorance and a desire to meet their human needs in what they perceive as finite opportunities.

Evil also manifests in the distorted concept of masculinity. Gerda Lerner's definition of patriarchy is succinct; she writes that it is "the manifestation and institutionalization of male dominance over women and children in the family and the extension of male dominance over women in society in general."[30] Masculinity and paternalism derive support from the system of patriarchy. In what Lerner describes as paternalistic dominance, the dominant group (men) are considered superior to the subordinate group (women and children). Lerner states that "the dominance is mitigated by mutual obligations and reciprocal rights. The dominated exchange submission for protection, unpaid labor for maintenance."[31] She notes that the same relationship occurred in slavery.

In the South, paternalism existed in the relationship between white men and black men. Unfortunately, this flawed paradigm of gender relations—flawed because it is based on duality, on inferior/superior type of thinking—was not interrogated by newly freed blacks when it concerned gender and family relationships. Instead it was embraced by those least capable of enacting its requirements. The requirements for the masculine head of the family were economic support and protection in exchange for submission in all matters, "sexual service and unpaid domestic service"[32] given by the woman.

As have many other writers, Barbara Christian noted the effect on black men who could neither provide economically nor offer physical protection for their wives and children. This "masculine urge to power" (Christian's term) appears to be acceptable. Christian writes that when the "masculine urge is blocked [it] therefore turns in on itself,"[33] which she offers as explanation for the Copeland men's behavior. Christian is correct in that not only do the men embrace the concept of masculine dominance, but so do the women, and their acceptance leads directly to their undoing. Masculine rage turned in on itself harms not only the self but spills over onto everyone in close range. A rejection of white patriarchy and a reordering of gender roles could have saved the Copelands.

Instead, Mem, Brownfield's wife, whose name means every woman, apologizes for her strength. When finally she asserts herself by finding a job and moving from the shack in which Brownfield has placed the family, Christian notes that she has stepped outside of her feminine role: "her attack on him might be seen by many as a betrayal, as unwomanly."[34] Clearly, Christian refers to the era of the 1950s and 1960s, what young people nowadays refer to as "old school." Indeed, today's students (both female and male) cheer when Mem finally picks up the gun and threatens Brownfield. She acts in self-defense and is fed up with Brownfield's physical and mental abuse. Students often are not aware of the infamous Moynihan Report characterizing black women as emasculators. Walker's novel appeared during this national controversy. Many black women were made to feel ashamed of their strength. Walker exposes the stereotype of the emasculating black woman in an ironic and humorous way. In the scene in which Mem threatens Brownfield with the shotgun, she aims it between his legs and threatens to shoot should he move one inch.[35] In the definitions of manhood and womanhood that undergird various beliefs, Mem's actions, in threatening her husband, may have appeared inappropriate, even if necessary. Mem's aggression, her refusal to continue to be passive and willingly bolster the ego of her tormentor, her intelligence and ability to earn a living for herself and her children, nevertheless describe not manly or womanly behavior but the characteristics of a confident, self-protective, fully functioning adult of any sex.

Regarding Mem's actions, Christian says that she has no option. Clearly, Mem does indeed have alternatives. One example is the decision that she makes to threaten Brownfield. An option could have been to kill him before he killed her. Still another possibility could have been to leave him in the shack and take their children to the better life she can provide. Not becoming pregnant could have been another option. Birth control was available and, if she could not afford it, surely some old wives' remedies were available. Her husband even charges that she should have learned to not become pregnant.[36] Pregnancies ruin her health and help Brownfield to orchestrate her downfall. Perhaps Mem's most self-defeating decision was to tell Brownfield what she planned to do to leave him. Choice is at the center of every major issue in the novel. Christian raises a pertinent question when she asks whether the characters are victims only because they allow themselves to be. She does not attempt to answer, but Walker does. The novel demonstrates that the possibility for self-realization and transformation exists for all who are willing to search their own souls.

THE LIFE YOU SAVE MIGHT BE YOUR OWN

Grange ceases to be a victim when he chooses to journey north and encounters a white girl in the park. The ambiguity of the entire episode is provocative. Grange claims it is murder, but it is also the girl's choice. The incident takes place in New York's Central Park on a day when Grange is cold, starving, and penniless. He watches two lovers in the process of breaking up. The young woman is pregnant. The man, a soldier, is married and cannot wed his pregnant girlfriend. He leaves her sitting on the park bench. Deserted, she breaks down and cries. For the first time in his life, Grange glimpses the humanity of whites. He feels compassion for the young woman as well as for the man. This pivotal scene illustrates the vulnerability of someone white, and Grange begins to understand that he is not the only person who suffers. Once he makes this connection, however, the situation quickly changes. Grange fears that the woman will harm herself. He is about to offer his assistance when she suddenly composes herself. She is presented as one too haughty to suffer.[37] Grange sees her change as typical of whites in the United States. The woman intentionally drops the money and the ring that the lover has given her, and Grange picks it up. The narrator says that he has stolen before, but this time, apparently still moved by the scene and the fact that the woman is pregnant, he chooses to offer her part of the money back. His decision might have been to take all the money and the ring and run away. Seven hundred dollars and an expensive ring will keep him from starving. Unable to turn away, however, Grange chooses to approach the woman.

Walker sets the scene that focuses on external appearances, just as she uses the shiny new car in the opening of the novel, to say, look beyond form to substance. Grange's effort to survive has forced his attention away from the external to the essence of himself. The narrator says he never considered his appearance or the fact that he smelled bad and had stinking breath.[38] He did not think that the woman would object to his appearance or to the audacity of a black vagrant offering her solace. He thought suffering was humanizing. He divided the money, four hundred for himself and three hundred for her plus the ring. The scene is dismal, with ice on the pond, and the night is freezing.[39] The color gray suggests each character's complicity in his or her own failures. Before the woman sees him, she smells him; then seeing him, she looks through him. When Grange offers her the money and ring, she denies that it belongs to her. Instead of leaving, Grange insists that it does indeed belong to her. When he tells her what he has witnessed, she demands that he give her all the money. Throwing part of the money into the pond, she laughs at Grange when he is unable to retrieve the lost twenty. It becomes clear to Grange that she has learned nothing from her own pain. Her fatal error comes in her racist response when she demands the money, calls him nigger,[40] and kicks him. Grange cannot bring himself to hit her, although he does shake her. Continuing to call him nigger, she missteps and falls into the ice pond. Grange immediately rushes to save her. His actions provide a context in which to understand the motivation of enslaved men and women who would save their enslavers from burning houses. Here too Walker alludes to Richard Wright's *The Long Dream*, in which Fishbelly leaves the bleeding white man to die under the overturned Oldsmobile for calling him a nigger. Preserving life regardless of whose life it is or appears to be, is humane, but Walker contends all life is one; metaphysically speaking, she links the moral impulse in Grange to self-preservation, which often is a subconscious saving of the self. Grange extends his hand and she grabs hold, only to release it when she sees that it is his. He tries to comprehend her rejection of him, as he examines his hand.[41] Calling him nigger with her last breath, she sinks to her death.

Faced with his inability to save her, Grange believes that her death is murder, overlooks the woman's choice in the matter, and focuses only on his own choice. Walker directs the attention to Grange's, rather than to the woman's, choice, because that action is one that he controls. Murder, generally, is deliberately killing someone, but not in self-defense or other extenuating factors. Grange's culpability is ambiguous and ironic. The woman's choice to abjure Grange's offer to save her is what kills her. One could also conclude that had Grange never approached her, she might not have lost her footing and slipped into the pond. Therefore, Grange certainly must share in the responsibility for her lost life. What is ironic, however, is Grange's need to claim murder. For the first time in his life, he takes responsibility for his actions, and as ambiguous and distorted as his thinking might be, nevertheless his action is empowering. Murder is power. To take what he cannot give back bolsters Grange's will to live. He is like Bigger Thomas in that he believed that killing was a necessary act to gain his self-respect. Nevertheless, unlike Bigger, who is driven by fear when he smothers Mary Dalton, Grange makes a choice to walk away from the dying woman, much like Fish's choice in Wright's later novel. Walker alludes to Wright's apparent acceptance of the white American concept of manhood—one steeped in violence and a lust for power—by having Grange claim the murder. In his later years, Grange would modify his belief about murder by thinking that because he had killed someone, he should not avoid death in turn,[42] an idea Walker also would have encountered in the writings of Albert Camus.

Grange converts from self-hating to hating the oppressor. Walker employs the rhetoric of the Black Power movement as a trope for Grange's transformation. The context of the movement was anger, and the texts of the movement include Nikki Giovanni's poem, "The True Import of Present Dialogue, Black vs. Negro," which asks if the Negro can kill. The poem ends by linking manhood with violence.[43] Amiri Baraka's poem, "Black Art," was also part of the Black Power text that embraced violence.

Grange, on Harlem streets, shouts messages of hate.[44] He believes that hate, not love, is the key to survival. The paradox is that Grange's statements are both true and untrue. The Sunday rhetoric of preachers who say, love your enemy and do good to those who abuse,[45] justified the acceptance of cruelty and exploitation. Walker makes the point by describing the church-going deacons who beat their wives to death when they could not feed them. Clearly, love of oppression is not the answer. Love of the self is. The thin line between hatred of oppression and the oppressor does exist. To stand in that space and separate the deed from the doer is beyond Grange's current capacity. When told that hatred is not good for the mind, he retorts that he does not just live with his mind. To live, people need respect and pride.[46] The Christian rhetoric has not worked as far as he can see. The spiritual message is that hatred is unnatural. Walker reiterated the unnatural character of hating in a 2015 talk she gave at the University of Georgia. Love is a natural phenomenon. When people hate, Walker asserts, they bring negative energy to themselves.

The issue of killing versus murder occupied Walker's thinking from the time she was an undergraduate, and she turns to the topic often in her fiction. In *Meridian*, killing versus murder is the seminal question Walker poses. Studying philosophy at Sarah Lawrence, Walker wrote in her notebook: "To kill in war is not murder."[47] She studied Plato's theory of forms, as well as East Indian metaphysics, and while she did not completely understand the Principle of Sufficient Reason, she was impressed by Schopenhauer's explanations by analogy. Walker also studied Albert Camus and admired his ethics of suicide as well as his position on terrorism and political violence. In college, she comprehended the unity of all life. In her notebook she writes: "What we consider individuality is simply different manifestations of the same will."[48] Ernest Holmes called it Mind. Crucial to Walker's understanding of life is her concept of death. Life, she knows, is eternal and death "inconsequential,"[49] since the will would neither gain nor lose. Like Grange, Walker herself has wrestled with racism. In part of an unpublished poem, she writes: "dear god/ she prayed/ make me stop/ hating them/ for what they did/ to my father and/ mother."[50]

Grange embraces violence and mirrors the actions of so-called militant black people of the 1960s. The Black Panthers armed themselves, and the Black Muslims rejected Christianity and nonviolence for active self-defense. Grange literally fights whites individually. He did not recognize various ethnicities. If they appeared white, he hit them.[51] Realizing that he could not fight all whites, Grange concludes, like members of the Nation of Islam, he will withdraw from white society, segregate himself completely, and defend his sanctuary with his life. Thus begins his third life.

Grange returns to the South. Interestingly, in the 1960s, the Muslims of the Nation of Islam demanded several southern states for their homeland. Their reasoning was that the South was the land that slave labor had built. Grange returns to Baker County because its southern landscape feels like home to him. Metaphysically and metaphorically, returning home is a return to self, introspection required for self-knowledge and spiritual development. Grange also knows that Josie, a prostitute and his former mistress, loves him and has the money that he needs to accomplish his plan. With his money and Josie's money from the sale of her Dew Drop Inn, he purchases an isolated farm. On the farm with his innocent young granddaughter, Ruth, Grange begins a sincere path toward self-awareness. He learns from his granddaughter about the danger of hate. He cannot teach hate without inspiring it. Grange finally learns to love, and he saves Ruth's life from her sadistic and perhaps insane father, Brownfield.

In notes on *The Third Life of Grange Copeland*, Walker says the story is about "a man whose intense hatred of whites makes him an intense lover of himself."[52] He is selfish because he cares only for himself and Ruth. The unpublished manuscript differs from the novel in that both Grange and Ruth regret the way they treat Josie. Other significant differences are that Grange stops Ruth from attending school, and Brownfield becomes quite ill and Ruth takes care of him. Brownfield dies a more peaceful and loving man, in one version. Instead of having both men transform, Walker apparently decides that some people do not change, at least not in a single lifetime. Walker's notes contain a sketch for the development of the novel that begins with hatred, moves toward self-love, and next moves to selfishness, to guilt and possessiveness, and finally into loveliness. Perhaps she meant into the sublime. Whether the progressions concerned Grange or if they included Brownfield, is unclear because in the alternate story Grange dies, and Brownfield takes custody of Ruth. Brownfield and Josie live together with Ruth, who refuses to speak to them. After three years of silence Ruth speaks: "I'm eighteen today, she said, softly, watching Josie's fear. I don't have to stay here anymore."[53] The ending of the novel is exceedingly more powerful than the early draft, in which Brownfield dies and Ruth's future is unclear.

Henry Louis Gates Jr. discusses acts of formal revision in African American texts and states that they need not be antagonistic: rather they might be "loving acts of bonding."⁵⁴ Such appears to be the case with August Wilson's award-winning play, *Fences*. The title parallels the fence that Grange and Ruth erect to keep others out and to keep Ruth in the safety of Grange's place. Wilson's text signifies upon Walker's in the character of Troy Maxson, who mirrors Grange in terms of his background of poverty and illiteracy.⁵⁵ Troy is the son of a sharecropper, though not one himself. Instead, he collects garbage in a northern city. Because he believes himself a failure, he is unfaithful to his wife, as Grange is with Josie in his first life. Both male characters appear to feel entitled to be unfaithful to inflate their egos. However, Rose, Troy's wife, is not like Margaret, who commits suicide. Rose commits to rearing Troy's love child, but not forgiving or accepting Troy. Like Grange, Troy destroys his relationship with his youngest son, and, like Grange, Rose lavishes her attention on Raynell, the motherless girl like Ruth, the daughter she never had. Wilson's revisions of Walker's motifs extend the meaning of choice and the disaster of blaming others for an unsuccessful life. Whereas Grange can change, Troy remains stuck in the moment of his great disappointment: his inability to play professional ball because of his race. He cannot see that life for his son can be different and, in this way, he mirrors Brownfield. Unwilling to change, see in a new way, or think a new thought, they perish.

In the preface to his play, Wilson writes: "When the sins of our fathers visit us/ We do not have to play host. We can banish them with forgiveness/ As God, in His Largeness and Laws."⁵⁶ Walker posits the same idea when Grange asks Brownfield for forgiveness, which Brownfield is unable to grant. Brownfield is not only governed by self-loathing, he is angry, and anger rests in the bosom of a fool, who is more than just an ignorant person. The word *fool* traced to its Hebrew root, *nabhal*, denotes a wicked person, shamelessly immoral with an evil character. Grange, upon his return to Baker County, tries to explain his actions to his son. Even though Brownfield suffers in similar circumstances as his father had, he refuses to understand. His thoughts are stuck in yesterday. Ironically, Brownfield wants Ruth to forgive him as well, and it appears that she, too, is unable. Forgiveness is a crucial issue in the novel.

Spiritual awakening is Grange's recognition that his life, his true essence, is beyond his ego. His true self transcends personality and the experiences that have shaped him. "Life shrinks or expands in proportion to one's courage,"⁵⁷ says writer Anais Nin. Grange is courageous, whereas his son is not. To leave one's home and venture into the unknown takes courage. To admit one's faults also requires bravery. In the final published version of the novel, Grange clearly is the hero, flawed, yet in his imperfection, more fully human.

BROWN FIELDS AND TOXIC WASTE SITES

Grange Copeland demonstrates one way that a person can cope with negative external conditions. In his first life, Grange enacts the "fatal shrug,"[58] deadly because a shrug indicates resignation, a giving up of the power to choose, a crucial component that makes one human. Grange's behavior in his first life poisons Brownfield. Grange is an angry, frustrated, ignorant, and violent man. He terrorizes his family with his shotgun and is unfaithful to Margaret, his wife, with Josie, a prostitute. The behavior that Grange models for his son creates just the type of man that Brownfield becomes. August Wilson's words, nevertheless, are not void: the sins of the father do not have to become the lifestyle of the son. A range of possibilities is available—and one that both Wilson and Walker suggest is forgiveness.

Brownfield cannot forget nor forgive his father's actions when Grange deserts the family. As a fifteen-year-old, Brownfield probably is incapable of understanding what Grange is experiencing when he walks out. In Brownfield's mind, his father's inability to touch him means a lack of love and a total rejection of his only child. Brownfield pretended to be asleep, and saw his father hover over his face but stop short of touching him.[59] Brownfield concludes that his father does not love him because even in the dark, his father does not touch him. As an adolescent, Brownfield did not understand his father's behavior, but he might have understood Grange's pain when he experienced a similar situation on the day he was forced to put his little daughter, Daphne, in the cotton fields to put arsenic on the cotton. Sometimes it is easier to disengage from a loved one than to fully engage when one believes that he is powerless to feel anything but pain as a result. Brownfield's own effort to protect himself from the searing pain of having his children worked like slaves mirrors his father's. To his own daughters, Brownfield was not loving but accusing, calling them names, and his youngest daughter, "he never *touched*."[60]

As an adult in the same situation as his father had been in, Brownfield could have empathized with Grange but chooses not to. Grange hoped that Brownfield would understand and be forgiving. He says that he tried to make up for the mistakes he made, but Brownfield will not let him. Brownfield blames rather than forgives. Grange declares that Brownfield is weak, and his brains are made of noodles.[61] The inability to assume responsibility for personal behavior is fatal to the soul, and Grange's pertinent question about owning our own souls[62] raises the issue of individual accountability in the face of oppression. Grange does not deny the power of racism and oppression to destroy the human will; he admits his own failures, but the key word in his treatise on manhood is "let." Racism and oppression can destroy if allowed to. Grange tells his son to hold on to a place inside where racism and oppression cannot enter.[63] Brownfield ignores Grange's lesson that no matter how bad situations appear to be, choice always is possible.

As his name suggests, Grange Copeland chooses to cope with the southern land that he loves and isolate himself as completely as possible from white people, racism, and oppression. His son resents his success. In league with Josie, who leaves Grange and Ruth to live with Brownfield when he is released from prison after serving only seven years for murder, he plans trouble for Grange. Brownfield plots against his father and plans to use the law to force Grange to relinquish Ruth to him. He believes white law will disempower Grange.[64] Brownfield brings the white racist law into Grange's life when he sues for custody of Ruth. Walker makes clear that even in dire circumstances, there are alternatives. Viktor Frankl has said: "Everything can be taken from a man but one thing: the last of human freedoms—to choose one's attitude in any given set of circumstances, to choose one's own way."[65] Grange assumes the cloak of manhood by deciding to protect his granddaughter from the monster that he has created. He accepts responsibility for Brownfield when Brownfield cannot or will not accept responsibility for himself.

Grange recognizes that the numbing of emotions to protect oneself from pain is a defense mechanism that cuts two ways. He recalls that as a child, he was sensitive to the natural environment. He liked the feeling and wonders how those warm and wonderful feelings were eliminated.[66] The feelings Grange describes are considered feminine, but Grange recognizes them as fully human. Walker has been criticized for feminizing her male characters but, rather, she makes them more fully human. Grange observes that the hardening of the heart spoils the soul and makes forgiveness impossible.[67] Not only does racism spoil the soul, but the concept of manhood that denies the feminine principle does so as well.

In the final chapter of the novel, Grange faces several options. He wants Ruth to survive whole, and live life as a fully human person. He wants her to live each day as "past, present and future."[68] Grange is wise in his contemplation of Ruth's life. Her knowledge of the past will prevent her from making old mistakes, and her present, her gift of now, creates her future, even at the quantum level of life. Einstein and other physicists have shown that the universe is fluid; what we look for determines what we see. This new worldview posits that instead of victims, people create the experience of reality through the subtle power of observation. Grange can comply with the law and return Ruth to Brownfield, an unrepentant murderer; he can flee to some unknown territory, abandoning the safe place that he has created for Ruth; or he can defend her with his own life, which is what he decides to do.

Inside the so-called house of justice, Judge Harry gives Brownfield custody of Ruth, and she resigns herself to the ruling.[69] Grange, however, refuses the unjust decision of white law. Instead he kills his son, making a choice that he knows will free Ruth but will demand his own life in return. Grange decides to die, not in despair like Margaret or Mem, but for a cause greater than himself. His choice enables Ruth's future.

WOMEN IN THE NOVEL

The women in *The Third Life of Grange Copeland* are signifiers—signs of suffering and not full characters. Elliott Butler-Evans refers to the women characters as "the subordinate discourse"[70] in the novel. While race is central to the story, so are gender issues. The problems that both Grange and Brownfield endure are grounded equally in race and gender. Had father and son not accepted the sexist idea of manhood, they could have avoided condemnation of themselves as failures. Brownfield could have lovingly accepted the help that Mem provided without believing that she had usurped his manhood.

The women in the novel are equally guilty of believing in the corrupted idea of gender roles. Not only do they hold themselves responsible for enhancing the men's egos, they reject their own strength, and believe and strive to achieve the outdated white idea of feminine frailty, submissiveness, and dependence. The women pay with their lives for their choices. In the process of striving to be what they are not, the women lose the respect of their children. What emerges is a recurring character in Walker's canon—the unprotecting mother.

Margaret Copeland is a harrowing excuse for a mother. She takes her son to work and allows him to fall into piles of squirming bait. She then leaves him at home alone. Under different circumstances, Margaret would be charged with child neglect and abuse of her son because he was covered with sores on his head and his legs. He has pus-filled boils under his arms.[71] Margaret may not have had good choices, and whether she did is not clear within the context of the narrative. Perhaps factory work was not all that was available. Work alongside her husband in the cotton field might have enabled her to keep her baby with her, even strapped to her back, as did some women. Work in some white woman's kitchen might also have been available. Taking in laundry and staying home with her child might have been another alternative. Margaret chose none of these, however. From a narrative viewpoint, Walker does not offer these options, perhaps, to stress the severity of the situation. Her point is clear: poverty is life threatening, but so is an unprotective mother.

Margaret's suicide is further evidence that she thinks only of herself. When it becomes clear to her that Grange is not going to return, she thinks nothing of leaving Brownfield alone to fend for himself. Not only does he see her conciliation to Grange as dog-like behavior (he is ten years old when he notices her behavior), as a teenager Brownfield says what he could not forgive is that his parents behaved as if he did not exist.[72] Margaret neglects Star, the child that she has outside of her marriage to Grange. Her suicide and infanticide left Brownfield with a profound sense of abandonment. He blames Grange for his mother's drinking and promiscuity, but the choices she made were hers alone.

Josie's mother, a shadow figure in the novel, is another un-protecting mother who permits her husband to abuse their daughter. She is described as meek and unassuming, a woman who never stood up to her husband.[73] The unnamed mother condones her daughter's sexual abuse, and based on Josie's dreams, the worst abuser is her own father, the reverend, the man of God who cannot forgive his daughter for becoming pregnant and embarrassing him. In Josie's nightmares, this unnamed "He" rides her. The narrator indicates, however, that it is indeed her father who rides her. Josie cannot bring herself to name him, and claims that she cannot remember him.[74] At sixteen, pregnant and expelled from her father's house, Josie becomes a prostitute to survive. She makes the choice to turn tricks as surely as her father decides to turn her out of the home. The men of her father's church have had sexual relations with Josie, but none claim the child, which leads to the horror in the father's eyes.[75] A scene at the father's birthday party is highly symbolic of maternal powerlessness under patriarchal rule. At the party Josie plans for her father, to earn his forgiveness, she becomes intoxicated and falls. Her father refuses to allow anyone to pick her up. The mother stood outside the ringed pack of men standing over her daughter's pregnant body, and cried. She did not intercede. The mother's submissiveness leaves her daughter at the mercy of the pack of men and the cruel father.

Walker's description of Josie and her ugly daughter do not allow for the platitude of victim. Both Josie and Lorene are survivors. Lauret complains that both are examples of "overdetermined characterization."[76] She insists that Lorene is described as "some kind of monster who would not be out of place in a horror film."[77] Lorene's grotesqueness—with a mustache and beard, malevolent eyes, and lips of a snake—cause one to question Walker's motives for creating such a character. In a 1983 interview with Claudia Tate, Walker explains that the effects of racism, oppression, and abuse are ugly and create the grotesque. She believes that the psychic pain produced by negative experiences and behavior shows up in physical form.[78] Both mother and daughter whores therefore are misshapen by the lives they live.

The women in Walker's works are either ineffective mothers, or dead, or both. Mem's mother, Josie's sister, is caught in the same trap Josie had been in—pregnant and banished from her father's house. She gives birth to Mem and dies shortly thereafter. Mem's father, like her maternal grandfather, is a preacher, married with a family in the North. He abandons Mem's mother. Her death leaves Mem at the mercy of a prostitute—Aunt Josie.

Josie also is an unfit mother. She leaves her daughter Lorene unprotected from the customers in her house of prostitution and competes with her as though she were her peer. Mem escapes by staying out of her aunt's and her cousin's way, but also by attending school in Atlanta, for which her guilty father pays the tuition. Mem represents choice. Her name was selected because it represents all women; in French *la meme*[79] means "the same" and is a signifier of freedom and education possible for women who make correct choices. Josie says that Lorene also could have attended school, but she refused. Choice for Lorene, however, is not a simple matter. Lorene's dilemma is complex. She had two babies by the time she was of high school age.

Mem clearly makes the wrong choice when she passes up the teacher she dates and marries Brownfield. The marriage is not the single choice that leads to her destruction, but the start of the many that follow. She allows Brownfield to abuse her. Feeling embarrassed when he makes fun of her speech, she *chooses* to speak the way he does. Mem, and not Brownfield, burns her books. She chooses to remain with Brownfield even after she knows that he has murdered their albino son. Her single choice to remain with Brownfield and not to kill him prevents her from protecting her daughters. In an early draft, the children were not just daughters but a daughter and son.[80] Mem was Mandy and, prior to that, Sadye. John Henry becomes Ornette in later drafts. That Walker settles finally on only daughters is significant in demonstrating the degree to which mothers work in the service of patriarchy by socializing their daughters to serve men. More than any other mother in the novel, Mem makes the greatest effort on behalf of her children, but her efforts are not enough. Ultimately, she deserts them when she walks headlong into Brownfield's shotgun.

The novel ends with ambiguity. What will become of Ruth is unclear, although presumably her life will be a good one because of her grandfather's plans. In the manuscript collection, Ruth Copeland is a character in an early draft of *Meridian*. The early draft of *Meridian* provides insight into the maturing Ruth. She dreams about Brownfield and, in the dream, she loves him. In a letter she writes that the dreams are depressing because in them she feels guilty for not forgiving and loving a man who appears to be the "incarnation of cruelty."[81] The operative word in this passage is "seemed." Brownfield's behavior is a mask, not the reality of the good father, the essence of Spirit. Ruth feels guilty for her inability to see beyond the mask. The spiritual context of Ruth's maturation would have rendered *Meridian* quite a different book. In the final version, Walker eliminates Ruth to focus fully on the new character of Meridian.

While the ending of *The Third Life of Grange Copeland* is appropriate, the manuscript notes are more satisfying. In college Ruth participates in the civil rights movement, but she also goes to Africa to find Quincy Long, the civil rights worker who came to Grange's home with his pregnant wife and the white couple to register him to vote. Quincy's wife has a miscarriage from the beating she endures by a mob in Alabama. Ruth hears about it and learns that they are divorcing. She finds Quincy (a math teacher who sounds a lot like Bob Moses) in Blelki, but he does not remember her. A collection of letters exchanged between Ruth and her college friend Winsome reveals the details. Walker leaves Ruth behind in the pages of her manuscript notebook, whereas Celie, Shug, Fanny, Olivia, and Adam appear in more than one novel.

The Third Life of Grange Copeland is not a spectacular technical achievement. Hortense Spillers[82] has dubbed it an apprentice novel. Lauret believes that the novel does "not quite work in the realist terms that the text seems to set up for itself."[83] She claims that the novel is incoherent, with conflicting character portrayals. Rather than displaying conflicted portrayals, the characters appear conflicted, as they should be. More significant than form is the content. The novel not only is an indictment of the southern sharecropping system, capitalism, racism, sexism, and hypocritical religion, but also a sermon on individual choice and responsibility. Circumstances, genetics, environment, oppressive people, and conditions may control people; however, Walker shows that the truth is otherwise. Acknowledging personal power can prevent victimhood.

In an essay titled "How to Change Your Life," Donald Curtis writes: "We need not be victims of environment or circumstances. We can rise above them. We can be transformed by the renewing of our minds. When we fully realize this, we will do something about it."[84] *The Third Life of Grange Copeland* is a demonstration of faith over fear, success over failure, abundance over lack, and life over death. Written in 1966 when Walker was just twenty-two years old, the spiritual context of the novel reveals her, even at so young an age, to be a natural mystic.

NOTES

1. Maria Lauret, *Alice Walker* (New York: Palgrave Macmillan, 2000).
2. Oscar Lewis, *The Children of Sanchez: Autobiography of a Mexican Family* (New York: Random House, 1961).
3. Bill Moyers, "A Conversation with Alice Walker," June 24, 2004. https://billmoyers.com/content/a-conversation-with-alice-walker/.
4. Ibid.
5. Donna Haisty Winchell, *Alice Walker.* (New York: Twayne, 1992), 47.
6. Walker, *The Third Life of Grange Copeland,* 38.
7. Ibid., 39.
8. Ibid., frontmatter.
9. Constance Webb, *Richard Wright: A Biography* (New York: Putnam, 1968).
10. Ibid., 5.
11. Ibid.
12. Gerri Bates, *Alice Walker: A Critical Companion* (Westport, CT: Greenwood Press, 2005).

13. Ernest Holmes, *The Science of Mind* (New York: Tarcher/Putnam, 1998), 281.
14. Walker, *The Third Life*, 9.
15. Moyers, "A Conversation with Alice Walker."
16. Bates, *Alice Walker*.
17. Walker, *The Third Life*, 227.
18. Moyers, "A Conversation with Alice Walker."
19. Ibid.
20. Clarissa Pinkola Estes, *Women Who Run with the Wolves* (New York: Random House, 1992), 63.
21. Ibid., 64.
22. Holmes, 438 (italics in the original).
23. Ibid., 64.
24. M. Scott Peck, *People of the Lie* (New York: Touchstone, 1985), 39.
25. Ibid., 41.
26. Ibid., 42.
27. Moyers, "A Conversation with Alice Walker."
28. Walker, *The Third Life*, 207.
29. Peck, *People of the Lie*, 43.
30. Gerda Lerner, *The Creation of Patriarchy* (New York: Oxford, 1986), 239.
31. Ibid.
32. Ibid.
33. Barbara Christian, *Black Women Novelists: The Development of a Tradition, 1892–1976* (Westport, CT: Greenwood, 1980), 188.
34. Ibid., 61.
35. Walker, *The Third Life*, 93.
36. Ibid., 107.
37. Ibid., 148.
38. Ibid., 149.
39. Ibid., 150.
40. Ibid., 151.
41. Ibid., 152.
42. Ibid., 153.
43. Nikki Giovanni, *Collected Poems* (New York: William Morrow, 2003), 19–20.
44. Walker, *Third Life*, 107.
45. Ibid.,154.
46. Ibid., 155.
47. Alice Walker Archive, Stuart A. Rose Manuscript, Archives, and Rare Book Library, Emory University (MSS 1061, Box 35).
48. Ibid.
49. Ibid.
50. Ibid. (Box 37/folder 20).
51. Walker, *The Third Life*, 151.
52. Alice Walker Archive, Stuart A. Rose Manuscript, Archives, and Rare Book Library, Emory University (MSS 1061, Box 35).
53. Ibid.
54. Henry Louis Gates Jr., *The Signifying Monkey: A Theory of Afro-American Literary Criticism* (New York: Oxford University Press, 1988), xxviii.
55. August Wilson, *Fences* (New York: Plume, 1986).
56. Ibid., preface.
57. Anais Nin, *Memorable Quotations of French Writers of the Past*, ed. Carol A. Dingle (Lincoln, NE: iuniverse, 2000).
58. Walker, *The Third Life*, 15.
59. Ibid., 21.
60. Ibid., 74 (emphasis added).
61. Ibid., 206.
62. Ibid., 207.

63. Ibid., 209.
64. Ibid., 169.
65. Viktor Frankl, *Man's Search for Meaning* (Boston: Beacon, 1959), 66.
66. Walker, *The Third Life*, 211.
67. Ibid., 214.
68. Ibid., 272.
69. Ibid., 245.
70. Elliott Butler-Evans, "History and Genealogy in Walker's *The Third Life of Grange Copeland* and *Meridian*," in *Alice Walker: Critical Perspectives Past and Present*, eds. Henry Louis Gates and K. A. Appiah (New York: Amistad, 1993), 106.
71. Walker, *The Third Life*, 7.
72. Ibid., 20.
73. Ibid., 39.
74. Ibid., 38.
75. Ibid., 40.
76. Lauret, *Alice Walker*, 33.
77. Ibid.
78. Claudia Tate (ed.), *Black Women Writers at Work* (New York: Continuum, 1984), 175–87.
79. Walker, *The Third Life*, 344.
80. Alice Walker Archive, Stuart A. Rose Manuscript, Archives, and Rare Book Library, Emory University (MSS 1061, Box 35).
81. Ibid.
82. Hortense Spillers and Majorie Pryse, *Conjuring: Black Women, Fiction and Literary Tradition* (Bloomington: Indiana University Press, 1985), 34.
83. Lauret, *Alice Walker*, 28.
84. Donald Curtis, "How to Change Your Life," in *Your Thoughts Can Change Your Life* (New York: Warner Books, 1996), 153.

Chapter Three

What We Love, We Save

The heart has its reasons where of Reason knows nothing.
—Pascal

Love is mystical. Scientists have not adequately defined love, or why we fall in love and need to love to develop and to thrive. Some psychologists have written that love is irrational. In *A General Theory of Love*, Thomas Lewis and his fellow researchers acknowledge that science is beginning to unravel the meaning and various aspects of love, and admit that poets and mystics have been closer to revealing the mystery all along. The stories of Alice Walker examined in this chapter interrogate the emotional lives of black women and, in so doing, seek to understand the human heart. Lewis states that people who do not follow the "Laws of acceleration and momentum break bones, those who do not grasp the principles of love waste their lives and break their hearts."[1] Walker provides examples of hurtful relationships, thwarted dreams and ambitions, neglect and abuse. The core of her message, however, is that love is the way to truth.

In her introduction to *Letters of Love and Hope: The Story of the Cuban Five*, Walker focuses on familial love and devotion, and how neither slavery nor incarceration can subdue or destroy.[2] Love, the need for it and its mystery, constitutes the single thread that connects all of Walker's works and her to the mystics of all ages. Joel Goldsmith, author of *The Foundation of Mysticism*,[3] defines mysticism as a conscious union with God, what Walker might identify as a conscious union with the universe, a unification with Spirit, the manifest universe or Love.

When Walker wrote *Anything We Love Can Be Saved*, from which the title of this chapter comes, she was referring to a writer's activism—hers. Her collection of essays reveals a deep belief in love.[4] Her credo governs the works examined here. The idea of love is a conundrum, at least for some critics. For instance, Alice Hall Petry begins her essay on Walker's short stories by posing the question, "Why is *You Can't Keep a Good Woman Down* so consistently less satisfying than the earlier *In Love & Trouble?*"[5] while other critics simply ask about either book: Where is the love? Walker writes that she believes in the goodness of the earth and the Divinity in all people and in the animals, bugs, insects, snakes and the goodness of Nature.[6] Nevertheless, she says that evil for her is a great disappointment, but that she has learned that every act carries the risk of disappointment, disillusion, and even despair. The stories and poems analyzed here run the gamut from disappointment to despair. The ultimate issue is that, with the power of love, all can be saved from destruction. Her stories and poems do not suggest that love is easy. Often it is excruciatingly difficult and, ironically for too many black women, acts of self-love appear impossible.

IN LOVE & TROUBLE

In this chapter I employ Organic Inquiry as a method for discussing Walker's two short story collections and poetry. Organic Inquiry is a research method developed in 1998 by transpersonal psychologists Jennifer Clements, Dorothy Ettling, Dianne Jenett, and Lisa Shields. A blend of research and spiritual inquiry, it values the researcher's own story. The psyche of the researcher acknowledges liminal and spiritual influences. Of this method Clements writes, "Organic Inquiry invites transformative change, which includes not only information, but also a transformation that consists of both changes of mind and changes of heart."[7] Organic Inquiry promotes the flow of intuition and synchronicity, which I experienced while working on this chapter. I was invited to give a poetry reading on Sapelo Island, one of the Georgia Golden Isles. I had mixed feelings about accepting the invitation. On the one hand, I welcomed the opportunity to promote my books, but on the other hand, I did not want to take time away from my writing. Agreeing to go, I stopped work on "Roselily" and packed my bags for a weekend away from writing. I thought it interesting that the place where I was to stay was owned by Cornelia Walker. While it turned out she was not related to Alice Walker, she told me that they claimed to be cousins but had yet to find the family link. Alice Walker had recently spent time at the place where I stayed. This guesthouse had a long hallway with a shelf filled with books, mostly *Reader's Digest Condensed Books*. My grandmother had been an avid collector of these hardback books, and the sight brought a flood of memories. As I scanned the shelves, my hand reached for the autumn 1962 *Digest* that contained the abridged version of *Dearly Beloved* by Anne Morrow Lindbergh. The title is the opening line in Walker's story, "Roselily."

There are striking parallels and, as far as I know, the novel was never banned, as was Walker's short story. The wedding in Lindberg's story takes place in a house, not on a porch, and it reveals the thoughts of those in attendance. Lindberg critiques marriage "a step toward death; a pace to eternity."[8] The women in Lindberg's story are white and upper middle class. Walker writes the missing part, adding a black unwed mother enmeshed in poverty. Walker's southern porch wedding is like Lindbergh's in form, utilizing the marriage vows throughout as statements set off from the text, retaining the narrative pattern while transforming the content. The white wedding takes place in "a rose-cold season."[9] Walker signifies on "rose-cold" with the name she selects for her character. Roselily is not privileged like the young bride, Sally, in *Dearly Beloved*; nevertheless, they face a similar question: What will married life be like? For Roselily, it does not promise freedom, just a respectable oppression, standing behind her husband who looks straight ahead.[10] For Walker, marriage in general does not represent freedom but entrapment. The very words used to describe the wedding are fraught with negative implications; wedlock suggests lock down or lock up, and marriage, mirage or a marring or mangling of the self.

Roselily represents the first of Walker's women in the collection of stories to juxtapose love, the positive emotion and/or behavior, with trouble, the negative emotion, concern, problem, or danger. Walker's title does not posit either/or but both/and. Therefore, one can conclude that love is trouble. *In Love & Trouble*'s subtitle, *Stories of Black Women*, states the criteria by which to perceive how being in love is trouble.

Roselily for a variety of reasons wants to be married; love does not appear to be one of them, however. She thinks of herself as a cornered rat, trapped in poverty and alone.[11] Marriage to the Black Muslim man from Chicago with the shiny car might bring freedom, but his religion that requires her to cover her head and to sit apart from him in service might present just another kind of entrapment. Roselily, like the cast of women in the thirteen stories included in Walker's first collection, is not the strong black woman stereotype. Her vulnerability shows. She is not the mythical black mother. She gives one child away to his father, and her other three children are without the benefit or presence of a father. She is their sole support, is tired, and desires to be cared for. She is not a black churchwoman, as many theologians seem to assume that black women are.[12] Roselily visualizes "God, a small black boy, timidly pulling the preacher's coattail,"[13] and near the end of the story, she sees the preacher as odious and wants to smack him out of her way. She does not believe he is a man of God, although tradition has taught her to do so, as well as to "force humility into her eyes."[14]

Psychologists have not defined exactly what love is or what people mean when they use the term. Within a theological context, *agape*-love is defined as wholly selfless, spiritual, and Divine, that is, the love of God. Psychology professor Robert Sternberg provides a useful definition and triangular theory of love that includes intimacy, passion, and decision/commitment. Intimacy includes feelings of closeness and connectedness that one experiences in a loving relationship. Passion includes romance, sexual attraction, and consummation. The most intriguing component is decision, deciding that one loves another, and the commitment to maintain that love.[15] None of Walker's stories represent successful triangular love.

Walker scrutinizes black love in these thirteen stories. In a 1993 essay, "Phallus(ies) of Interpretation: Toward R=Engendering the Black Critical 'I,'" literary scholar and critic Ann duCille quotes song lyrics: "Love, Oh, love, Oh careless love." She observes that everybody knows the song, but "the only problem is that the story almost everybody knows is almost totally false."[16] The truth set forth by mainly black male writers of fiction and nonfiction is that gender relations are fine. DuCille quotes historian Lerone Bennett who wrote that "Black men and women—despite slavery, despite segregation, despite everything—created a modern love song in life and art that is the loveliest thing dreamed or sung this side of the seas."[17] His comments, made in 1981, challenge Walker's portrayal of love in *In Love & Trouble*. Bennett's statement is appealing because it is positive, but it denies sexism and violence experienced by black women at the hands of black men. Whitewashing black love might be advantageous to black men, as duCille posits, but "for women the costs of sustaining such myths are continued harassment, brutalization, insanity, suicide, or even death."[18] Walker's stories present a truth about love that is seldom recognized by black male writers.

Walker anchors her texts with lengthy quotations that center and direct the reader to the core issues in the stories. The first epigraph is from Elechi Amadi's novel *The Concubine*. Too lengthy to quote here, the gist is this: Ahurole is a young girl under the influence of an *agwu*, her personal spirit. Her parents try to nullify or at least control this contrary spirit, which in the West might be identified as her ego or individuality. Such an individual spirit is problematic in a society where communalism is paramount, and where individual choice is not freely given, especially to women. The final sentence of the quotation reveals that Ahurole is promised in marriage to a man when she is only eight days old.[19] Thus, love and trouble are at the heart of Amadi's novel, as it is in Walker's collection.

The second epigraph included in *In Love & Trouble* comes from Rainer Maria Rilke's *Letters to a Young Poet*. In the excerpt that Walker chose, convention is condemned as an enabler for people choosing to take the path of least resistance. Rilke insists that "we must hold to what is difficult; everything in Nature grows and defends itself in its own way and is characteristically and spontaneously itself, seeks at all costs to be so against all opposition"[20] (frontmatter). Clearly this epigraph supports the first, as Ahurole's spirit encourages her to resist all opposition. Unfortunately, most of the women in Walker's collection of stories do not have the courage to be themselves or pay dearly for it when they do insist on following their own spirit.

The problem with most of the women characters in Walker's stories is not, as some critics surmise, their love and loyalty to black men, but rather their lack of love and loyalty to themselves. Walker has written that the women in her stories run the gamut from angry, strong, hateful, loving, and physically attractive to grotesque.[21] When they commit to black men instead of themselves, it leads them to dead ends with few options. The ultimate issue for women and for men in the stories is choice. As a college student, Walker was not only influenced by Camus' and Nietzsche's thoughts regarding suicide; she apparently accepted many of their existentialist ideas about personal responsibility. Roselily chooses to marry a Muslim man. While some might argue that her life will be better off in Chicago than in Panther Burn, Mississippi, the issue is whether she is jumping from the frying pan into the fire.

Walker, a great admirer of the works of Zora Neale Hurston and Jean Toomer, dedicates *In Love & Trouble* to both and also to Nella Larsen. She calls them the three mysteries. Hurston's and Toomer's fingerprints are in another story from the collection. In "Really, Doesn't Crime Pay?" Mordecai Rich could well be a trope for Toomer—an itinerant writer recording his impressions of the South and the people in it.[22] Mordecai, like Toomer, was both sensitive to and condescending toward women. He is responsive to Myrna in ways that her husband is not, but he also patronizes her when, after reading her story, he asks if she thinks about serious ideas.[23] When Mordecai questions Myrna's marriage to an old man,[24] Hurston's Joe Starks comes to mind. If this is not enough to signify the presence of Hurston, a few lines later we are informed that, like Joe Starks, Ruel works in a store and owns acres of peanuts. Joe owned 200 acres. The parallels continue in that Joe has also chosen Janie because of her physical appearance, just as Ruel has married Myrna for hers.

Myrna wants to be a writer but does not have the courage to openly defy her husband, who forbids her from becoming one. Recognizing her own fault, she says that cowardice has stopped her writing and that she has the heart of an odalisque.[25] She is a coward, but she is not stupid. From the beginning she knows intuitively that Mordecai Rich is unscrupulous.[26] She perceives his smile is deceiving, and describes him as cold-blooded and untrustworthy. Still she allows him to seduce her, and he steals her work, publishing it under his name. Here the Toomer parallel is clear. In "The Divided Life of Jean Toomer," Walker says that Jean Toomer used black people to write *Cane*, then cut his connections by passing as white.[27] Mordecai is an opportunist, and Walker says that some might take Toomer as a racial opportunist.

The story that Mordecai plagiarizes, "The One-Legged Woman," is reminiscent of Flannery O'Connor's short story, "Good Country People." Myrna, Walker's character in "Really, Doesn't Crime Pay?" has written a story set on a dairy farm, as in O'Connor's "The Displaced Person." Myrna's lover steals her intellectual property, whereas in O'Connor's story, Hulga's leg is taken by Manley Pointer after he seduces her in the hay loft. Unlike O'Connor, Walker is not concerned with the Christian conundrum of good and evil; rather, she illustrates the problem of self-sacrifice. The wife in Myrna's story has sacrificed her leg to protect her husband's ego. Without her leg he is no longer physically attracted to her. The husband's rejection makes it clear to the wife that her sacrifice was useless.[28] She goes to the barn and commits suicide.

Instead of committing an act of violence against herself, Myrna tries to behead her husband, Ruel. He awakens in time to save himself and blames Mordecai Rich for his wife's bizarre behavior. She blames her husband instead of assuming responsibility for her own unhappiness. Her passive-aggressive behavior mirrors the adage of cutting off her nose to spite her face. Her choice to be false to herself and to others comes back in the same energy that her choice sets in motion when she marries Ruel, accepts the role of wife that he expects, or pretends to accept it, and becomes intimate with a vagabond. She is false to her husband, spends his money, benefits from whatever security the marriage provides, and endures his lovemaking; she is little more than a prostitute. No love in this story. Regarding her relationship with Mordecai, Myrna admits love had nothing to do with it.[29] The end of the story foreshadows the opening of *Meridian*. Myrna describes herself being "like a drowned body washed to shore,"[30] which conjures Marilene O'Shay, murdered for cuckolding her husband and whom he turns into a prostitute by placing her dead body on display and charging people to view it. The title of the story, "Really, Doesn't Crime Pay?" applies to the husband who kills his wife as well as to the crime of theft that Mordecai Rich commits.

"Her Sweet Jerome," a story first titled "Trust," is a fascinating play on the grotesque and demonstrates how without love, nothing can be saved, and even revolutions will fail. The husbands in the first two stories are limited by the culture in which they live. While they are responsible for their own limited and sexist visions, Walker does not blame them for their wives' shortcomings. They are not physically abusive and at least one, Ruel, tries to do what he thinks will make his wife happy. Both men are sexist and believe that the women will be satisfied with having and taking care of children, but they do not appear as villains. They are egocentric, insensitive, and basically clueless as to the creative and intellectual needs of their wives. Conversely, Jerome Franklin Washington III is another matter. He is a wife-beater, arrogant and cruel. His name represents the opposite of who he appears to be. Jerome is a Greek name, meaning sacred. A saint and a scholar, St. Jerome prepared from Latin a standard text of the Bible. Jerome Washington is a schoolteacher turned revolutionary. The woman in this story remains nameless except for assuming her husband's name, first and last. She is a hairdresser and has money. She buys Jerome, just as Ruel bought Myrna. Both Jerome and Myrna allow themselves to be purchased, and then respond with cruelty and violence toward their spouses.

Literary scholar Donna Winchell calls Mrs. Jerome Franklin Washington tragic.[31] On the contrary, she is grotesque. The narrator says that falling in love with a teacher is the beginning of her troubles.[32] However, her troubles began long before she ever fell in love. She is unloved. Her mother is not mentioned, but her father disinherits her for no apparent reason except perhaps her sex. He is excited to have a son-in-law. Her concept of love, like those of the men in the previous stories, is one of ownership. On first seeing Jerome, she thinks that if he were hers, she would buy him a car, and she does. Her behavior, however, is not what makes her grotesque. Walker describes her as a woman with big bones who is decidedly unattractive.[33] Before writing that, she had ham hands in a draft Walker wrote: "her short wrists ended in wrinkled and grooved miniature car tires"![34] A roll of fat sits on the woman's neck, and her skin is described as rough.[35]

The woman's physical appearance can only indicate the state of her consciousness, except that she at first appears to be unaware of herself, then in complete denial. Her lack of self-awareness is evident when the narrator states that she could not decide if she was lovelier than the other women in town. By the time she had cooked breakfast, she had convinced herself that she was.[36] Her self-delusion is clear when her husband ridicules her, and she pretends he compliments her. The woman is so utterly repulsive, so ignorant—telling her clients that she does not miss her "eddicashion"[37] because she has money—and because she chooses to accept the physical abuse from Jerome, she is not a sympathetic character. Perhaps Walker is playing an O'Connor joke on the reader, forcing the reader to judge Mrs. Washington in the same way that her husband judges her, being repulsed as he is repulsed, and guilty as he is guilty. Walker may be warning, avoid judging by external appearances.

Mrs. Washington suspects her husband of cheating, and it drives her insane. Her rival turns out to be a combination of black books, revolutionary meetings, and the black is beautiful rhetoric and changing aesthetic. She is all wrong for the new world order, but Walker has made her so repulsive that she is even wrong for the old aesthetic. The most significant point of this story is the hypocrisy of the intellectual revolutionaries and their inability to relate to ordinary folk, or even to folk like Mrs. Washington. Her looks should not matter. The choices she makes, however, create her situation and lead to her physical demise, when she burns up her husband's books and herself in the process.

"Everyday Use" is the most popular story in *In Love & Trouble*. On first reading it, I had thoroughly mixed emotions. Having come of age during the late 1960s and early 1970s, I was enamored of Africa, changed my name that came from my deceased grandfather to an African name, dressed in traditional African attire (still do), and cut my flipped hair and wore it natural. While a student at Howard University in 1975, I pierced four holes in my ears and put a ring in my nose. In a seminar with Professor Leon Damas (one of the founders of Negritude), I was shocked when he said my nose ring was unbecoming and asked me why I wanted to look like an African. He conducted class in a three-piece suit.[38] To this day I wear multiple earrings and my nose piece.

Reviewing the literature on "Everyday Use," I felt at odds with what most critics were saying. They judged Dee Johnson's name change to Wangero Leewanika Kemanjo as faddish and superficial. In most of the critical essays, Dee is the villain, which is a misreading of Walker's most popular story. One essay concurs with my reading of the text. In "Fight vs. Flight: a re-evaluation of Dee in Alice Walker's 'Everyday Use,'" Susan Farrell writes: "While Dee is certainly insensitive and selfish to a certain degree, she nevertheless offers a view of heritage and strategy for contemporary African Americans to cope with an oppressive society that is, in some ways, more valid than that offered by Mama and Maggie."[39] The image of Dee/Wangero filtered through the mind of her mother, the narrator, is unappealing, but Walker gives more substance and determination to Wangero than she is given credit for in the story.

The voice and the viewpoint from which the story is told is suspect. The mother's narrative is neither omniscient nor infallible. In fact, she is incorrect about Maggie and cannot possibly know what Maggie thinks, such as when she says Maggie thought the world never said no to her sister.[40] Wangero apparently never accepted what the world had to say to her, and good that she did not, otherwise her education and upward mobility would have been doomed. The world indeed has said no to her: no, she is not supposed to succeed; no, she is not beautiful; no, she is not intelligent. The world has said that her heritage is one of poverty and enslavement, and the way most critics read the story, in order to be true to her heritage, she must remain that way. David Cowart, in "Heritage and Deracination in Walker's 'Everyday Use,'" states that "Chief among the little gestures that collectively add up to a profound betrayal is the changing of her name."[41] Cowart points out that Mrs. Johnson could trace the name "back beyond the Civil War,"[42] in other words back to slavery, which is precisely the reason for the name change. Cowart appears to assume that Wangero is American (whatever that is) without any other cultural connections and no sense of history beyond slavery. Of her hairstyle and dress, he writes: "She now styles and dresses herself according to the dictates of a faddish Africanism and thereby demonstrates a cultural catch-22: an American who attempts to become an African succeeds only in becoming a phony."[43] In the first place, the power to name oneself is a central aspect of self-determination, and clearly Wangero is a self-determining individual bent on reinventing herself, which is her prerogative. Second, she is not insensitive to her mother when she announces her new name. She tells her mother not to call her by her new name if she does not want to.

Critics of the black aesthetic movement were never quite able to grasp the significance of African heritage to African Americans, pointing out that many of the names were not authentic, that even Africans on the continent did not wear traditional dress, and that the Afro was inauthentic. Literature professor Michael Cooke noted that the Afro was banned in Tanzania,[44] as if that made any difference. African American people were aware of the damage to the African psyche that colonialism had perpetrated. What they might not have been prepared for, as I was not prepared for the criticism from a veteran Negritude poet, was the rejection from African nationalists and socialists who saw the efforts of African Americans to embrace a black identity as arrogant, imperialist, and capitalistic. The reason it did not matter whether Africans embraced the Afro hairstyle is that, regardless of what anyone said, when a person of African descent refused to alter the texture of her natural hair, this by nature is African, and people wearing their hair natural knew this. Another issue that seemed irrelevant coming from American whites and conservative blacks was the charge that African hair and dress were not genuine, without ever challenging the authenticity of black people donning European hair and fashion.

The unresolved conflict in this story is not what today would be the embrace of Afrocentric culture, but rather the daughter's inability to simultaneously embrace and reject a culture that is rich and sustaining but also debilitating and limiting. People who have never endured dire poverty have the tendency to romanticize it. What is "nurturing" (Cowart's word) about a three-room shack with a tin roof in the middle of a pasture, with no real windows and rawhide holding up the shutters, may be the desire to escape. The mother thinks that Wangero will want to tear it down, but again she is incorrect. She misjudges this daughter because the daughter has changed. Dee would have wanted to destroy the house, but Dee is dead. Wangero has undergone a cultural rebirth. The problem is that most read her transformation as insincere. We have no way of judging, other than by taking the mother's word.

The mother complains that Dee often read to them about lifestyles different from their own.[45] Winchell sees this act as Wangero trying to force knowledge on her sister and mother that they "probably do not need."[46] Knowledge is never useless. Winchell further states that "Mrs. Johnson can take an objective look at who and what she is and find not disillusionment but an easy satisfaction. Simple pleasures—a dip of snuff, a cooling breeze across a clean swept yard, church songs, the soothing movement of milk cows—are enough."[47] Somehow, in the United States, the land of opportunity, this "ignorance is bliss, 'tis folly to be wise" idea rings untrue. Neither is it supported by the text. When the mother thinks of Maggie's marriage, she thinks she will be alone and just sing church songs to herself.[48] She admits that she is not even a good singer. Her statement does not sound like a future to which she is looking forward. The other indications that her poverty is not an easy satisfaction include her turning her back on the shack[49] and taking exception to a letter from Wangero suggesting that her mother and sister chose to live there.[50] The mother emphasizes the word choose. Apparently the circumstances, she believes, are not of her choosing, but in Walker's existential dialectic, choice matters greatly. In this letter from Dee/Wangero, another statement indicates her change: she has grown in an awareness and appreciation of home. Earlier in a letter she says she will never bring her friends home. Her arrival with a friend indicates that she has moved beyond her previous feelings.

Dee/Wangero's attempt to educate her mother and sister could be compared to Nettie trying to teach Celie to read and, therefore, can be viewed positively, as Farrell points out.[51] The coupling of this story with the poem "For My Sister Molly Who in the Fifties" provides more support for reading Dee/Wangero's effort as positive. The difference between the poem and the story is that in the poem, Molly's efforts are not resented. The poem's narrator appreciates learning about Hamlet and songs from Africa. The poem ends with regret because the sister left them.[52] There is no resentment, just a sense of loss.

The extent to which Wangero is alienated from her culture is not as clear as critics have stated. In "Patches: Quilts and Community in Alice Walker's 'Everyday Use,'" Houston Baker and Charlotte Pierce-Baker characterize Dee/Wangero as a "sellout to fashion and fantasy in a television-manipulated world of 'artistic' frames."[53] Mrs. Johnson—but not her daughter—is manipulated by television. The mother dreams of shows she has seen and imagines herself on the *Johnny Carson Show*.[54] She thinks her daughter would want her to be slim, "with lighter skin and straight hair."[55] But she is incorrect in what she imagines. Wangero has embraced nappy hair, evidenced by her own Afro. There is no evidence in the text to compel us to conclude that Wangero is insincere. The Black is Beautiful aesthetic that affects Wangero's choices makes concern about her mother's complexion highly unlikely. Mrs. Johnson is the one still stuck in the Negro aesthetic, saying that Dee is light with "*nicer hair*."[56] Her comment about Wangero's hair is before she sees the Afro. Clearly the mother feels unappreciated, but when Wangero arrives, the daughter's critical eye that the mother warns about, has turned artistic. She can now see quaintness in the pastoral setting. But even her photographs are suspect. Winchell believes that Wangero takes the photographs based on a "desire to show off the primitive lifestyle of those whose name she rejects."[57] Critics appear more concerned with the African name than does the mother, who makes a good faith effort to accept it. Some have argued that the name is not authentically African but invented; whatever it is, it is not a slave name. Most critics fail to use the name and continue to use Dee. Naming is defining, and they appear unable to relinquish their power to name—a situation that mirrors the power struggle that ensued in making Kunta Kinte into Toby, except in this instance the tables are reversed.

The Bakers call Wangero "'unconventionally' black"[58] without defining what is typically or traditionally black. Surely it is not poverty and ignorance. Sam Whitsitt's essay, "In Spite of It All: A Reading of Alice Walker's 'Everyday Use,'" is a perceptive analysis that looks at Walker's poem, "The Girl Who Died #2," and compares the judgment and identity politics that cause her despair and lead to her suicide to the way the Bakers condemn Wangero. Whitsitt concludes: "Walker has little sympathy for identity politics whose logic turns the contrary and the wayward into traitors."[59] He continues by stating that "Walker calls her [Wangero] an 'autonomous person,' and she tells us that she, like Dee, has an 'African name . . . and I love it and use it when I want to . . . it's part of me."[60] Whitsitt mistakenly claims that Wangero's name is the same as Walker's. It is not. Walker's African name is Wangari, authentically Kikuyu.[61]

Whitsitt argues compellingly that the mother experiences an epiphany when she decides to take the quilts from Wangero and place them in Maggie's lap. From the beginning of the story, the mother clearly admires Wangero. She likes her style, her bright-colored dress that the daughter has designed and sewed herself, contrary to those who read Wangero's style as inauthentic. The mother also likes the fact that Wangero can go eye to eye with anybody, black or white, especially white. She even prefers Wangero's lighter complexion and nicer grade of hair. The mother's description of Maggie is revealing. She compares her to a "lame animal, perhaps a dog run over by some careless person,"[62] and later the mother says that Maggie's face has "a kind of dopey, hangdog look,"[63] twice comparing her to a dog. Even more significant than her descriptions of Maggie is her embrace. She had never before hugged her daughter![64] When the mother says that she once thought that Wangero hated Maggie, she may have projected her own conflicted emotions. There is nothing to indicate that Wangero hated her sister. That she hated the house that burned down is apparent. Her intense look as she watched it burn says as much.[65]

Mrs. Johnson experiences a change that comes over her like the Holy Spirit when she is in church, gets happy and shouts, causing her to value Maggie in a new way. Wangero also experiences a cultural awakening that is not false. She overcomes the shame that their poverty inspired. She brings home a friend and has a new appreciation for the items she once disdained. She is just the opposite of what the mother has anticipated. Wangero sees, perhaps for the first time, that she has a heritage other than poverty. She has come seeking her inheritance, which she needs in a way that Maggie does not. Precisely because Maggie knows how to quilt and can make more quilts, and can remember the folk without any mnemonic devices, Wangero asks for and needs the old quilts. When she says old, she is not using the term disparagingly but as one would say of antiques or heirlooms. The conundrum here is that an heirloom loses its value when it is used up. It cannot be passed from one generation to the next. Wanting to preserve the quilts by hanging them does not traduce her heritage, as Cowart argues. Wangero is not incorrect when she says that Maggie and her mother fail to understand. The mother believes that Wangero looks at her with hatred, but the mother's interpretation is untrustworthy. Wangero says they just do not understand. New quilts will not suffice. The quilt pieces from people who are dead, such as from old dresses, a tiny piece from a Civil War uniform worn by Grandpa Ezra, once used up, can never be replaced. Maggie can make more quilts, but they will not be the same. The difference between everyday use and art may hinge on the issue of what can be reproduced versus the irreplaceable.

While she is disappointed by her mother's refusal to give her the quilts, Wangero does not appear to be angry. She kisses her sister and urges her to take advantage of the progress that black people have made. Her statement that they do not understand their heritage, while sounding condescending, is not false. Black heritage is vast, extending far beyond the Civil War back to Africa. Maggie and Mama may know their culture (black and southern), but their heritage is beyond that culture. Culture is what one does, how one lives, what one eats, how one talks, sings, dances. Heritage, on the other hand, can be thought of as what one has, what tangible thing one inherits, as an heirloom to be treasured. Black hair is heritage: kinks inherited from generation to generation, or a drum, Benin art, or an Ashanti stool, artifacts.

Walker has commented on the three characters, Mama, Wangero, and Maggie. She "really see[s] that story as almost about one person, the old woman and two daughters being one. The one who stays and sustains—this is the older woman—who has on the one hand a daughter who is the same way, who stays and abides and loves, plus the part of them—this autonomous person, the part of them that also wants to go out into the world to see change and be changed."[66] Walker's comments bring us back to the metaphysical concept of unity and her effort to tell all parts of a story.[67] Her statement also points to the need to love all parts of the self.

The story "Strong Horse Tea" demonstrates how the absence of love results in the destruction of so much human potential. The mother in the narrative wants a white doctor from town to treat her infant son, who is dying from double pneumonia and whooping cough. She rejects the help of Aunt Sarah's folk remedies, which she calls "nigger magic."[68] Desperate, the mother asks the white postman to send the doctor; instead he delivers the message to black Aunt Sarah.

The story pays homage to Jean Toomer and might allude to Toomer's effort to capture the strong horse tea of black southern culture. Rannie Toomer, the central character, is another of Walker's grotesque women, described as having a hanging bottom lip.[69] She is unmarried and unattractive. The baby is all that she possesses. One might wonder how the story would have differed had she been pretty. For one thing, instead of the postman wanting to be rid of her, he might have tried to seduce her. Her life would have been different in terms of the attention men would have paid to her. In a patriarchal society to be female is a handicap, to be black and female is a double bind, but to be female, black, and ugly "is the rust on the razor that threatens the throat."[70]

Scholar and folklorist Trudier Harris recognizes feminist politics in the folk culture in Walker's story, but argues that Walker draws Rannie Toomer in a way that "show(s) the futility of her position as a lone female, with a child, in the middle of nowhere. Walker *imposes* feminist politics upon folk culture and makes it one of the villains . . . a monster used to degrade Rannie."[71] On the contrary, it is not folk culture that Walker denounces, but poverty, capitalism, and patriarchy. These are issues that Walker does not impose because they are intrinsic to the lived experience of a single, impoverished, black mother in the southern United States at a point in time. In an interview, Walker says that a Rannie Toomer might no longer be found in the American South, but somewhere in the world—perhaps in Africa or in India—she is alive and suffering.[72] Walker does not indict folk culture; she condemns sexism, racism, and economic systems of commercialism that advertise to people like Rannie, who have no money to purchase goods, trapping her on the outside looking in on a culture that cares nothing about whether she or her baby son lives or dies. In her naiveté, Rannie believes that the white doctor will come to save her baby.[73] The white doctor does not come, and her baby dies from lack of medical care.

The pastoral setting of this story—Rannie and her son live in the middle of a cow's pasture—is significant. Critic Deborah Anne Hooker believes that Walker's "compassion for the earth"[74] is first evident in this story, but I suspect Walker's worldview has always been ecocritical, before there was even a name for it. Clearly illustrated in her poetry collection, *Once*, written when she was still an undergraduate, is a paean to southern landscapes. In "South: The Name of Home," Walker writes of her love of trees. In another poem, magnolia is intoxicating.[75] In notes from her manuscript collection, dated 1965, she has written "my love of music is like my love of trees, complete, natural and worshipful."[76] Walker's love for the southern landscape as well as for the earth and the universe in general is clear. What is not clear is the meaning of this short story.

Hooker refers to the ambiguity in the story, and links Rannie's rejection of Aunt Sarah and her folk remedies to the influence of the advertisement circulars the mailman gives to her. While the circulars represent the capitalist, materialist world beyond her reach, they may not inform Rannie about the advances in Western medicine. I say Western instead of white as many critics have chosen to do, because white erases the contributions of blacks and other people of color who have made significant contributions to Western medicine. To say white also obliterates the significant folk medicine tradition among whites. Therefore, the difference is not necessarily between black culture and white, but between the haves and the have-nots. Somehow Rannie has learned about medicine that is more exact and provides more reliable results than that which is offered by Aunt Sarah. Rannie wants this medicine for her baby.[77] The story raises the question of the meaning of folk culture: Are we to believe "a sugar tit soaked in cat's blood?"[78] constitutes the pharmacopeia of black folk medicine? Walker could have easily selected some actual remedies for pneumonia and whooping cough. Harris points out that neither Newbell Niles Puckett's nor Daniel and Lucy Thomas's works on superstitions refer to mare urine as a cure for anything.

Aunt Sarah might have suggested some actual cures for Rannie's baby. Modern medicine is based on the use of many flowers and herbs, of which Walker is aware. A book given to me by my grandmother contained several remedies for whooping cough that include red clover blossoms boiled, strained, and mixed with sugar, sunflower tea, and chestnut leaves tea with sweet oil. There was no mention of cat blood or urine. Sassafras, which Aunt Sarah does mention, is a medicinal for stomach ailments. Arrowroot, also mentioned, can be used to treat fungal infections.

My grandmother, who lived from 1905 to 2004, had an interesting relationship with folk medicine. One of twelve children, all but four died of childhood diseases that she often said could have been cured or prevented had her parents been able to afford something other than folk medicine. Nevertheless, sometimes the folk medicine worked. My grandmother had scarlet fever, diphtheria, whooping cough, and mumps. They used what was at hand, and it worked for her. She never forgot, however, that those same diseases killed her eight siblings. Their deaths motivated her to encourage her only child, my mother, to become a registered nurse. Ironically, while my grandmother was cautious of folk medicine, she respected it, but my mother completely rejected it as sheer quackery, a conundrum that Walker presents in the story of Rannie Toomer. Walker points out that faith must only be placed in those who would respond.[79] A difficult choice is to know of the existence of something better for your child and simultaneously accept what is available, when what is available is not what is best.

When Rannie realizes the white doctor is not coming and allows Aunt Sarah to examine Snooks, Sarah informs her that only strong horse tea (mare urine) will save him. Rannie's effort to collect the tea in the brutal thunder storm adds to the absurdity of the situation, especially since the child dies while she is running behind the mare trying to catch the urine in her plastic shoe that has a hole that she must stop up with her mouth. Aunt Sarah identifies herself as the doctor.[80] Aunt Sarah is not even clean; her clothes are heavily stained.[81] That she is dirty could indicate that she plays a nasty trick on Rannie.

The ambiguity in Walker's stories stems not from her feminist bias, as Harris suggests, but from her own ambivalent relationship with poverty. No wonder she is conflicted, given that her father died at the age of sixty-three from complications of emphysema, diabetes, and pneumonia and that she herself lost the sight in her right eye because her family was too poor to go for a doctor. Folk culture is not the villain or "a monster used to degrade Rannie";[82] rather, it is the society in which a mother is forced to view what is available without having access to it. The real monster is a society without love for all people. Rannie's choice is almost no choice at all. If choice means the ability to accept or reject a variety of possibilities, her possibilities are severely limited. Walker's story demonstrates how, in certain situations, choice becomes the absurd.

"The Diary of an African Nun" is the best example from *In Love & Trouble* to reveal what critic Hedda Ben-Bassat calls Walker's rebellious metaphysics.[83] In a few short pages, Walker condemns the ascetic self-denial of the Christian order by pointing to the life-affirming pagan tradition symbolized in the dance, "the oldest dance" of copulation, "the dance of life" that "breaks finally to the acclaiming cries of babies."[84] Ben-Bassat understands Walker's metaphysics to challenge not just Christian, but also pagan, ideas. She writes: "Paganism as an official institutional system is no more viable a faith for Walker than it was for the Gnostics, who abused Homer as freely as they did Moses."[85] She is correct in noting that an official institutional system does not make for a viable faith. She is, however, incorrect in stating that "Walker abuses African paganism just as freely as she does Christian sacramentalism."[86] Her statement is not supported by the text.

In what begins as a highly intuitive analysis of Walker's work, Ben-Bassat ends with a glaring misreading of "The Diary of an African Nun." The mistake occurs on two levels. In Ben-Bassat's reading of the story she states: "After participating in a Christian ritual and the pagan dance, [the nun] learns that people are just as imitative in either frame."[87] The nun does not participate in the dance; she simply recalls it and, in doing so, highlights the Manichaean dualism of the black/white and Christian/pagan symbolism. In part three of her diary entry, the nun clearly writes that she goes to bed at seven but can hear "the drums, smell the roasting goat's meat."[88] The people only become imitative after, and then only if she is successful in converting them from their pagan ways. The nun worries about her role as the white man's wedge, the one Tashi applies to Olivia and her missionary family come to save the Olinka in *Possessing the Secret of Joy*.[89] The nun is clear about her role and writes: "I must be among the lying ones and teach them how to die."[90]

In this story, Walker castigates colonial and imperialist invasions of indigenous culture. True to her existentialist dialectic, everyone involved is responsible for the breakdown of ethnic values. The nun does not escape for allowing herself to be used. If the people subsume their traditional beliefs for ones that offer suffering and death, then indeed they are partially responsible for their own destruction. What is life-generating is repressed and even censured by the critic, though certainly not by Walker. Ben-Bassat writes of the "jungle" scene: "Obviously, the violently physical and orgiastic nature of the dance in the jungle appears diametrically opposed to the ascetic and barren spiritual sacrament in the mission school. . . . Walker's depiction of the pagan ritual does not leave out its threat of intoxication and violent conquest of passion."[91] On the contrary, there appears to be no threat of violence. The critic inserts a stereotype into the narrative with her reading of the setting, a reading clouded by her own cultural myths.

The story itself is straightforward. An African nun is lonely and imprisoned in a stark white habit. She has embraced Western religion, and it stands in opposition to her culture. She is expected to bring converts from her fellow Africans to join the church, which looks askance at sex and embraces an immaculate conception, simply denying life as the Africans know it. This reading is literal. Ben-Bassat correctly points out that Walker writes in layered allegory. The spiritual aspect of the story is found in its unstated aspects, the silences between each entry, and in the philosophical questions the nun raises. Where Walker is going with this story is beyond the literal to the mystical conclusion of the absolute unity where the sexual healing encountered in the dance lures the insipid lover into the circle of life—where all truth is one.

The nun knows the truth of her pagan culture. Clearly, she is in touch with the earth and all its holiness because she writes of the snowcapped mountains melting in spring. The black mountain capped with white snow is her habit that chills.[92] The allegory here is the ecospirituality that critics recognize in Walker's later works, that has been present from the start. The image of the snowcapped black mountains melting in the warmth of spring is a parable for unity, the coming together of spirit. The pagans recognize the resurrection in the spring, understand and celebrate new life and life forms, including bugs and bees, but the nun is made melancholy by the Christian's faith only in the resurrection of Jesus. The nun claims that her pagan belief is more fruitful.[93] Wholeness is Walker's intended goal, but contradictions divide the world.

The nun wants to teach the world to dance.[94] To see that the sacred and the secular are one in the same is the message of this story.

Walker's message is not to blame but to expose the fact that the horrendous acts that we commit against each other should cause people to transform their behavior. "Elethia" is a story from *You Can't Keep a Good Woman Down*, and mirrors the psychic sickness of racism and one woman's response to it, her activism. The name Elethia is important because it speaks to Walker's unending engagement with Spirit. Elethia means healer. Elethia's friends call her Thia, which means "Divine One." Spelled differently, but synonymous, Thea means gift of God. Transposed, *thai* means freedom in the Thai language. The layers of meaning add to the mystery of this story, which focuses on the freedom to act and juxtaposes the actions of the young generation against those of the old. The story represents one of the rare instances in which Walker appears to criticize the older generation. They are described as grateful to the white man, even though they could not enter the eating establishment by the front door.[95]

Elethia works in a white restaurant that displays a statue of Uncle Albert, a black man cast in the stereotypical role of Uncle Ben on the box of rice, grinning and happy to serve white people. Elethia discovers that Uncle Albert is not a wax figure but stuffed, like a taxidermy. Once she makes the discovery by noticing that his fingernails are real, she and her friends liberate the dead man by breaking in, cremating him, and carrying his ashes with them as a constant reminder of their U.S. history, even as some of the guys join the army. Elethia goes to college and discovers that there are more stuffed people, Native Americans displayed in museums, a chilling portrayal of some historic realities. The homily here is that the young woman makes the life-altering discovery. Once she does, she takes the initiative to act.

Theologians often characterize evil as natural evil and moral evil. The former results from what are called natural disasters, floods, earthquakes, or hurricanes. The evil within the context of Walker's story is moral evil that results from the exercise of human choice. Within this context, Jamie T. Phelps, a professor of systematic theology, points to socially constructed evil that "involves patterns of relationships that are directed toward the denial of human dignity and value of some human beings for the benefit of other human beings."[96] Those who take part in the oppression and murder of their fellow men and women are not just perpetrators of an individual evil act. They are part of a system, a social structure that enables them to commit such acts. The social constructs "primarily benefit a white male power elite."[97] Walker's stories present an age-old theological problem, that of evil in the face of a good and omnipotent Spirit. Freedom appears to be the one likely explanation for the existence of evil. Human behavior and freedom of choice enable people to behave in almost any way they choose. Without choice, people would not be free. Walker's theological position aligns with the concept that human behavior results from freedom of choice.

Walker's poetry collected in *Good Night Willie Lee, I'll See You in the Morning* calls romantic love into question. Lines that say love has made her sick and point to the futility of loving someone who is undeserving[98] interrogate the sacrifices often made in the name of love. The poem "More Love in His Life" states that the woman is responsible for adding love to the man's life.[99] The overriding message is reflected in the poem, "Never Offer Your Heart to Someone Who Eats Hearts." The poem ends on a hopeful note by having the hearts replaced with God and song. God and song are the bridge into the metaphysical meaning of Walker's poems. "Never Offer Your Heart to Someone Who Eats Hearts" warns against embracing false prophets, and of submitting free thinking to a dogma. The demand of being true to God demands that we sing our own song. Walker concludes in the final poem of the book that love and forgiveness are all that matter. The title poem, "Goodnight Willie Lee, I'll See You in the Morning," records the words of Walker's mother saying good-bye to Walker's father at his funeral. Her mother's words produced an epiphany. Walker understands how forgiveness permits, even enables, rebirth.

Walker's volume of poems titled *Revolutionary Petunias* won the 1974 National Book Award. The poems are autospiritual. They are inward-looking and reveal Walker's distillation of the civil rights revolution in the South, her slowly unraveling marriage, and her memories of herself as the child of southern black sharecroppers. Her dedications make clear her allegiance to the bygone era of the Student Nonviolent Coordinating Committee (SNCC), Bob Moses, and other Mississippi leaders. The poems canonize revolutionaries and lovers, but looks askance at pseudo-revolutionaries and their militant posturing.

The opening poem, "In These Dissenting Times," establishes the autospiritual tone of the book. It acknowledges the ancestors and traces the self back to God or to gods. Walker places the movement within the context of everlasting life; she is not fooled as were so many about the fight for freedom. Her words capture precisely what is easy to forget: that young people were not the first to struggle, win, or lose.[100] Walker reaches back in time to recall the women who strong-armed them to church. In church there are the funerals, old men singing and lifting the casket with a gentle swing, being awkward with flowers, standing in their brown suits waiting for what is sure to come. Death. But for the young, "Winking at a Funeral," romantic love blossoms. They do not know or care that the flowers are fading and think nothing of the arsonist. This poem evokes the bombing of 16th Street Baptist Church during the height of the civil rights movement. Walker's poem winks at the gruesome horror of the church bombing, just as those who are young wink at death and fall in love while old men stand and wait. Within the context of the poem, winking maintains its flirtatious meaning, but it also means to shine, as Shine on Me in the "Hymns" let the light from the lighthouse shine on me. The poem's muted progression explodes in the last two lines, asking who the arsonist was.[101] Church is so much a part of the movement for freedom, of Walker's childhood activities and memories, but in her spiritual development it expands far beyond four walls. The poem "You Had to Go to Funerals" resembles an unpublished story about the tradition of attending funerals. Death is a constant for the people who struggle to survive without proper health care and, later, for those who defy the laws of segregation circumscribing their lives.

"Uncles" is a poem mirrored in the opening chapter of *The Third Life of Grange Copeland*. Thadious Davis has written that Walker's poetry is a preface to her fiction, which appears to be the case with "Uncles."[102] They come home from the North to brag of their jobs and opportunities in Denver, Jersey City, and Philadelphia, the city mentioned in *Third Life*. Also expanded upon in the novel is the way that Uncle Silas seemed womanish in his headties.[103] In the novel, Brownfield admires his uncle, but says he would not wear a headrag. The poem introduces what the novel completes—the freedom the uncles claim is just a façade.

Many of the poems alternate between church, Wards Chapel AME, and burials. In "Sunday School, Circa 1950," the question is always the same: Who created you?[104] The answer also is invariable. The I of the poem forgets the catechism, but savors the memory of the human touch. The loving relationships constitute the religion the poet recalls. The poem "Burial," as Davis points out, contains the pattern from which Celie is drawn. The misspelled gravestone that reads "Racher" and not "Rachel" is reminiscent of the marker for the murdered wife in *Meridian*'s opening chapter, the loving wife and mother, but leaves out gone wrong.[105] "Baptism" and "View from Rosehill Cemetery: Vicksburg," dedicated to Aaron Henry, one of the founders of the Mississippi Freedom Democratic Party, round out the first section of the book.

Section 2 opens with a quotation from Albert Camus' *The Rebel*. Camus concludes that the time will come when revolutions will need beauty. In "Revolutionary Petunias," Sammy Lou of Rue, probably Ruleville, Mississippi, in Sunflower County, is the prototype of what Walker calls incorrect, meaning so wrong regarding the image of the black queen or princess popularized by nationalists. Her incorrectness is the very core of her being and provides what many armchair revolutionaries lacked, the courage to take a hoe and send the man who murdered her husband to meet his maker. She is the mother of five children, all ironically named for U.S. presidents and their wives.[106] The last child is named for the founder of the Methodist movement, John Wesley, as was her husband. Perhaps Walker chose these names to show the woman's patriotism as well as her Christianity, also part of her incorrectness. The power of the poem lies in accepting the incorrectness while embracing the woman's heroic actions. Within the context of the Black Power movement there was the tendency to dismiss the older generation and to question their failure to respond correctly to segregation. On her way to the electric chair for killing a murderer, Sammy reminds her family to honor God's word.[107] Her final words, however, are to remind those left to water her purple petunias. Regardless of life's circumstances one must take care of the flowers, one must keep beauty alive. The need for beauty is not diminished in the woman who kills, and therefore her humanity remains intact. What we love, we save, regardless of the circumstances we face.

Walker's stories and collections of poems enable one to glimpse her psychic and mystical development. In one poem she admits that love is old-fashioned but urges to love anyway.[108] The takeaway from these early works can be summarized in the words *love* and *forgiveness*.

NOTES

1. Thomas Lewis, *A General Theory of Love* (New York: Random House, 2000), 13.
2. Alice Walker, "Introduction," in Nancy Morejon, *Letters of Love & Hope: The Story of the Cuban Five* (Melbourne: Ocean Press, 2005).
3. Joel Goldsmith, *The Foundation of Mysticism* (Longboat Key, FL: Acropolis Books, 1998).
4. Walker, *Anything We Love Can Be Saved*, introduction (n.p.).
5. Alice Hall Petry, "Alice Walker: The Achievement of the Short Fiction," *Modern Language Studies*, 19, no. 1 (Winter 1989), 193.
6. *Anything We Love Can Be Saved*, xxv.
7. Jennifer Clements, "Organic Inquiry: Toward Research in Partnership with Spirit," *Journal of Transpersonal Psychology* 36, no. 1 (2004): 26.
8. Anne Morrow Lindbergh, *Dearly Beloved* (New York: Harcourt, Brace & World, 1962), 17 (page refers to the *Readers Digest* edition).
9. Ibid., 10.
10. Walker, "Roselily," in *In Love & Trouble*, 8.
11. Ibid., 9.
12. See Katie Cannon, "The Bible Is the Highest Source of Authority for Most Black Women," in *Katie's Canon* (New York: Continuum, 1996), 56.
13. Walker, "Roselily," 4.
14. Ibid.
15. Robert Sternberg, "A Triangular Theory of Love," *Psychological Review* 93 (1986), 119.
16. Ann duCille, "Phallus(ies) of Interpretation: Toward R=Engendering the Black Critical 'I,'" *Callaloo* 16, no. 3 (Summer 1993): 443.
17. Ibid., 444.
18. Ibid., 446.
19. From Elechi Amadi, *The Concubine* (New York: Heinemann, 1966).
20. From Rainer Maria Rilke, *Letters to a Young Poet* (New York: Norton, 1993).
21. Walker, *In Search of Our Mothers' Gardens*, 251.
22. Walker, "Really, Doesn't Crime Pay?" in *Love & Trouble*, 12.
23. Ibid., 17.
24. Ibid., 12.
25. Ibid., 16.

26. Ibid., 14.
27. Walker, "The Divided Life of Jean Toomer," in *In Search of our Mother's Gardens*, 64.
28. "Really, Doesn't Crime Pay?" 17.
29. Ibid.
30. Ibid., 22–23.
31. Donna Haisty Winchell, *Alice Walker* (New York: Twyne, 1992).
32. Walker, "Her Sweet Jerome," in *In Love & Trouble*, 25.
33. Ibid.
34. Alice Walker Archive, Stuart A. Rose Manuscript, Archives, and Rare Book Library, Emory University.
35. Walker, "Her Sweet Jerome," 25.
36. Ibid., 27.
37. Ibid., 26.
38. Damas's poem in *Pigments* proclaims: "I feel ridiculous/ in their shoes/ in their tuxedo/ in their dress shirt/" but not in their three-piece suit?
39. Susan Farrell, "Fight vs. Flight: A Re-evaluation of Dee in Alice Walker's 'Everyday Use,'" *Studies in Short Fiction* 35, no. 2 (Spring 1998): 179.
40. Walker, "Everyday Use," in *In Love & Trouble*, 47.
41. David Cowart, "Heritage and Deracination in Walker's 'Everyday Use,'" *Studies in Short Fiction* 33, no. 2 (Spring 1996): 171.
42. Ibid.
43. Ibid.
44. Quoted in Henry Louis Gates. Jr., *The Signifying Monkey: A Theory of Afro-American Literary Criticism* (New York: Oxford University Press, 1988), 153. See also Stanley Meisler, "Afro Hairdo Riles Africa's Blacks," *Milwaukee Journal*, September 22, 1970.
45. Walker, "Everyday Use," 50.
46. Winchell, *Alice Walker*, 82.
47. Ibid.
48. Walker, "Everyday Use," 50.
49. Ibid., 51.
50. Ibid.
51. Farrell, "Fight vs. Flight."
52. Walker, "For My Sister Molly Who in the Fifties," in *Revolutionary Petunias*, reprinted in *Her Blue Body: Everything We Know*, 175.
53. Houston Baker and Charlette Pierce Baker, "Patches: Quilts and Community in 'Everyday Use,'" *Southern Review* 21, no. 3 (July 1, 1985): 705–20.
54. Walker, "Everyday Use," 48.
55. Ibid.
56. Ibid, 49 (emphasis added).
57. Winchell, *Alice Walker*, 81.
58. Baker and Baker, "Patches," 714.
59. Sam Whitsitt, "In Spite of It All: A Reading of Alice Walker's 'Everyday Use,'" *African American Review* 34, no. 3 (2000), 443–49.
60. Ibid., 449.
61. Rudolph P. Byrd, ed., *The World Has Changed* (New York: New Press, 2010), 11.
62. Walker, "Everyday Use," 49.
63. Ibid., 49.
64. Ibid., 58.
65. Ibid., 58.
66. Quoted in Barbara Christian, ed., *Everyday Use: Alice Walker* (New Brunswick, NJ: Rutgers University Press, 1994), 101–2.
67. See Walker's comments in "Saving the Life That Is Your Own," in *In Search of Our Mother's Gardens*, 3–14.
68. Walker, "Strong Horse Tea," in *In Love & Trouble*, 93.
69. Ibid., 88.

70. Maya Angelou, *I Know Why the Caged Bird Sings* (New York: Random House, 1969), 3.

71. Trudier Harris, "Folklore in the Fiction of Alice Walker: A Perpetuation of Historical and Literary Traditions," *Black American Literature Forum* 34, no. 3 (1977), 443 (emphasis added).

72. Quoted in Claudia Tate, ed., *Black Women Writers at Work* (New York: Continuum, 1986), 175–87.

73. Walker, "Strong Horse Tea," 89.

74. Deborah Anne Hooker, "Strong Horse Tea," *Southern Literary Journal* 37 (2005): 81–103.

75. Walker, *Once*, 99–100.

76. Alice Walker Archive, Stuart A. Rose Manuscript, Archives, and Rare Book Library, Emory University.

77. Walker, "Strong Horse Tea," 90.

78. Ibid., 89.

79. Ibid., 93.

80. Ibid., 94.

81. Ibid., 89.

82. Harris, "Folklore in the Fiction of Alice Walker," 443.

83. Hedda Ben-Bassat, *Prophets without Vision: Subjectivity and the Sacred in Contemporary American Writing* (Lewisburg: Bucknell University Press, 2000), 161.

84. Ibid., 163.

85. Ibid., 165.

86. Ibid.

87. Ibid.

88. Walker, "Diary of an African Nun," in *In Love & Trouble*, 115.

89. Walker, *Possessing the Secret of Joy*, 22.

90. Walker, "Diary of an African Nun," 118.

91. Ben-Bassat, *Prophets without Vision*, 166.

92. Walker, "Diary of an African Nun," 117.

93. Ibid., 118.

94. Ibid.

95. Walker, "Elethia," in *You Can't Keep a Good Woman Down*, 28.

96. Jamie T. Phelps, "Joy Came in the Morning: Risking Death for Resurrection," in *A Troubling in My Soul*, ed. Emilie Townes (Maryknoll, NY: Orbis Books, 1993), 48.

97. Ibid., 52.

98. Walker, *Good Night Willie Lee, I'll See You in the Morning*, 237 (page numbers refer to the reprint in *Her Blue Body*).

99. Ibid., 247.

100. Walker, "In These Dissenting Times," in *Her Blue Body*, 155.

101. Ibid., 158.

102. Thadious Davis, "Poetry as Preface to Fiction," in *Alice Walker Critical Perspectives Past and Present*, ed. Henry Louis Gates Jr. and K. A. Appiah (New York: Amistad Press, 1993), 275–283.

103. Ibid., 164.

104. Ibid., 168.

105. Ibid., 171.

106. Ibid., 189.

107. Ibid.

108. Ibid., 233.

Chapter Four

Amazing Grace

Walker's experience in the civil rights movement provides grist for the mill of her powerful works. In the years following the assassinations of John and Robert Kennedy, Malcolm X, Viola Liuzzo, Martin Luther King Jr., and all the others named on the final page of *Meridian*'s chapter 1, "The Last Return," Walker gathers the memories and grinds them into flour that makes up the metaphysical bread of life and death, as it were, for those absent or too quickly forgotten. Walker has written in her notebooks of the importance of keeping records, for without a written account, people can and will deny events. The decade of death, the 1960s, is unique only because, as Walker notes, television made it so. Grieving became a solitary act.[1] People grieved alone as they watched the evening news. Death in the segregated South was no stranger to the black people who lived there under the constant threat of violence.

Spiritual unity in *Meridian* takes inspiration from Black Elk, whose memory of the 1876 Battle of the Little Big Horn parallels Walker's memory of the twentieth-century battle for human and civil rights. Black Elk's statement, "I did not know then how much was ended,"[2] speaks for Meridian, Truman, Anne-Marion, and for all the characters and people swept up in great change.

The novel's subtext is the expansive definition of the word *meridian*. Walker's notes indicate that Anne-Marion initially was the central character in the first drafts of the novel, and working titles included "The Girl Who Forgives Everything," "Atonement," "Meridian Hill," "The Atonement of Meridian Hill," "Premium Salt," and "The One Who Walked Away."[3] Walker takes great care in titling the book and naming the central character. Meridian Hill, as Rudolph Byrd points out, alludes to Jean Toomer, who was born in Washington, DC, near the Potomac and not far from Meridian Hill,[4] a park in northwest DC now known as Malcolm X Park. Toomer's poem, "The Blue Meridian,"[5] refers to the park but, even more significantly, the poem itself is about a new United States that the poet imagines, but one that Walker witnesses.

The lines in Toomer's poem may have inspired Walker to change her title. Given the relevance of Toomer's poem to the content of the novel, the extensive dictionary definition for the word *meridian* seems unnecessary. Greil Marcus recognizes in his review of the book that Walker pays homage to Camus, whose 1951 essay, "The Rebel," contains a section titled "Thought at the Meridian."[6] The philosophical issue for Camus was whether the end justifies the means and, if it does, what will justify the end. Walker echoes Camus when her Meridian asks, if she killed someone, what would the music sound like?[7] Toomer's poem introduces Meridian's connection to the South with the line that states life is waiting there. Meridian, Mississippi, also is meaningful as the home of the slain 1964 civil rights worker, James Chaney. Walker's extensive definition points to the middle—Camus's idea of moderation. The denotative meaning adds that meridian is prime, "the highest point of prosperity, splendor, or power"[8] and refers to Meridian's evolution from fractured psyche to wholeness.

Marcus says that *Meridian* "tries to make itself a parable."[9] The novel succeeds. Beginning with death and ending with resurrection—the dead Marilene O'Shay, and the "strong enough to go and owned nothing to pack"[10] Meridian who returns to the world cleansed of sickness—contains a powerful spiritual lesson. Meridian poses many issues, a reason some critics select only one issue to dissect rather than the entire novel. Walker has complained that reviewers have failed to treat the novel as a whole.[11] Given the complexity of the book, full treatment in a review is unlikely. Far more than the classic novel of the civil rights movement, encompassing women's issues including motherhood, spirituality, land rights, issues of class and color, sex and sexuality, *Meridian* is a paean to the flawed warriors who persevered—to the one, Meridian, who walked away.

Walker integrates the civil rights movement and the women's movement in the novel. The opening chapter positions Meridian as a war-worn civil rights worker still marching for justice, still leading those willing to follow. Set in an imaginary town, Chicokema, in rural Georgia, the novel addresses the issue of discrimination complicated by economic class. Meridian leads the children of the guano plant workers, most (but not all) of whom are black, to see a carnival sideshow. The plant workers and their children are discriminated against because those who do not work in the plant claim that the workers stink. They are segregated and prevented from seeing the sideshow on any but their designated day. In a single paragraph, Walker introduces the issues of class (the plant workers are poor), race (most are black people), and gender (the woman on display). The sideshow is a white woman, Marilene

O'Shay, whose dead body her husband displays because even in death he owns her. Here also is an example of maternal support of patriarchy. Marilene O'Shay was unfaithful to her husband, and he killed her. Her mother does not hold him accountable. One of the townsmen explains that her husband killed the wife and her lover and was acquitted by the law, the church, and even forgiven by the wife's mother.[12] The issues of motherhood, women's right to ownership of their own bodies, civil and human rights, revolutionaries versus those who just look like Che, philosophical questions of violence versus nonviolence, the difference between right and correct, and guilt that masks as love, appear in the novel's first twenty pages.

The chapter titled "The Last Return" begins with Truman Held, a significant name that Walker settles on after "Ben, Justin, and John," which she used in the early drafts of the novel.[13] Truman Held personifies a man held by the same cultural and political history that holds Meridian. Walker has said that Meridian is structured like a Bearden collage,[14] a collection of images, an assemblage that creates a new whole. The new picture is of the civil rights and Black Power movements, women, motherhood, guilt, forgiveness, and a new way to view history as nonlinear. The end of the novel is the beginning of Truman's last return. The beginning starts with the decade marked by death, 1963. Through a series of flashbacks, Walker indicates how Meridian arrives at the place where Truman finds her.

Truman finds Meridian in a small southern town, and she is still enacting what some call the outdated activities of a movement long deceased. Barbara Christian observes that the novel "begins with a point of time in the seventies when the strategy of non-violent resistance is no longer widespread, at a time when the dramatic demonstrations of the Civil Rights Movement have ended, and when most observers would say that the Movement was over."[15] Meridian is like the old lady from Mississippi in Walker's essay about the woman who refused to let the movement die.[16] Karen Stein has stated that Walker reappraised the civil rights movement after she wrote the award-winning essay, "The Civil Rights Movement: What Good Was It?" Stein contends that "while [Walker] wrote of the Civil Rights Movement with unreserved approval in 1967, she would later contend that it continued to oppress women and so failed in its mission of human liberation,"[17] and that Meridian is Walker's critique of the movement. What appears to occur in *Meridian*, however, is not so much a critique of the civil rights movement as a criticism of the Black Power movement that followed.

Walker's essay is not an unreserved approval of the civil rights movement, and does not suggest that it was without flaws. She says the movement ignited a renewed faith in the human spirit and the ability for blacks and whites to work together.[18] Walker also admits that the movement was not perfect, but what it accomplished was enough.[19] People were awakened, and the movement ignited the fire for the second-wave feminist and Black Power movements.

The opening section of *Meridian* articulates the rhetoric of the Black Power movement. The scene in New York takes place after the civil rights movement, with Meridian admitting that nonviolence has failed.[20] She plans to go live among the people in the South, like when she worked on voter registration.[21] Assuming the timeline of the novel begins, as Christian suggests, in the late 1970s, the "ten years ago"[22] that Meridian refers to would place her in New York circa 1968, after the assassinations of Malcolm X and King, and at the time when the Black Panther Party organization opened its New York City office in 1968; after the publication of Carmichael and Hamilton's *Black Power: The Politics of Liberation in America* (1967) and perhaps following the 1968 Black Power salute at the Olympic Games in Mexico City. The question the revolutionaries pose is: Will she die and kill for the revolution? Meridian cannot accept the group's question as rhetorical. She answers yes to the first part—she would die—but she cannot say that she will kill. To say yes would be contradictory to the integrity of who she is and what she believes. She thinks that perhaps the group will never find it necessary to kill; however, her conscience says she is avoiding the issue.[23] The point is to be truthful.

In an early draft of the novel, Ruth, who becomes Meridian, recites a poem reminiscent of Giovanni's poem asking whether a black person can kill. Walker's poem asks: "Who will hold the knives/ we need/ to hold/ to castrate the beast?/ to cut the tits off his women?/ to break under our heels/ the false teeth of his grandmother?/ who will sodomize his sons?" The poem ends by asking: "who will be men?"[24] As a young girl, Meridian not only rejected her mother's urging to profess a religion in which she did not believe; in an oratorical competition, she also refused to complete her speech the minute she realized the untruth of what she was saying. Meridian cannot truthfully respond to the revolutionary group; she remains silent. In her silence she recalls when she was thirteen, and her mother wanted her to join the Christian church, and to make statements that she did not believe. She refused, just as she refuses to say yes to the revolutionary group. Saying no, always a choice, is not without consequences. One penalty for refusing without understanding the right (unalienable) to say no, is guilt. Meridian says no to her mother's religion, to motherhood, to revolutionary murder and violence, but then she suffers from self-imposed guilt.

Meridian's guilt is multifaceted, as Winchell observes, noting that Meridian spends years attempting to rid herself of the guilt for having failed her mother.[25] The source of her guilt, however, appears to be more sinister than just a belief that she has failed to be the perfect daughter. Meridian hates her mother. She employs the defense mechanism of reaction formation to avoid the anxiety the emotion produces. Even though Meridian embraces a defense against hatred, it does not disappear. Rather, her guilt reappears as a debilitating physical and psychic pain. The following quotation demonstrates the conflicted relationship Meridian has with her mother: "it is death not to love one's mother."[26] Meridian thought her mother ignorant and cruel. To compensate, she professed to love her deeply. Her claim is unconvincing. If Meridian loves her mother because she is afraid not to, it is fear and not love. This same section makes it apparent that her mother's love is conditional, predicated on her children's behavior. Meridian's mother should have said no to motherhood.

The historical imperative for black women to become mothers is paradoxical. Enslaved women forced to breed like cattle could not enjoy motherhood, and when regardless of the circumstances, they bonded with and loved their children of rape or forced impregnation, the children were sold away from them. One of the benefits of freedom was the opportunity for black mothers to keep their children. Within the cultural paradigm of this maternal history there is no option for women to reject having children. Meridian is charting new territory when she rejects motherhood. Her mother's response to Meridian giving away her son is to say that God gave her the child and it is her duty to care for it.[27] This idea is typical of that time and reflects what Christian women in particular believed to be their obligation. Mrs. Hill is a self-righteous Christian whose position is supported by her reading of the Bible but undercut by her own behavior, because the biblical verses say that mothers should love their children and husbands.[28] She does neither.

Meridian not only is too immature to be a wife, but she suffers from the same malady as Margaret and Mem in her expectations of manhood. In a revealing paragraph about why she does not love her husband, she thinks that Eddie will never grow up, that he will always be a boy running errands for others, a gofer instead of a man with power and authority.[29] Rife with stereotype and political innuendo, Walker's novel calls into question the Western concept of true manhood, an issue rarely questioned regarding white men but one at the core of black female-male relationships. The impetus for black women to step back, step over, or step aside, to allow black men to lead as Mem did when, clearly, she was the most competent one, relies on the false assumption that men by their very nature are leaders. Both women and men adhere to this false belief. In Meridian's mind, a man has power and authority. Walker circumvents Meridian's definition when the narrator says Meridian did not know what a man was.[30] Walker has written in her notes that "Perhaps black men are frightened of black women because we demand that they become something for which there is—as yet—no model. Certainly, we do not want them to remain slaves. Certainly, we do not want them to be slave owners, i.e., white men. (Husbands.) Or the white man's idea of what a man is."[31] New definitions are needed for both men and women. Whether one accepted the gender roles projected by the larger society, especially in the South of the 1950s, there was a concerted effort, through the Jim Crow laws and southern customs, to prevent black people from becoming men and women and to ensure that they functioned only as boys and girls.

Unable to decipher what her mother means when she says, "Be sweet,"[32] Meridian becomes sexually active and pregnant as a teenage high school student. In the chapter ironically titled "The Happy Mother," the extent to which Meridian despises motherhood becomes clear when she dreams of murdering her child.[33] In an early draft of the novel, when Meridian is still named Ruth, the baby is crying and Ruth rushes into the child's room with a huge knife, plunging it into the baby's abdomen. Had Walker retained this scene, it would have produced outrage. In still another draft, the murder turns out to be just a dream. Meridian fails to love her son or her husband.[34] Anthropologist Sidney Greenfield believes that romantic love motivates people "to occupy the positions husband-father and wife-mother and form nuclear families that are essential not only for reproduction and socialization but also to maintain the existing arrangements for distributing and consuming goods and services."[35] Further, he says that love must motivate people to assume these roles because the burden outweighs the gain to individuals. No one in her or his right mind would assume such a responsibility. Romantic love is the opiate. Meridian's youth, her lack of preparation for engaging in sex and married life, mitigate harsh judgment of her behavior.

Extenuating circumstances do not, however, alleviate criticism of Mrs. Hill who, unlike her daughter, has grown to adulthood unencumbered, and was able to complete school. She had freedom and a career as a teacher.[36] She chose to marry and to have children. She is solely responsible for misreading the look in the eyes of her students' mothers, a look she thought meant that she was missing something wonderful in her life. That she might have been deliberately tricked by a society that depends on women to accept their roles as wives and mothers is clear, but equally clear is her responsibility to educate herself. Like Brownfield in terms of accepting personal responsibility, she never admits that the error is hers because she became uncertain that living (single) was enjoyable to her.[37] Instead she blames others for not warning her against motherhood.[38] Mrs. Hill married a man she did not love. There is no opiate at work. She mistook tolerance for love. Without love, as Greenfield insists, the drawbacks of marriage and motherhood far outweigh the advantages. Mrs. Hill is another of Walker's un-protective, incompetent mothers.

The chapter titled "The Attainment of Good" may be a realization of God. Walker exposes, as she has done in *The Third Life of Grange Copeland* when Grange strikes a bargain with God and his uncle swallows the fly, the fundamental illogic of essentialist belief. Part of Christian precepts involve sacrifice. Steeped in violence and bloodshed, biblical teachings say, for instance, that "almost all things are by the law purged with blood; and without shedding of blood is no remission,"[39] and "For then must he often have suffered since the foundation of the world: but now once in the end of the world hath he appeared to put away sin by the sacrifice of himself."[40] Central to Christianity is the martyr, the one who sacrifices for all. Walker addresses the idea of sacrifice later in *Meridian*. In this chapter she opens with the line: "Her [Meridian's] mother's life was sacrifice."[41] The mother's belief, one that Meridian has rejected, is not unusual. Mrs. Hill was a fundamentalist who believed God was in the church building. She never questioned the preacher, whom she did not understand. She never complained.[42]

This three-page chapter sets forth not only the problems with the church, but the responsibility of those who wish to attain good or the reality of God. Knowledge and understanding, neither of which Mrs. Hill can acquire in church because the preacher did not make sense, can only be attained through self-knowledge. She learned only about the birth and crucifixion of Jesus.[43] She relies on the preacher in the same irresponsible way that she places her belief in schoolteachers. She believes in their infallibility;[44] otherwise, she might have to assume the responsibility of teaching her own children and finding God for herself and in herself.

Meridian's decision to give her son up for adoption is the first inkling of love that she expresses for the child. Her guilt is compounded by her hatred of her mother, not caused by her mother's constant query, asking if Meridian has stolen anything. The narrator says Meridian has stolen her mother's peace, but Meridian's paralysis and guilt are not from stealing her mother's serenity, because she has no way of knowing that she has done so. What Meridian does know is that her mother refuses to help her. Meridian sublimates her desire to kill her son into thoughts of suicide, and the hatred of her mother into thoughts of her mother's maternal perfection. When, finally, Meridian emerges from her deep depression in mid-April 1960—a significant date because April 15–17 marks the foundation of the SNCC (Student Nonviolent Coordinating Committee), she takes a spiritual approach to her situation. She begins, at first unaware of what she is doing, to meditate on her condition. Then she volunteers with the voter registration and civil rights workers in her town and meets Truman Held.

When her marriage falls apart in an early version of the novel, Meridian gives her son to her in-laws. After the civil rights movement she comes back to claim him. In the published version, Meridian gives her son to a well-to-do family who can take better care of him than either she or her in-laws can. Of Meridian's choice, the narrator reminds us that she might have killed her child and taken her own life[45] as Margaret does in *The Third Life of Grange Copeland*. Instead of recognizing what is best for the grandson whom she does not want to take care of, Mrs. Hill believes that her daughter should accept the cross of motherhood,[46] and that she is a monster for not wanting Eddie Jr. Meridian accepts, along with the resentment that she already harbors, the guilt that Mrs. Hill lays on her for accepting the college scholarship.[47]

Even though Meridian recognizes the correctness of her choice for herself and her son, subconsciously she feels condemned to repentance for the rest of her life.[48] The fundamental expectation of society that women make others instead of themselves, and that women naturally want to sacrifice their own freedom to nurture children and husbands, is a myth without logical explanation. The prevalence of such beliefs and what follows is not just the history of the civil rights movement but also a redefining of womanhood through grappling with guilt and sublimating hatred into spiritual atrophy.[49] Recovery, healing, and wholeness follow.

Meridian is characterized as "failed revolutionary," compared to the "Anne-Marion type revolutionary."[50] Meridian is the most revolutionary of all, as Anne-Marion recognizes by her need to keep writing to Meridian. Even though Meridian gives away one child and aborts another when she becomes pregnant by Truman, Winchell says: "Her mothering instincts surface."[51] Christian also suggests that Meridian gives "some part of herself as a mother."[52] Perhaps a mothering instinct does not come into play, but rather a human response to help the helpless children who are the most vulnerable of all. The reason for Meridian's work on behalf of the children is explained in the revolutionary sermon into which she wanders. The minister chastised the older members for not joining in the battle and allowing the children to fight for them.[53] Children were at the forefront of many demonstrations in the civil rights movement. A Children's Crusade in 1962 brought criticism from Malcolm X and other leaders for putting children at risk.[54] Meridian does not prioritize motherhood but, like Toni Cade, she privileges "self-hood."[55]

Meridian has doubts about her role as a revolutionary. In the chapter titled "Questions," Walker's theological position is articulated through Meridian's thoughts. In the new black church with the B. B. King stained-glass window, Meridian concludes that the church must use what is sustaining: the music, which has always brought comfort and strength.[56] This kind of worship, she believes, will lead the people to protect themselves and, by extension, to protect others. Meridian knows that she will fight and even kill to protect her own life, and that because the black experience in the United States had created of them one existence, she will protect the people.[57] Meridian concludes that she would kill to protect others. Her resolve is soon lost, however, and she thinks of herself as a failure. Although she waivers in her commitment to kill, the revolutionary group that expelled her does nothing radical, and Anne-Marion becomes a well-known poet with two children and a home with a lake. Indeed, Meridian is not an Anne-Marion type of revolutionary.

Revolutionary killing becomes an ethical rather than a revolutionary question. For Meridian the issue is what is right versus what is correct; what is right is just, ethical, and moral. That which is correct does not carry the same type of value judgment. What is correct is what is acceptable or appropriate. Meridian decides it is never right to kill, but it might be correct when necessary.[58] Camus argued in *The Rebel* that killing is a question that must be answered in this century, meaning the twentieth century.[59] Whether murder is rational or not is an issue still alive in this new century.

Meridian, perhaps unknowingly, chooses the path to sainthood. Following her graduation from Saxon, she and Anne-Marion share an apartment. Once, while meditating on the ceiling, Meridian becomes enraptured. She refuses to eat and feels her oneness with the universe. At first Anne-Marion ignores her strange behavior, but she becomes frightened when she sees the halo surrounding Meridian's head. She seeks the help of Miss Winter, the Saxon music professor. Listening to Meridian rambling in dream-sleep, Miss Winter whispers: "I forgive you."[60] These three words open the door of the painful guilt she has felt not only for giving away her son, but for hating her mother and denying it with her self-talk saying that she loves her mother. Miss Winter releases Meridian from shame, the lowest level in spiritual growth. Forgiveness is always an inside job; it is the self that must accept and forgive. Meridian must release shame and blame to move from being a victim into a higher consciousness. Celeste Frazier, director of the Power of Oneness Center, states: "Duality is actually the position we are in when we are stuck between where we are and what we are becoming. When we are mesmerized by fear, we become paralyzed."[61] Often paralyzed by fear, Meridian is on her way to becoming what some have called a saint. Walker, however, makes her into a flawed one, and therefore more real.

The pathway to sainthood for Meridian moves from the romantic love of Truman[62] to a recognition of her oneness with him, which culminates in *agape* love: they were totally unified in Spirit.[63] Meridian articulates Walker's mysticism, for a mystic "sees beyond the illusion of separation into the intricate web of life in which all things are expressions of a single whole."[64] In a draft of the novel, a version in which Anne-Marion faces down the tank, Walker writes that Meridian, "Like a woman from Cane, she became a virgin. Her nickname was saint. Said with irony, said—sometimes—with amazement and contempt—sometimes with admiration and love."[65] Walker defines a virgin as a person who derives no pleasure from sexual intercourse. Shug says that Celie is still a virgin because she never experienced orgasm. Meridian, in the published manuscript, never enjoys sex; however, in several drafts of the manuscript she meets someone who satisfies her sexually.

An editor critiqued two sections of a late draft of the novel, and said that the "Treasure" and "The Lady Who Had Puppies" chapters should both be deleted. "The Lady Who Had Puppies" was excised, but Walker retained "Treasure." The editor had written: "In theory the story of a seventy-two-year-old virgin having a passionate love affair and is now fearful she is pregnant should be tearily funny and moving. Unfortunately, it doesn't come off. The writing is synthetic and sentimental and sometimes even portentous and pretentious as the opening with Meridian's eyes are like ears."[66] Walker eliminated the opening of "Treasure," but retained the story itself. Rims Mott, a forty-five-year-old house painter, makes love to Margaret Treasure. Walker's description of Margaret presents a clue to the importance of this section. Walker represents fat women as repulsive. Her work does not contain descriptions of fat men. But fat Josie, fat Mrs. Jerome, fat Miss Margaret Treasure, all call attention to the judgment of women by society. Described by her sister as a stereotypical Aunt Jemima figure—black, obese, and old[67]—Margaret Treasure defies the preconceived ideas.

Margaret Treasure is the antithesis of society's ideal of beauty, age, and sex. Perhaps this is a parable, one that resonates with Giovanni's "Woman" poem stating that if women are attractive, they become sex objects; if they are fat and black they receive no love and no sex, but are expected to be mothers and grandmothers.[68] Walker probably never intended for the vignette of Miss Margaret Treasure's affair with a younger man to be laughable, and Margaret Treasure's belief that she is pregnant at seventy-two is no funnier than Sarah's becoming pregnant at ninety.[69] "Treasure" and the cryptic chapter "Gold" offer lessons on self-worth. At seven, Meridian discovered gold that no one appreciated but her, and finally she buries it and forgets its worth. Perhaps Miss Margaret Treasure is a parallel, and to people's dismay, at seventy-two she discovers sex.

Rape is an issue for Walker that she continues to interrogate in *Meridian*. Margaret and Josie are rape victims in *The Third Life of Grange Copeland*. Someone is raped in each novel thereafter. The rape in *Meridian* is complicated by race. In the classroom setting, only about half of the students believe that Lynne has been raped by Tommy Odds. Even Christian states that Lynne "allows Tommy Odds to rape her, because she feels the guilt of being a white woman."[70] Many of the male students believe the sex is consensual because Lynne does not continue to resist. Some of the women students are resentful of her presence, which they believe caused Tommy to be shot by white racists. They are quick to point out that she, like everyone else, had choices. According to the dictionary, rape is the crime of forcing someone to have sexual intercourse. The male argument that Lynne was not forced gains significance.

The chapter on the rape is titled "Lynne" and begins by saying that Tommy Odds raped Lynne.[71] Walker is not ambiguous in this statement. What follows, however, is not as clear. The very next sentence challenges the first, saying that it was not rape, and Tommy Odds points out that Lynne had not resisted. She had not screamed because she was white, and he was black, a situation that surely would have resulted in his murder. The crux of the issue for most students is this sentence that states there was a point at which Lynne knew she could prevent him from raping her.[72] She fails to do so.

Instead, she thinks of his feelings and no longer resists, puts her arm around his neck, tells him she forgives him, and kisses the stump of his amputated arm.

Before date rape entered the popular vocabulary, situations like those of Lynne and Tommy Odds occurred with frequency and with little, if any, consequences to the rapist. Walker uses this scenario to point to the issues surrounding date/acquaintance rape. The term *date rape* was first used in a 1980 article published in *Mademoiselle* magazine. Dr. Mary Koss, however, began a study in the 1970s in which she interviewed college women about nonconsensual sexual encounters and published her findings in *Ms.* magazine in 1987; she coined the term *acquaintance rape*.[73] What takes place between Lynne and Tommy Odds today would be called gray rape. Students sometimes define rape as the crime of forcing a person to have sexual intercourse without consent. The definition leads students back to their original camps; some say that Lynne gave consent when she ceased to fight back,[74] others say that she was not actually forced. The confusion and the gray areas stem from the myths surrounding rape. The rapist is characterized as a stranger with a knife or gun, but more than half of all women who are raped are attacked by someone whom they know. Another element of the myth is that rape victims "are women who ask for it."[75] The "Lynne" chapter presents a classic case of acquaintance rape complicated by race.

The idea of force does not necessarily mean physical violence. A person can use the power of fear alone to commit rape. Lynne is afraid to scream because of what her scream entails within the southern racial/sexual context. A most insidious component of acquaintance rape is that the victim trusts the perpetrator. After Tommy Odds violates Lynne, he brings three other black men whom she knows to her house. She has not locked her door because she recognized the guys she thought were her friends.[76] She trusted them. In gray rape, victims often think that the rape is their fault because they were not forceful enough, but instead of resisting, many women freeze, only later to ask themselves why they did not scream. Bruises become a badge of credibility, and when none exist, the credibility of the rape victim is diminished. Walker knows well the mind-set of men who have accepted the myths surrounding rape. What Tommy Odds describes, and what the writer of the *Time* article, "When Is It Rape?" call "real rape," is part of the mythology. Tommy Odds describes what rape is to him: "nine-year-old black girl . . . raped by a white animal last week in Tchula . . . they pulled her out of the river, dead, with a stick shoved up her,"[77] he says to Lynne. Although the three men refuse to rape Lynne as Tommy Odds urges them to do, at least one of them, Altuna Jones, does not believe that Lynne has been raped because he had been told the only way to rape a woman was to kill her.[78] A final injury to women or to anyone who is sexually violated is to not be believed. When Lynne tells Truman what has happened, he chooses not to believe her. The emotional results of rape include all the symptoms Lynne exhibits: shame, fear of becoming pregnant, and feelings of worthlessness. Lynne's low self-esteem and loneliness result from her fear and Truman's emotional abandonment of her, and lead to her promiscuity. Elliott Butler-Evans writes that "Lynne's sole response is an abstraction from self, from her own degradation and humiliation to an 'understanding' of the feelings of her rapist, destroys whatever feminist argument the text attempted to advance."[79] He further states that Lynne's status as victim is problematic, exactly as it should be. The feminist position is not necessarily to focus on the victim status of women, but to make women aware of their power and choice.

While Walker acknowledges Tommy's anger at whites for his attack, clearly, he has no justification for raping a white woman, any more than he could justify raping or physically assaulting a black woman because of the displaced anger caused by racism. The description of Tommy enraged but powerless—"Tommy Odds was impotent. He spat in her face, urinated on the floor, and left her lying there"[80]—creates an epiphany for Lynne: she realizes that black people do not suffer without hatred, as she had thought. She also recognizes that all too often the hatred that black people experience is directed inward. Walker's description of Tommy Odds as small, dirty, and lifeless[81] indicates that hatred, like acid, can destroy the hated and the hater.

The way that society thinks about rape changed to an extent with the 1975 publication of Susan Brownmiller's *Against Our Will: Men, Women and Rape*. Instead of viewing rape as a sex crime, Brownmiller introduced the idea that it was a crime of violence and power.[82] For students on college campuses where an unfortunate number of acquaintance/date rapes take place, Walker's novels engender meaningful discussions.

The end of *Meridian* has been called a "minor failure"[83] because Walker rejects death and martyrdom and allows Meridian to walk away. Marge Piercy believes, "Some act is needed to make real the change"[84] in Meridian. The novel addresses Piercy's critique before she utters it: "All those characters," Walker writes, "in all those novels that require death to end the book should refuse. All saints should walk away. Do their bit, then—just walk away."[85] Walking away is the act, and a significant one, that makes real the change in Meridian. By having Meridian refuse martyrdom, Walker critiques a core value of the Christian church at the center of the civil rights movement. In early Christianity, the Eastern Church taught a peaceful and joyous embrace of God. The Western church devised a more frightening God and "demanded hideous death as a condition of salvation."[86] Salvation, like Mrs. Hill's love for her daughter, is not free. There are conditions to be met. Meridian says no to those conditions.

A WOMANIST THEOLOGICAL READING OF *MERIDIAN*

In some respects, Meridian resembles the Greek definition of martyr, that is, a witness. The act of bearing witness did not necessarily lead to death, and in the Baha'i faith, a martyr is a person who devotes oneself to service. Meridian's physical death is not required for her to be a martyr. Her time on the cross ends and she chooses to walk on. Jacquelyn Grant, one of the initiators of Womanist theology, has stated that Christology is a central doctrine in Christian theology, and is an issue inconsistent with Walker's writings. Christology is the belief that God is incarnate in one person, Jesus whom Christians recognize as the Christ, often using Christ as his last name. Black liberation theologians in the 1960s challenged "the concept of a God and Christ who allow the evils of a socially unjust society"[87] and called it "White supremacist ideology."[88] In the 1970s feminists would also challenge the concept of Christology based on the maleness of Jesus, seeing the idea of Christology as an oppressive tool of patriarchy.

The Christological construction does not coincide with Walker's theology. Grant argues that black women have the capacity for developing a wholistic theological and Christological construction that distinguishes between the white feminist and black feminist experiences. She asserts that black women "scholars should follow Alice Walker by describing our theological activity as 'Womanist theology.'"[89] In Walker's own God talk, she has said she does not believe in the conventional concept of God. For her God is Spirit in everything, everywhere.[90] Meridian represents a womanist like Walker who possesses a God-consciousness that reaches beyond the confines of southern black Christianity, that rejects what Deborah McDowell calls "a comforting myth which dimmed the horrors and brutalities of oppression."[91]

In the chapter titled "Camara" (not Camera, as McDowell mistakenly quotes), the name of Truman and Lynne's daughter refers to Camara Laye, author of the novel *The Radiance of the King*. Meridian acknowledges the change that has taken place in the black church. Walker introduces black liberation theology in the prayer, sermon, and songs of the service Meridian attends. Liberation theology, whether feminist, womanist, or black, claims that God is on the side of the oppressed. Grant says they "mean that God is in solidarity with the struggles of those on the underside of humanity."[92] A God that chooses sides, that judges, that responds to some and not to others, appears too close to man for comfort. The anthropomorphic deity is what Shug in *The Color Purple* instructs Celie to remove from her eyeball—the old white man with the long white beard.

The problem with Christology, whether it comes from a liberation/feminist/womanist paradigm or a traditional/fundamentalist orientation, is that the revolutionary person, Jesus, viewed as God incarnate becomes the exception. Walker's theology affirms God incarnate in everyone and in everything. Hers is a significantly different way of seeing the world. Writing about the role of Jesus in the womanist tradition, Grant makes the point that for black people, "Jesus was all things"[93] except them. By placing the divinity in Jesus only, they in many ways disempowered themselves. They waited for a savior instead of becoming one, and waited for power that was theirs already.

Meridian enacts both the crucifixion and the resurrection with her life. In her example, her crucifixion is self-imposed, as are many painful ordeals and victimization. The resurrection also is self-generated. Meridian's walking away is not unlike the ascension, and what she does, others must do. The parallel with Christology is unmistakable. In the final chapter, "Release," the last words are that Meridian's self-imposed experience of the terror must now be experienced by the rest. Christology includes embracing martyrdom, the crucifixion, and the resurrection, which for some Christians means a literal acceptance. Grant maintains that evangelical theology includes the belief of the sacrificial death of Christ for the sins of humanity.[94] Not all Christians interpret Christology in the same way and, for many, the issue simply is a question of who Jesus was, human, Divine, or both. Walker's works defy the idea of sacrificial death and expose suffering as a choice. Her homiletic emphasizes the need to examine politics and social issues to reach the spirit of individual persons. She endows Meridian in the end with spiritual health and transcendent energy that empowers her walking away.

Suffering in the Science of Mind philosophy is entirely man created. Holmes writes: "The Universe does not demand suffering! . . . Someday we shall decide that we have had enough suffering."[95] In her refusal to accept death as glorified, Meridian reflects not only Walker's choice to live when she was most vulnerable to suicide, but she, like many spiritual thinkers, embraces the idea that "The world has learned all it should through suffering."[96] The philosophy does not deny that suffering is an experience, but believes that reality is beyond it. In that reality, suffering is "not even an illusion or hallucination; there is a part of us that is never fooled. That is why in the greatest trial, death, or any human suffering, something rises up from within and says with Job: 'Though I die, yet shall I live.'"[97] Meridian duplicates this metaphysical message in the life she chooses to live.

Walker challenges the glorification of death on the cross by having Meridian walk away from death, and she exposes suffering as a choice. A. Elaine Crawford, in "Womanist Christology: Where Have We Come from and Where Are We Going?" notes that womanist theologians are questioning, as Walker implies in *Meridian*, crucial theological issues that include these: "Does the death on the cross glorify violence? Does the cross sacralize abuse? How does one teach and preach healing through the life, death, resurrection of Christ without romanticizing suffering?"[98] Walker outright refuses to romanticize suffering, although Meridian suffers and, in Walker's own experience, she and the civil rights workers suffered. The focus nonetheless is on choice and how to experience the consequences of those choices, and work through the effects of those decisions, die as the old person, and emerge as a new self that the experiences have wrought. Glorifying the cross renders suffering sacred. A theology of the cross is one Christian symbol that is a shrine to violence. Walker's next novel, *The Color Purple*, which earns her the Pulitzer Prize and the National Book Award, extends her theology of freedom and rejection of suffering further into the mystical realm.

NOTES

1. Walker, *Meridian*, 21.
2. Ibid., preface.
3. Alice Walker Archive, Stuart A. Rose Manuscript, Archives, and Rare Book Library, Emory University.
4. Jean Toomer, "The Blue Meridian," in *The Collected Poems of Jean Toomer*, ed. Robert B. Jones and Margery Toomer Latimer (Chapel Hill: University of North Carolina Press, 2014), 50.
5. Ibid.
6. Albert Camus, "Thought at the Meridian," *The Rebel* (New York: Alfred Knopf [1956] 1991), 297.
7. Walker, *Meridian*, 14.
8. Ibid., frontispiece.
9. Quoted in Henry Louis Gates Jr. and Anthony Appiah (eds.), *Alice Walker: Critical Perspectives Past and Present* (New York: Amistad, 1993), 14.
10. Walker, *Meridian*, 241.
11. Quoted in "Interview with Claudia Tate," in Rudolph Byrd (ed.), *The World Has Changed* (New York: New Press), 60.
12. Walker, *Meridian*, 7.
13. Alice Walker Archive, Stuart A. Rose Manuscript, Archives, and Rare Book Library, Emory University.
14. "Interview with Claudia Tate," 60.
15. Barbara Christian, "Novels for Everyday Use," in Gates and Appiah, *Alice Walker*, 74.
16. Walker, "The Civil Rights Movement, What Good Was It?" in *In Search of Our Mothers' Gardens*, 120.
17. Karen Stein, "*Meridian*: Alice Walker's Critique of Revolution," *Black American Literature Forum* 20, no. 1–2 (1986): 129.
18. Walker, "The Civil Rights Movement," 125.
19. Ibid., 121.
20. Walker, *Meridian*, 18.
21. Ibid., 19.
22. Ibid., 13.
23. Ibid., 15.
24. Alice Walker Archive, Stuart A. Rose Manuscript, Archives, and Rare Book Library, Emory University.
25. Donna Haisty Winchell, *Alice Walker* (New York: Twayne, 1992).
26. Walker, *Meridian*, 17.
27. Ibid., 77.
28. See Titus 2:4.
29. Walker, *Meridian*, 85.
30. Ibid., 66–67.
31. Alice Walker Archive, Stuart A. Rose Manuscript, Archives, and Rare Book Library, Emory University (Notebook 10).
32. Walker, *Meridian*, 86.

33. Ibid., 65.
34. Ibid., 66.
35. Sidney Greenfield, "Love and Marriage in Modern America: A Functional Analysis," *Sociological Quarterly* 6 (1965): 377.
36. Walker, *Meridian*, 40.
37. Ibid.
38. Ibid., 41.
39. Hebrews 9:22.
40. Hebrews 9:26.
41. Walker, *Meridian*, 74.
42. Ibid.
43. Ibid., 75.
44. Ibid., 76.
45. Ibid., 89.
46. Ibid., 86.
47. Ibid., 89.
48. Ibid., 90.
49. Ibid., 91.
50. Winchell, *Alice Walker*, 64.
51. Ibid.
52. Christian, "Novels for Everyday Use," 87.
53. Walker, *Meridian*, 214.
54. See Andrew Manis, *A Fire You Can't Put Out* (Tuscaloosa: University of Alabama Press, 1999).
55. Toni Cade, *The Black Woman* (New York: New American Library, 1979), 105.
56. Walker, *Meridian*, 219.
57. Ibid., 220.
58. Ibid., 207.
59. Camus, *The Rebel*.
60. Walker, *Meridian*, 131.
61. Celeste Frazier, *The Science of Mind* magazine (June 2010): 48.
62. Walker, *Meridian*, 81.
63. Ibid.
64. Joan Borysenko, *The Way of the Mystic: Seven Paths to God* (Carlsbad, CA: Hay House, 1997), xi.
65. Alice Walker Archive, Stuart A. Rose Manuscript, Archives, and Rare Book Library, Emory University (Box 48/14).
66. Ibid.
67. Walker, *Meridian*, 230.
68. Nikki Giovanni, *The Collected Poems* (New York: William Morrow, 2003), 71.
69. See Genesis 17:17.
70. Christian, "Novels for Everyday Use," 96.
71. Walker, *Meridian*, 171.
72. Ibid., 172.
73. Mary Koss, *The Rape Victim: Clinical and Community Approaches* (Battleboro, VT: Stephen Greene Press, 1987).
74. Ibid., 173.
75. Nancy Gibbs et al., "When Is It Rape?" *Time* (June 3, 1991), 1.
76. Walker, *Meridian*, 173.
77. Ibid., 174.
78. Ibid., 175.
79. Elliott Butler-Evans, "History and Genealogy in *The Third Life of Grange Copeland* and *Meridian*," in Gates and Appiah, *Alice Walker*, 123.
80. Walker, *Meridian*, 176.
81. Ibid., 179.

82. Susan Brownmiller, *Against Our Will: Men, Women and Rape* (New York: Simon and Schuster, 1975).
83. Marge Piercy, "*Meridian*," in Gates and Appiah, *Alice Walker*, 11.
84. Ibid.
85. "Interview with Claudia Tate," 62.
86. Karen Armstrong, *The History of God* (New York: Ballantine Books, 1993), 105.
87. Jacqueline Grant, *White Women's Christ and Black Women's Jesus: Feminist Christology and Womanist Response* (Atlanta: Scholars Press, 1989), 1–2.
88. Ibid.
89. Ibid., 209.
90. Walker, *In Search of Our Mother's Gardens*, 265.
91. Deborah McDowell, "The Self in Bloom: Alice Walker's *Meridian*," in Gates and Appiah, *Alice Walker*, 171.
92. Grant, *White Women's Christ*, 209.
93. Ibid., 212.
94. Ibid., 110.
95. Ernest Holmes, *The Science of Mind* (New York: Tarcher, 1999), 336.
96. Walker, *Meridian*, 107.
97. Ibid., 108.
98. A. Elaine Crawford, "Womanist Christology: Where Have We Come from and Where Are We Going?" *Review and Expositor* 95, no. 3 (1998): 367–82.

Chapter Five

Dear God

In the 1992 preface to *The Color Purple*, Walker declares the novel a theological work that moves from the religious to the spiritual. *The Color Purple*, discussed from many angles, praised and condemned, is a canonical work. Gerri Bates has called the book "a novel about womanhood and the awakening of consciousness and spirit,"[1] which certainly is true. More than womanhood, however, Walker's novel is about peoplehood, and Spirit with a capital S. *The Color Purple* is the signifying monkey, and critics are the three blind men trying to describe an elephant. Yes, the novel has negative images of some black men, but that is not the whole story. Just as the trunk is not the entire elephant. Yes, Celie is excruciatingly passive, but neither is she the entire book, no more than the elephant is just its rump. The challenge is to see the novel in its entirety.

More than any of her previous works, *The Color Purple*—Walker's third novel—is her paean to Spirit. In 1972, Walker stated that her attraction to purple is its deep color, suggestive of mysticism.[2] Felipe Smith identifies Walker's use of purple as a revision of tropes found in Toomer's *Cane*. *Cane* contains "purple haze" "pale purple shadows" and "blue-black" purple skin, and from Toomer's poem "Song of the Son" the dark purple plums[3] of the enslaved ancestors. Smith concludes that Walker's title and Toomer's intent in focusing on the purple is a figuration signifying colored people.

In this novel, Walker lays the theological groundwork for ideas that she expands and clarifies in her later works. This work exposes the sexism embedded in Western theology. Walker declares that organized religion is "an elaborate excuse for what man has done to woman and to the earth."[4] *The Color Purple* posits a clear theology of transformation. Walker seeks to dismantle the structures of society still mired in patriarchy—one of which is that churches still, for the most part, promote the worship of an anthropomorphic male—a god who punishes evildoers and rewards those lucky enough to please him—a god that judges human actions but does not intercede—and one who lives apart from and looks down on his creation. Walker brings a mature and thoughtful rendering of Divinity, one that incorporates the best from all spiritual traditions and sees God in creation as creation, a loving, nonjudgmental presence in us and within the earth. The color of purple is holy, as is the earth and all that is within it. People have the holy obligation to take care of the earth.

The Pulitzer Prize– and National Book Award–winning novel generated more than its share of negative reviews. Trudier Harris "felt [the novel] had done a great disservice . . . to southern black communities"[5] and thought that it should not have been canonized. She found the story incredulous and stated that she could "not imagine Celie existing in any black community [she] knew or any that [she] could conceive of."[6] Walker's frame for her story comes from her own family's history and her paternal grandfather's lifelong love for Shug Perry, even though he was married to someone else named Rachel. Clearly, the favorable responses to the work outweigh the unenthusiastic reactions; otherwise Walker would not have been awarded the prizes and received the recognition.

What makes the novel so compelling is the simplicity of the story—the universality of suffering that appears to be embedded within the human condition but involves choice, and the thrilling example of the rising of the spirit and the transformative power of love to transmute suffering into triumph. Celie is everywoman, and Albert is everyman, black, white, rich, or poor. The words of the Prophet make clear Walker's theological message in her presentation of the likes of Celie and Albert and all the characters condemned as immoral in the novel: "And if any of you would punish in the name of righteousness and lay the ax unto the evil tree let him see it to its roots; and verily he would find the roots of the good and the bad, the fruitful and the fruitless, all entwined together in the silent heart of the earth."[7] Unfortunately, because some of Walker's detractors focused on the issues of race and racism regarding the characters, they missed the message of the universal collective condition. Harris has written: "The effect of the novel's popularity has been detrimental in two significant and related ways. Response to its unequaled popularity, first of all, has created a cadre of spectator readers. . . . For them, the book reinforces racist stereotypes they may have been heir to and others of which they may have only dreamed."[8] Further, she points out that Celie's path, which leads to ultimate triumph, is unrealistic and that the abuse is too excessive. Ironically, what Harris objects to is the quality that helps to make the novel a classic. Celie's achievement is remarkable because of what she overcomes—a fractured and fearful child becomes whole. Often it turns out that truth is stranger than fiction. In the ensuing years since the publication of Walker's book, documented cases of abuse of women and girls, not just black women by black men, but by all kinds of men to all kinds of women and girls, has revealed that far from stereotypical, *The Color Purple* revealed a truth. Admittedly and thankfully Celie's story is not the truth for everyone, but if the story is the truth for just one child and one woman, then the story is worth telling and affects all. For Walker, the story is an archetypal frame that comes once again from her personal knowledge.

The issue of stereotypes and white reaction to both the novel and the film centered on economic class. People wanted to believe that all black people in the South were impoverished like the Copelands, and that the Johnson's house and land and Celie's fortune were unrealistic. Nothing could be further from the truth. Information about black farmers and landowners is readily available for anyone who doubts. Walker could have researched the subject but found it unnecessary, because she knew black landowners from having grown up in rural Georgia. The other concern stems from what may be African American supersensitivity regarding what white people think and is expressed in Harris's critique of the novel. The fear of white disapproval is not lost on Walker, who writes: "I was called 'liar' and 'whore' and 'traitor' for no other reason than that people who have been made to depend on the approval of the powerful grow afraid of criticizing themselves, because the powerful may hear, amplify their distress, and hold them up to censure and ridicule."[9] In an early interview with Claudia Tate before the writing of *The Color Purple*, when asked about white perception, Walker responded that she could not think of any black women writers who were interested in white opinion.[10] Walker's insistence on truth telling transcends the boundaries of race and class.

WALKER'S MEN FINDING THE SACRED MASCULINE

The novel's greatest controversy swirled around Albert's (Mr. ____) character. Critics seemed to think Walker characterized him as a brute. They fail to examine Walker's deeply human and spiritual characterization of Albert. As a young man, Albert falls in love with Lillie (Shug Avery) but cannot marry her because his color-conscious, dictatorial father chooses Annie Julia for him to marry. Walker fails to explain why Old Mister prefers Annie Julia, as she appears to be just as dark complexioned as Shug. The details are unimportant because this is a woman's story, not a man's. Walker in her characterization of men has not been careless, or worse, intentionally meanspirited, as some have claimed. Critic Bernard Bell claims that Walker's male characters only become human when she feminizes them. He writes that it is "problematic . . . the implied author and protagonist's hostility toward black men, who are humanized only upon adopting womanist principles of sexual egalitarianism."[11] Clearly sexual egalitarianism appears to spell feminized to some men, but means the loss of male privilege, which is what they fear. To be fully human is to embrace both the masculine and feminine sides, and what sexual egalitarianism means to Bell is unclear, but for Walker the lack of sexual egalitarianism certainly did mean that male privilege is in the same category with white privilege. Bell seems to miss the larger issue, and that is how Albert becomes less than fully mature in his failure to stand up to his father. His physical violence toward Celie diminishes his manhood, not his sensitivity, which humanizes him. When he learns to sew, or finds beauty in nature, evidenced by his admiration for seashells, and when he realizes he is not superior to women because of his male anatomy, he embraces the sacred masculine. Albert's problem, aside from being steeped in the culture of male hegemony and patriarchal rule, is that he is deeply unhappy. He is oppressed by the senior patriarch. Walker demonstrates how oppression breeds cruelty. Furthermore, she understands that some black men were too wounded to "value the truth of [her] work."[12]

In her first novel, Walker exposed how the outside forces of racism and poverty can work to destroy black families, but she insists that these external stressors are no excuse for individual misbehavior. In this novel she removes the stress of poverty. As landowners, neither Albert, his father, nor Pa experience the racism that Grange and his family endured. The focus is clearly on family dynamics. Albert's resentment is not toward some overbearing white man but his father, whom he has allowed to prevent him from becoming his own man. Like a child, he rebels by continuing his affair with the woman he loves. Even though his father's behavior causes Albert much pain, it does not sensitize him to his own son Harpo's situation. When Harpo wants to marry Sofia, Albert forbids him for no reason other than his power to do so. Albert wants Harpo to suffer in the same way that he is suffering. Harpo, unlike his father, has the courage to resist, although passively. He goes on strike. Since Albert himself does very little work, and Celie can only do so much in the fields, Harpo's resistance severely constricts Albert's income when he sells his crop. Harpo forces his father to negotiate, and Harpo comes out the winner. He marries the woman he loves and acquires a salary and a place to live.

As Albert matures, he views the actions of his own father with a critical eye. After Celie leaves Albert, and he is at his nadir, his father tells him that what he needs is to find a young woman to clean his house, cook his meals, and provide him with sex, the same spiel he offered Albert when he went looking for a wife/slave and ended up with Celie. This time Albert ignores the advice. Albert suffers from a soul sickness. Had the novel been about him, the reader might have guessed that he was clinically depressed. Celie's description of Albert's daily activities suggests as much. She says he gets up, sits on the porch and stares out at nothing. He does, however notice trees and butterflies.[13] Even in this early description from Celie's observant viewpoint, a quality of humanness emerges that is not captured in stereotypes. Albert seeing the butterfly that lights on the rail speaks to what kind of man Albert could be. Later in the novel, he notices other living creatures besides butterflies. He says to Celie that she reminded him of a timid bird poised to take flight whenever she was frightened.[14] Celie is surprised that he noticed, and he admits that he was too foolish to care. As a young man, Albert is afraid to challenge the prevailing stereotypes that expect him to be stoic and rule his home with an iron fist.

After Celie leaves, Albert's deterioration is rapid and brings him close to death, an experience that usually is transformative. Sofia describes his condition to Celie, saying that he could not sleep; thought he heard bats outside his door, wouldn't bathe, and wouldn't eat. Finally, Harpo takes the situation in hand to save his father. His father was too weak to resist.[15] Clearly, his conscience is killing him. To recover he must make amends to Celie, whom he has hurt by withholding Nettie's letters, a mean-spirited, petty action, among his other transgressions. At Harpo's urging, Albert gives Celie all the letters, and in return he is reborn.

Albert begins where all must, just where we are. His existential questions regarding why we were born, why we have a particular sex, where we came from, and where we are going[16] all point to his central question: Why do we need love? While he does not know the answers, he is clear that we all do need love, and he knows that he has suffered because of his failure to marry the one that he loved. His choice, to allow his father to be the boss, affected not only his own life but the life of the woman he loved, his first wife Annie Julia, and his second wife, Celie. He made both wives miserable to match his own misery.

The transformation of Albert from villain to a deeply reflective and caring human being is clear. Walker transforms him like Nicodemus, who is born again. Alluding to John 3:1–7, in which Nicodemus asks how a man can be born when he is old, Walker introduces Albert's seashells as trope for water, implying that he can be born of water and of Spirit, as in the biblical text. After Albert's change, he views himself as "a natural man."[17] Celie says he takes care of himself. He works in the fields, cleans the house, cooks, and washes the dishes when he finishes dinner. Celie compares his behavior to being like a woman.[18] Instead he takes care of himself as all adults should do. He cares for others—again, not necessarily a feminine trait, but a human one.

Albert remains a natural man also in his sensuality. For Walker, sex and desire are not sinful. The key feature in the entire drama is love. Celie is capable of forgiving Albert because she says he loved Shug Avery and was loved by her.[19] Love is the redeeming quality. Love, for Shug, Henrietta, Harpo, and even Sofia and Celie, brings Albert into his best self. Love in Walker's work recognizes no gender, nor does it conform to man-made rules and regulations. In his mature years, Albert finally expresses his true self. He confesses to Celie that as a young boy watching his mother sew, he wanted to learn how to sew but was ridiculed by those who believed such activity was women's work. Women's work is an arbitrary assignment of value to genderless tasks, because whenever men are brave enough to go against the prevailing trends and stake a claim to the job, ironically it becomes acceptable but distinguished from women's work by the financial compensation. For instance, a man who likes sewing might become a tailor. A man who enjoys cooking might well become a chef. The confinement of gender roles will only engender frustration and anger, as in the case of Albert.

Albert reveals his admiration for Shug and her resistance to gender typing when he says that Shug acts manly. He means that she is brave, honest, and confrontational. In his estimation, to be womanly is to be timid, submissive, and perhaps even dishonest.[20] Clearly, forthrightness is the kind of freedom thought to belong only to men. Albert as Mr. _____ behaves like a stereotypical woman. He submits to Old Mr., and tells Celie that all he wanted was Shug Avery, but his father decided on another woman for him.[21] He accepts what he is given instead of fighting for what he wants, and that decision is a recipe for displaced anger and scapegoating. At one level Albert recognizes that Shug and Sofia are not like men or women.[22] Celie is quick to say that they are not like him or her. She also tells him that they are womanly, because it is women that possess the qualities he admires. Celie drives home her point by using Harpo as an example. Not as weak as his father, Harpo is passive-aggressive rather than confrontational until it comes to women, which makes him a coward. When Harpo becomes the unique person he was created to be, he wins back Sofia, his first love.

Walker seeks to heal divided humanity rather than divide it, and even make the masculine whole, which includes the feminine. Too many fully human qualities have received the designation either of masculine or feminine. One mistake that feminists made during the era of women's liberation in the late 1960s and 1970s, one that Walker avoids, was critiqued by Marianne Williamson in her spiritual analysis of that time. Williamson writes: "Certainly feminism has helped empower women, the women's movement has liberated us to actualize more of our human potential, and the modern view of women has helped us right injustices like the subjugation and oppression of females."[23] The central error, she insists, was to try to become like men. In doing so, women dishonor the sacred feminine. Walker escapes the tendency to dishonor the feminine but instead focuses on traits that are fully human. Strength, which is too often perceived as a masculine characteristic, is a part of Sofia, Shug, and all women who survive whole. Weakness, synonymous with the weaker sex, occurs in the male characters of Albert and Harpo. Walker's point is that strength is not governed by sex. Likewise, neither is modesty, a trait that Williamson identifies as feminine, and one that women should have maintained. Some would call chastity the modesty that she describes. For all the reasons that women might want to be chaste or modest, so should men. Characteristics or behaviors, in Walker's view, are neither masculine nor feminine, but uniquely human and governed by the ability to choose.

The critique of Harpo's character has mostly focused on his role in the Spielberg film rather than the novel. In the film he is a buffoon who falls through the roof; no such event takes place in the novel. Walker writes that she does not understand Spielberg's rendering of him unless he thought that Walker named Harpo for the comedian and clown, Harpo Marx. Walker states that he was not so named. Harpo tries as best he can to pattern his marriage after his father's, his only example. In some ways he is successful, but the problem is that he chooses the wrong woman to attempt to dominate. Like his father, he does have an affair with a woman to whom he is not married, Mary Agnes, and has a child with her. Unlike Celie, Sofia finds someone else as well, Henry Broadnax. Eventually, Harpo learns that his overbearing ways have driven the woman he loves away from him and possibly contributed to her troubles. Celie accuses him during the dinner at Sofia's sister's house, charging that if he had not tried to dominate Sofia, she would not have been vulnerable to the whites.[24] Harpo's effort to forbid Mary Agnes from going to Memphis and his reprimand of her about laughing indicates that he still has much to learn. He tells her it is bad luck to laugh at men.[25] His father's fall from grace when Celie leaves him, and Sofia, who laughs in his face, assist in Harpo's transformation.

The other men in the novel, while not central characters, are less hideous than critics claim. Grady is attracted to Mary Agnes, but he is neither an abuser nor a buffoon in the novel. The film scene with Grady and Albert smashing eggs on each other's heads is Hollywood idiocy, and not Walker's. Odessa's husband, Jack, is an upright man who supports his family and serves his country in the war. Henry Broadnax is supportive of Sofia and tries to please her.[26] On the other hand, the white men in the book do not fare as well. The warden is a rapist, and sexually assaults his own niece. In his vitriolic treatment of Sofia, the mayor is not much better. Walker successfully sexualizes racism by showing how it affects black women as blacks and as women. Sofia is kicked and beaten in the street because she is black. Similar treatment would not happen to a white woman. Squeak is raped because she is a woman.

WALKER'S WOMEN

The women are Walker's central text, and critics focus on her portrayal of the women as well. In her critique of Walker's women, Harris has stated that

Walker's portrayal of a character such as Celie is unrealistic, for she could not believe anyone could be so weak. Another point of view is that to deny suffering as unrealistic is to in fact deny some people's pain. Fortunately, in her 2001 book *Saints, Sinners, Saviors: Strong Black Women in African American Literature*, Harris admits that the idea of the strong black woman is a stereotype and often a harmful one because it sets unrealistic expectations for black women.[27] To be sure, when the novel begins, Celie is not a woman. She is a fourteen-year-old girl raped by a man she believes to be her father. Walker was chastised for this violent incestuous opening scene by critics who claimed she was airing dirty laundry, presumably to whites, because blacks surely already knew that acts of rape and incest existed within some families without regard to race, ethnicity, or economic class. Moreover, no such criticism is apparent of Ralph Ellison's highly acclaimed *Invisible Man*, in which Trueblood has sex with and impregnates his biological daughter while in bed with his wife, or of Mary Rambo's stereotyped portrayal in the same novel. In terms of incest, Walker certainly is not the first writer to broach the subject, not even for women writers; Toni Morrison's *The Bluest Eye* contains Cholly's rape of his daughter Pecola.[28] The anger and resentment directed toward Walker and *The Color Purple* do not stem from her portrayal of either male or female characters, but bear on her theology of transformation.

The Color Purple, in particular, calls to question a belief in God, and whether people should accept what they have been told as children or employ intelligence and intuition to arrive at a mature understanding. She poses questions, too, of what exactly this earth is, whether it is alive and sacred, and are we. Many people do not frequently contemplate these issues; for others, their scrutiny challenges traditional mythmakers—an act of sacrilege. Walker has been accused of having more concern with selfhood than with race and class issues. Race, class, and gender, however, comprise the self. Harris claims that Celie's letters to God require readers to stretch their imagination. She writes that she can imagine Celie talking to God—she says *with*, which suggests that God might talk back—and points to the example of Mariah Uphur in Sarah E. Wright's *This Child's Gonna Live*. But writing letters to God, Harris insists, is altogether another matter. She believes that "Even if we can suspend our disbelief long enough to get beyond that hurdle, what Celie records—degradation, abuse, dehumanization—is not only morally repulsive . . . it invites spectator readers to generalize about black people."[29] Harris further questions Celie's growth and maturation, saying it is incredible.

Writing to God is not so outlandish when one considers the example introduced by Toni Morrison in *The Bluest Eye*. Soaphead Church, the morally repulsive pedophile, writes to God. For spectator readers who embrace stereotypes and think in terms of broad generalizations, anything written may not change their views and, in any case, African American novelists are not obligated even to try to change their minds. The concern with external appearances too often becomes a roadblock to honest self-examination.

An even more curious criticism of Celie is that she is unrealistic for the setting of the novel. The novel takes place roughly between 1900 and 1945. Celie is fourteen when the novel opens in about 1914. By 1920 she is married to Albert, and the novel concludes during World War II. Celie's passivity is in step with the time, although individual personality accounts for large discrepancies in human behavior. Why some women submit (Celie) and others resist, like Nettie, Shug, and Sofia, is a mystery. Harris argues that Celie has knowledge of right and wrong. She writes: "And she does go to church; whether or not she believes what she hears, certainly something of the Christian philosophy seeps into her consciousness over the years."[30] Harris insists that there are guidelines for action, and indeed those do exist. For women, they might include Genesis 3:16: "Unto woman He said, I will greatly multiply thy sorrow and thy conception; in sorrow thou shalt bring forth children, and thy desire shall be unto thy husband and he shall rule over thee." This certainly appears to apply to Celie's situation, as does 1 Corinthians 14:34–35: "Let your women keep silence in churches for it is a shame for women to speak in church"; Celie does keep silent. Further, 1 Corinthians 11:3 states: "I would have you know, that the head of every man is Christ, and the head of the woman is the man; and the head of Christ is God." That Celie behaves like she has no head of her own is not surprising. Ephesians 5:22–24 instructs: "Wives, submit yourselves unto your husbands, as unto the Lord. For the husband is head of the wife, even as Christ is head of the church; and he is savior of the body . . . so wives should submit to their husbands in everything." Celie does. Furthermore, Celie states the dogma of the church to Sofia when she tells her Mr. is so abusive that she must talk to God, then justifies accepting the abuse by saying that he is her husband,[31] which means lord and master according to some biblical passages.

Wanting to maintain a marriage for the sake of children often is given as the reason some women stay in abusive relationships. Harris points out that Celie does not have any children with Albert. Given the time in which the novel is set, however, where would Celie go? No shelters for battered and abused women were available. She has no family to turn to for help. The church is not helpful, but rather is part of the problem. Society derives from a patriarchal legal system that afforded men the right to chastise their wives and children physically. Women and children were considered the property of men, and the term *domestic violence* was neither a crime nor a part of the vocabulary. Such is the case during the time of the novel.

Patriarchy has a long history dating back to antiquity. According to Walker, it dates to about five thousand years ago.[32] Under the Laws of Chastisement during the reign of Romulus in Rome (753 BCE), wife beating was acceptable and condoned. Under these laws, the husband had absolute rights to physically discipline his wife. Because by law a husband was held liable for crimes committed by his wife, these laws were designed to protect the husband from harm caused by the wife's actions; the husband was permitted to beat his wife with a rod or switch if its circumference was no greater than the girth of the base of the man's right thumb. The tradition of these laws was perpetuated in English common law and in much of Europe and in the United States.[33] The end of the Punic Wars brought more freedom to women, giving them property rights and the right to sue their husbands for unjustified beatings. However, in 300 CE, church fathers re-established the husband's patriarchal authority and the patriarchal values of Roman and Jewish laws. The Christian church has not led the fight for the fair and equal treatment of women any more than it fought for the liberation of black people. Roman emperor Constantine the Great had his wife burned alive when she was no longer of use to him.[34] In the Middle Ages, the church sanctioned the subjection of women. Priests advised abused wives to win their husbands' goodwill through increased devotion and obedience.

The habit of looking upon women as a species apart, without the same feelings and capacity for suffering that men possess, became inbred during the Middle Ages. In a medieval theological manual, a man is given permission to "castigate his wife and beat her for correction."[35] There is ample evidence illustrating the collusion between church and state regarding the abuse and control of women and children. While black people, for the most part, were not part of the law- and theology-making mechanism of Europe, the Moors may have been an exception. Nevertheless, the African patriarchal system was no better for women. Chinua Achebe's 1958 novel, *Things Fall Apart: The Story of a Strong Man*, is hailed for its description of pre-Christian African culture. Okonkwo, the strong man, beats his youngest wife, Ojiugo, for bringing him his dinner late. He is fined, not because he beat her, for that was his prerogative, but because he did so during the week of peace.[36]

Not until 1924 did a French court rule that a husband did not have the right to beat his wife. Prior to this, the Napoleonic Code was dominant in suggesting that "Women, like walnut trees, should be beaten every day."[37] This statement is echoed by Albert when he tells Harpo, "Wives is like children, you have to let 'em know who got the upper hand. Nothing can do that better than a good sound beating."[38] In the United States, many ignored wife beating and considered it a private issue under the cultural belief that a man's home is his castle, and that what goes on behind closed doors can remain in the dark. Not until brave souls like Alice Walker brought to light the physical battery and violence did the situation begin to change. In the 1970s, stories from women writers at once described what were then unfamiliar accounts of abuse to inform a disbelieving public of its widespread nature.[39] *Widespread* implicates violence toward women from men of all economic, social, racial, and ethnic backgrounds, and educational levels. Church-sanctioned subjugation of women is partly responsible for men's attitudes, and for women's acceptance. Only after the formation of Women against Abuse in 1976, and organizations like it, did the legal system in the United States begin to change.

Celie is a believable character whose story is told in a hundred different ways by a hundred different women in similar or worse situations. Prompted by Harris's essay containing anecdotal responses to *The Color Purple*, I decided to check statistics and compare the facts with Walker's depiction of Celie's abuse. I found that domestic violence is the leading cause of injury to women between the ages of fifteen and forty-four in the United States—more than car accidents, muggings, and rapes combined.[40] Three to four million women in the United States are beaten in their homes each year by their husbands, ex-husbands, or male lovers. One in every four women will experience domestic violence in her lifetime.[41]

In 1992, the American Medical Association reported that as many as one in three women will be assaulted by a domestic partner in her lifetime—four million in any given year.[42] An estimated 1.3 million women are victims of physical assault by an intimate partner each year.[43] The facts are clear; no exaggeration is necessary. Celie knows only how to stay alive, which is what she says to Nettie when Nettie tells her to fight.[44] Staying alive is more than a lot of women can manage. In Walker's fiction, Margaret cannot manage it, and neither can Mem.

The United Nations did not recognize domestic violence as an international human rights concern, and did not issue its Declaration on the Elimination of Violence against Women until 1993. The U.S. Congress passed the Violence against Women Act in 1994. Eighty-five percent of domestic violence victims are women.[45] The average prison sentence of men who kill women partners is two to six years, while women who kill their men partners are, on average, sentenced to fifteen years.[46] Women of all races are about equally vulnerable to violence by an intimate partner.[47]

Celie's lack of self-esteem, and the fact that Celie thinks she is ugly, are also of critical concern. After the publication of Morrison's *The Bluest Eye*, which exposed the pathology and tangled web of abuse that drives Pecola to desire white features and blue eyes to become beautiful, the issue of black beauty was exposed but unresolved in the literature of the 1970s. Harris states: "Nettie was there during Celie's early years, and Nettie apparently has a rather positive conception of herself."[48] The different experiences of the two sisters are striking. Nettie is not raped. Nettie is desired by the opposite sex and not rejected like Celie, and Nettie's intellect enables her to formulate a positive self-image. She is smart. As far as black beauty goes, in the late 1970s when *The Color Purple* was conceived and into the 1980s, the concept of beauty in North America had shifted back to traditional standards. The Black is Beautiful concept had become passé, and many black women and girls still struggled and even now wrestle with the issue of physical aesthetics.

"SOME PLACE WITH FUNNY STAMPS"

The letters from Nettie add substance to the novel, and place Celie's treatment and the abuse of women in a global context. A world exists beyond rural Georgia, and the letters give voice to that world and to the politics of race and gender. Walker situates Celie in the context of issues facing all black people in the diaspora. The letters represent the pervasive nature of oppression—the colonialism, sexism, racism, and Christian imperialism that Nettie eventually understands and shares. Nettie tells her sister about the framework on which patriarchy rests. In 1982, when *The Color Purple* was published, many women had not quite put together the relationship between all the -isms. Intersectionality was not yet in currency. Pan-Africanists and black nationalists who were aware of colonialism and imperialism either did not see or chose not to recognize the relationship between these forms of oppression and the treatment of women and girls.

David Bradley's 1984 article "Alice Walker: Telling the Black Woman's Story" suggests that Walker speaks for all black women, causing Harris to object. However, his assertion is not promoted by spectator readers/whites but by a black man, who surely must have known better. Walker responded to Bradley's *New York Times* article, an ad hominem claiming Walker's blind eye, which he mistakenly thinks is false, caused a distortion in her view of black men.[49] Walker wrote:

> Most of thinking humankind, even the totally blind, can now see quite clearly the oppression of women by sexist men, customs and laws, and I believe it is the prerogative of women to write freely (and as much) about their oppression by men (and to the same purpose) as men of color have written of their oppression by whites . . . "who would be free must . . . strike the blow," said our grandfather, Frederick Douglass. If he thought only his grandsons would act on this, he was mistaken.[50]

Others also criticized Walker: Audre Lorde, Pearl Cleage, and Mary Hoover, a San Francisco educator. Lorde claimed that Walker was chosen for the cover of *Time* magazine because she was not a lesbian and therefore posed no threat. Cleage wrote in the *Atlanta Journal-Constitution*: "The fact that *The Color Purple* is being hailed from *Ms.* Magazine to the *New York Times* . . . raises for me the question of whose vision of black life I am being prompted to accept and why."[51] Hoover claimed that Walker "went out of her way to make herself likable to white people."[52] Donna Green, an African American, led a movement in northern California to have the book banned from California high school English classes.[53] Maryemma Graham, writing in *Freedomways*, declared *The Color Purple* an outstanding novel but objected to Walker's portrayal of men, saying that Walker "identifies men as the sole source of female oppression."[54] Of course, women oppress themselves by adhering to male hegemony. Otherwise there is no one else to blame, but Walker does not place blame. Laws often oppress women, and men have made the laws. The economic system oppresses women, and women did not create that either. The church oppresses women and, until recently, women had no part in that either. Racism oppresses black women, but generally speaking, black women do not maintain intimate sexual and love relationships with racists. Herein lies the difference. Walker's critics may not see that her focus on personal change will result in the social and political changes they desire.

Walker has said that for her, writing is therapy. She recalls that as a lonely child, she wrote to comfort herself. When suffering from depression, she was able to write herself out of it because the act of creation is healing. The characters in *The Color Purple* heal through various creative acts. Celie creates folk pants for her therapy, Albert learns to sew, Harpo heals his broken heart by starting his own business when Sofia leaves, and Mary Agnes sings her way to wholeness. Walker's message about dysfunction, heartache, and pain is that within each person is the capacity to heal. She does not suggest, however, that people can achieve wholeness and well-being without support. Community, or what she has called a circle, is necessary for attaining balance.

In a *Writers Digest* interview, Walker states that writers should have a circle, a like-minded community to which they belong. In her works she clearly has the same intention for her characters.[55] She advocates for both solitude and community. The community of womenfolk in *The Color Purple* exemplifies the power of the circle. The scene in which the women close ranks against the men and announce that both Celie and Mary Agnes are leaving for Memphis with Shug is a turning point in the narrative. The men can either join the circle or be forever on the periphery. Slowly but surely, the men join hands, Albert as a friend to Celie, and Harpo as a companion to Sofia. When there is no circle of kinship in terms of like minds and friendship, it forebodes disaster. A circle of friends could have saved both Margaret and Mem in *The Third Life of Grange Copeland*. The lack of support so obvious in the lives of these abused and isolated women is present in *The Color Purple*.

While the need for friendship and community is apparent, so is the need for solitude. Walker's example of solitude as an enabler is Meridian. Celie also has a season of loneliness when Shug takes off with Germaine. The separation breaks her heart, but also enables her growth. Alone, she grows into her best self. She comes to the realization that she can live without Shug. Finally, Celie finds peace. She says she will be happy if Shug returns. However, should Shug fail to return, she will still be content.[56] Solitude can bring peace and self-acceptance, whereas circles can sometimes be constricting, as are the circle of militants in *Meridian*.

METAPHYSICAL READING OF *THE COLOR PURPLE*

> *Art is utterly dependent on philosophy; or ... on a metaphysic. The metaphysic or philosophy may not be anywhere very accurately stated and may be quite unconscious, in the artist, yet it is a metaphysic that governs.*
> —Lawrence, *Fantasia of the Unconscious*

Lindsey Tucker makes a compelling case for Walker's use of the epistolary form for *The Color Purple*: she employs the form to develop the individual by using language and to have a black woman write her own text to appropriate linguistic powers.[57] Gerri Bates traces the form back to seventeenth-century England and France and concludes that the form itself is indicative of the "culture of woman"[58] that contained diaries, letters, and journals. Some critics have pointed out that *The Color Purple* may be indebted to the African American slave narrative. While these observations are compelling, Walker may go further back than the seventeenth century for her narrative form. Hers is a parody of the Pauline text, or the Epistles of Paul to the Romans. While this idea may seem a stretch, a close reading reveals how Celie stands as sign and signifier of the content of Romans.

From the beginning Celie addresses her letters to God because, as the ultimate sign of the oppressed, according to her own husband, she is ugly, skinny, black, a woman, and that amounts to nothing.[59] The patriarchal power of the man in the role of her father, the gist of his message similar to Paul's injunction, silences her: "Let your women keep silence in the churches: for it is not permitted unto them to speak; but they are commanded to be under obedience, as also saith the law."[60] Walker is working in the tradition of the African American preacher, and she places this narrative squarely within Christian culture. With Celie's story, Walker interrogates every troubling aspect of Paul's letters and the other biblical texts that support his stance.

In terms of the form of her novel, Walker signifies on the apostle Paul, and with her opening chapter not only is Celie's silencing within the context of Christian tradition, but the letters describing Celie giving birth allude to Genesis 3:16, regarding the sorrow of childbirth. Celie's words accusing Harpo of making Sofia vulnerable to whites because he tried to rule her also relate to Paul's creed.[61] Walker is meticulous in her word choice. She shows the power of the biblical text in the lives of these people corrupted by the word, even as their actions corrupt the word in despicable ways. For examples, they force conception through the rape of a child, and force the child to take a husband she does not desire. The Bible not only enforces the submission of women, but also ensures the blind obedience of children with the Fifth Commandment instructing children to honor their father and mother, as well as with "Children, obey your parents in all things: for this is well pleasing unto the Lord."[62] Celie takes the biblical instructions to heart, as demonstrated in her response to Alphonso, the man she thinks is her father. Although Celie's mother dies cursing her, Celie refuses to hold it against her, even though the mother is the one responsible for protecting her daughter and has failed to do so.

When she was a small child saying Easter speeches at Ward's Chapel AME Church, Walker was attentive to the sermons grounded in biblical examples. In college, as she began to study various philosophies, she realized just how powerful theologies are in constricting the lives of the oppressed. In 1964–1965, as an undergraduate at Sarah Lawrence, she read Arthur Schopenhauer and exclaimed in her notebook: "What a way to look at individuality!!"[63] In this instance, Walker is responding to Schopenhauer's treatise, "Will." The French philosophers intrigued her; she wrote her honors thesis on Camus. She must have read more of Schopenhauer than her notebooks indicate, however, because she attributes to the character Albert, Schopenhauer's philosophy from "On Women," which states: "Women are directly adapted to act as the nurses and educators of our early childhood, for the simple reason that they themselves are childish, foolish, and short-sighted."[64] When Harpo asks Albert why Sofia won't obey, Albert's reply suggests that it is because she is like a child.[65] Albert's way of gaining the upper hand is through physical abuse. While philosophical misogyny does not spell out violence, the venomous ideas of male supremacy provide the rationale, just as white supremacy provided the impetus for the rape and lynching of black people.

Celie dies on the patriarchal cross of suffering—she even says that she knows she is dead[66]—and rises with the angry energy of the black god Kali. Celie affirms her way to wealth using her creative powers. Purple, used within the context of Christian liturgy, often during Lent season and for Easter, signifies pain and suffering and the royal resurrection. Purple as a color is also a gift within the non-Christian context of the novel. Ultimately, Celie's journey is one of choice. Some personalities would have responded to her circumstances with the chutzpah expressed in the Negro spiritual, "Before I'll be a Slave/ I'll be buried in my grave/ and go home to my God and be free," echoed in the poem by Frances Ellen Watkins Harper, "Bury Me in a Free Land." Celie accepts all sorts of abuse because she believes her submission will keep her alive. In one sense she is correct, physically alive but she is spiritually dead. When she is willing to die physically, she gives birth to herself spiritually.

Celie represents the least among us, and her narrative is a parable of spiritual evolution. She matures from a fundamentalist reader of the Bible to one who is enlightened, capable of reading between the lines and intuitive in her ways of knowing. When information arrives suggesting that her sister Nettie and the rest of her family are dead, Celie trusts her intuition. Celie continues to write to her sister, declaring that she expects her to arrive home safely.[67] Here the metaphysical lesson is not merely to trust in one's own spiritual wisdom, but that the act of setting expectations becomes a self-fulfilling prophecy. The same law or spiritual principle that operated when Celie expected the worst and received what she expected, still works for her when she changes her perspective. The law has not changed, but her use of it has.

Walker has been dubbed a student of New Age thinking. On the one hand, "New Age" is quite old, dating to the 1800s publication of Ralph Waldo Emerson's *Nature* and the beginning of the Transcendentalist movement. In a 2006 interview with Amy Goodman, Walker defines herself as a "Renegade, an Outlaw, a Pagan,"[68] and a lover of the earth. Her ideas align more closely with New Thought than with New Age, which dates from the hippie movement of the 1960s and 1970s. Critics have suggested that Walker's move to California may have led to hippie influences. Her college notebooks, however, reveal Walker to be greatly influenced by philosophy and not popular culture.

Both sociologist Robert K. Merton (1910–2003) and philosopher William James (1842–1910) postulated theories that might have influenced Walker's ideas that emerge in *The Color Purple* and in her later works. James's *The Will to Believe*, as well as Merton's coined phrase "self-fulfilling prophecy," apply to Celie. James wrote: "It is wrong always, everywhere, and for [*sic*] every one, to believe anything upon insufficient evidence."[69] Walker demonstrates that Celie's lack of self-confidence and self-worth acts as a catalyst for her experiences. She believes in the teachings of the church and a God for which she has no evidence. Celie accepts what others tell her, without question. Her sins of omission create the psychic environment that enables her oppression. The fact of her responsibility in no way excuses her oppressors. They are both culpable, the oppressed and the oppressor. Walker has stated that people are both.

Clearly Celie represents individuals everywhere, female or male. She stands for deep inertia. Harpo is Celie. Celie even recognizes that Harpo is afraid, just like she is.[70] Albert shelters his Celie-self by being a bully. Some people are so angered by Celie's inaction because she mirrors their shadow selves. Most people have been hurt by intentional abuse or even by unintentional slights that hurt their feelings, and unwisely take to heart fearful resentiments. From a Christian metaphysic, Jesus serves as example for spiritual growth and development, his crucifixion and resurrection a sign of the power humankind possesses. Celie also signifies the Divine feminine present in all women and men.

Walker questions the messages presented in the Bible. In the Beatitudes, Jesus is purported to have said that the meek shall inherit the earth. Celie is meek—quiet, submissive, easily imposed upon—and she does in a sense inherit the earth. Meekly accepting abuse as her lot, she sweats and works in the fields, the earth, from sunup until the close of day. To grow spiritually, she must move beyond her meekness and assert herself. She must believe that she is worthy. When she does rise from her grave of degradation, she inherits the material house and land, but more importantly, she comes into the possession of her spiritual vision, one that she thinks through on her own. Unorthodox and personal, her core beliefs fit well the woman she becomes.

The spiritual dimensions of *The Color Purple* form a highly significant component. Yes, the story is a rags-to-riches tale, but the transformative power of love moves the story from the particular to the universal. The prosperity that Celie enjoys, in what some critics label a fairy-tale ending, is part of the message that Walker conveys; that is, life continually expands and thrives. When people align with all of nature, notice purple the color, and see God in all, they too will thrive and benefit from the abundance of life. Humans appear to be the only creatures who struggle. Sai Maa (Divine Mother) believes that as humans we suffer because we resist change, preferring to hold onto the familiar.[71] Even in view of the highly detrimental, like Celie's environment, she is too afraid to let go and move into her best life. Her fear diminishes as her love for Shug increases and is reciprocated. Loving awakens her long-dead emotions, among them anger, a healthy wrath that enables her to assert herself. Anger in some ways requires a person to possess a certain amount of self-worth. For Celie, this feeling comes from Shug's affirmation of her physical self and knowing that she is not alone in the world, that her beloved sister is still among the living, as are her birth children.

An examination of the manuscript for *The Color Purple* reveals that this gift came to Walker as a whole. Unlike her other manuscripts, *The Color Purple* is a single handwritten document contained in spiral notebooks. It flows from beginning to end with few revisions. Walker recognizes that she has been a channel through which Spirit has spoken. She ends her novel acknowledging as much, by thanking everyone for appearing as characters. She is the author, but also a medium through which the ancestors have spoken.[72] *The Color Purple* is the turning point for Walker in that each work becomes more overtly spiritual. Walker states that she believes in change. Therefore, her major characters undergo alterations in their thinking and behavior. Walker also reveals that her existential concerns are related to questions of spirituality and religion.[73] She made this statement about religion at the beginning of her career, after the publication of her first novel. Her engagement with religious issues has only grown more profound.

When Celie tells God he must be asleep, it is her last letter to God until the final prayer/letter when she recognizes God as omnipresent. In the moment of her recognition of the unity of all, she is transformed. *The Color Purple* mirrors the passion of Jesus of Nazareth and his transformation into the Christ. Walker's novel raises the issue of how humanity can transform from helpless children into fully functional adults, and separate true belief from indoctrination. In the ultimate personal apotheosis, Walker's message is to embrace the power within, just as her characters Celie, Shug, Harpo, and Mr. do.

In her review of *The Color Purple*, Dinitia Smith complains of "its occasional preachiness."[74] That Walker preaches, and does so within the African American context of speaking the word, is arguably unarguable. There is a difference between the verb *preach*, however, and the adjective *preachy*. The difference is that preachy connotes self-righteousness, excessiveness, or tedious focus on a moral issue, none of which appears applicable to Walker even as *The Color Purple* is a sermon and preface to her next novel, leading into the temple of her deeper metaphysics.

NOTES

1. Gerri Bates, *Alice Walker: A Critical Companion* (Westport, CT: Greenwood Press, 2005), 88.
2. Walker, *In Search of Our Mothers' Gardens*, 39.
3. Felipe Smith, "Alice Walker's Redemptive Art," *Critical Essays on Alice Walker*, ed. Ikenna Dieke (Westport, CT: Greenwood Press, 1999), 120.
4. Quoted in Rudolph Byrd, ed., *The World has Changed*, 90.
5. Trudier Harris, "On *The Color Purple*: Stereotypes and Silences," *Black American Literature Forum* 18, no. 4 (Winter 1984): 155.
6. Ibid.
7. Kahlil Gibran, *The Prophet* (New York: Alfred A. Knopf, 1963), 42.
8. Harris, "On *The Color Purple*," 155.
9. Walker, *The Same River Twice: Honoring the Difficult—A Meditation on Life, Spirit, Art, and the Making of the Film*, The Color Purple, *Ten Years Later*, 33.
10. Claudia Tate, ed., *Black Women Writers at Work* (New York: Continuum, 1984), 180.
11. Bernard Bell, *The Afro-American Novel and Its Tradition* (Amherst: University of Massachusetts Press, 1989), 266.
12. Walker, *The Same River Twice*, 31.
13. Walker, *The Color Purple*, 27.
14. Ibid., 253.
15. Ibid., 224.
16. Ibid., 282.
17. Ibid., 260.
18. Ibid., 222.
19. Ibid., 260.
20. Ibid., 269.
21. Ibid., 282.

22. Ibid., 269, 270.
23. Marianne Williamson, *A Woman's Worth* (New York: Random House, 1993), 61.
24. Walker, *The Color Purple*, 200.
25. Ibid., 201.
26. Ibid., 82.
27. Trudier Harris, *Saints, Sinners, Saviors: Strong Black Women in African American Literature* (New York: Palgrave, 2001).
28. Toni Morrison, *The Bluest Eye* (New York: Holt, 1970).
29. Harris, "On *The Color Purple*," 156.
30. Ibid., 158.
31. Walker, *The Color Purple*, 42.
32. Michael Toms, "Gardening of the Soul" (interview with Alice Walker; New York Hay House Audiobooks, 2000).
33. See Emerson Dobash and Russell P. Dobash, *Women, Violence and Social Change* (New York: Routledge, 1992).
34. See Venessa Garcia and Patrick McManimon, *Gendered Justice: Intimate Partner Violence and the Criminal Justice System* (Lanham, MD: Rowman and Littlefield, 2012).
35. See Del Martin, *Battered Wives* (New York: Pocket Books, 1976), 34.
36. Chinua Achebe, *Things Fall Apart: The Story of a Strong Man* (New York: Heinemann, 1958).
37. Various sources, but see Mineke Schipper, *Never Marry a Woman with Big Feet* (New Haven: Yale University Press, 2004).
38. Walker, *The Color Purple*, 35.
39. Dobash and Dobash, *Women, Violence, and Social Change*, 2.
40. "Violence against Women, A Majority Staff Report," Committee on the Judiciary, United States Senate (October 1992), 3.
41. "Violence against Women, A Majority Staff Report," Committee on the Judiciary, United States Senate (August 29 and December 11, 1990), Senate Hearing 101-939, Pt. 1, page 12.
42. Patricia Tjaden and Nancy Thoennes, Full Report of the Prevalence, Incidence, and Consequences of Violence against Women. *Findings from the National Violence against Women Survey*. United States Department of Justice (November 2000).
43. Jill Smolowe, "When Violence Hits Home," *Time*, July 4, 1994.
44. Walker, *The Color Purple*, 17.
45. Bureau of Justice Statistics Crime Data Brief, Intimate Partner Violence, 1993–2001 (February 2003).
46. *Cost of Intimate Partner Violence against Women in the United States* (Atlanta: National Centers for Injury Control, 2003).
47. National Coalition against Domestic Violence, 1989.
48. Harris, "On *The Color Purple*," 157–58.
49. David Bradley, "Alice Walker: Telling the Black Woman's Story," *New York Times Magazine* (January 8, 1984): 25–37.
50. Walker, letter to the *Times*, *New York Times* (February 12, 1984).
51. Quoted in Evelyn White, *Alice Walker: A Life* (New York: Norton, 2004), 384.
52. Ibid.
53. Ibid.
54. Quoted in Rachel Lister, *Alice Walker, The Color Purple* (New York: Palgrave Macmillan, 2010), 12.
55. Jessica Strawser, "Interview: Alice Walker Offers Advice on Writing," *Writer's Digest* (August 31, 2010). www.writersdigest.com.
56. Walker, *The Color Purple*, 283.
57. Lindsey Tucker, "Alice Walker's *The Color Purple*," *Black American Literature Forum* 22, no. 1 (Spring 1988): 81–95.
58. Bates, *Alice Walker: A Critical Companion*.
59. Walker, *The Color Purple*, 206.
60. 1 Corinthians 14:34.
61. Walker, *The Color Purple*, 200.

62. Colossians 3:20.
63. Alice Walker Archive, Stuart A. Rose Manuscript, Archives, and Rare Book Library, Emory University (Box 35/1).
64. Schopenhauer, "Essay on Women," https://www.the-philosophy.com/schopenhauer-women.
65. Walker, *The Color Purple*, 35.
66. Ibid., 146.
67. Ibid., 280.
68. Amy Goodman, Pacificia recording. First Congregational Church, February 13, 2006.
69. William James, *The Will to Believe* (New York: Dover, 1960), 8.
70. Walker, *The Color Purple*, 27.
71. See Sai Maa, *Petals of Grace: Essential Teachings for Self-Mastery* (New York: Sai Maa publisher, 2005).
72. Walker, *The Color Purple*, 299.
73. Walker, *In Search of Our Mothers' Gardens*, 265.
74. Dinitia Smith, "Celie You a Tree," *The Nation* (September 4, 1982): 181.

Chapter Six

Entering the Temple

In 1996, *The Same River Twice: Honoring the Difficult* voiced Walker's hurt and frustration from the conflagration of criticism that followed *The Color Purple*, both the book and the film. Walker selected a spiritual title for her book, choosing what Clarissa Pinkola Estes calls the *Rio Abajo Rio*, the river beneath the river,[1] arrived at only through deep meditation and acts of creativity, with writing being one of those acts. River is a mascon[2] word in black religious and folk traditions. The River Jordan, where Jesus was baptized, projects the image of rebirth. The river is moving water or living water. The title is appropriate for Walker's narrative because she has, as Donna Seaman writing for *Booklist* reminds us, "paid dearly for her creativity and forthrightness about her belief in personal freedom on all fronts, from sexuality to spirituality."[3] The river in Walker's title symbolizes how she cuts her pathway to the sea. Like the river, she arrives at her destination only because she refused to compromise her truth despite physical or emotional impediments. Saying the same river twice is appropriately ironic, as no river is the same, and yet water is the changing same. From the beginning of time, or the time of no beginning, there is no new water, but ancient water that is seemingly changed by what it encounters. For Walker, writing the screenplay for *The Color Purple* was like trying to enter the same river water that had moved downstream.

The river is a familiar image and metaphor that represents life and mystery. One writer observes that a river succeeds "only because it finds its own way without short cuts, straight lines, or disregard of any physical impediments but in full acknowledgement of the reality of all that surrounds it, implying that the longest way round is the shortest and only safe way to the sea."[4] The statement provides the context for Walker's memoir, which chronicles the making of the movie *The Color Purple*. Her title, perhaps

Tree of Life. *Artist: James Perryman.*

taken from Heraclitus's statement, "You could not step into the same river twice," reminds one that it is impossible to step into yesterday. Equally important is the subtitle, *Honoring the Difficult*, which introduces Walker's understanding of *namaste*, the Sanskrit word that means to behold the Divinity in a person. Namaste is a greeting that also indicates the ability to see beyond physical appearances to the core that is Divine. The effort to honor the sacred in that which is difficult marks the significance of the subtitle. Walker can acknowledge the sacred even in the vitriol of her attackers. She understood that African Americans and, indeed, all black people have been so deeply wounded that many are unable to tolerate anything that approaches honest criticism. Honoring the difficult allowed her to face not only her own pain, but the collective pain of oppression.

The book begins with the journal entry titled "Fish and Bird Come to My House I Swim Away with Them." The short three-page writing sets the stage for what follows. Steven Spielberg (a Sagittarius) and Quincy Jones (a Pisces) represent bird and fish: Sagittarius refers to the secretarybird, *Sagittarius serpentarius*, and Pisces to fish. The essay records how they approached her for permission to turn *The Color Purple* into a movie. They came to her home on Galilee Lane in San Francisco on February 21, 1984. Walker agreed to write the screenplay, which she later realized would be like entering the same river twice. However, she set her mind to it, and on June 18, 1984, she mailed the first draft to Los Angeles.

The title of Walker's screenplay is "Watch for Me in the Sunset or the Color Purple." She confesses that fear drove her to change the name because she thought that Spielberg's film might not live up to the name of the novel. According to some students, the title sounds more like the name of a Western movie. The title appears in the film in Nettie's letter to Celie but does not appear in the novel. Walker was unable to produce a successful screenplay. By 1985, she realized that they needed to find a screenwriter. Walker met Dutch-born Menno Meyjes, and he was chosen for the job. He was apprehensive because he was not American, not black, and not a woman. He should have been nervous, because there were issues that he just did not seem to understand. Had Walker not been ill, suffering from Lyme disease, she would have objected more stringently to the weakening of Shug's character. Walker writes that "Shug's completely unapologetic self-acceptance as outlaw, renegade, rebel, and pagan; her *zest* in loving both women and men, younger and older,"[5] was completely avoided. In the film version, Shug becomes a woman dependent on her father's approval and forgiveness. The most jarring line in the entire movie, the one that unravels Shug as rebel, is when she says to Celie in the bathtub scene, "I never known a child yet to turn out right unless there's a man around!" At first irritated by the line, later I saw the glaring irony; for certainly, some children do not turn out right precisely *because* there is a man around. Celie is one example.

Walker laments the fact that Celie's and Shug's relationship is not erotic as it is in the novel. Students who view 1985 as the Stone Age believe that the audience would not have been able to tolerate eros between two women on-screen at that time. They probably are correct; still, I remind them of the 1968 mainstream film, *The Killing of Sister George*, which featured a lesbian couple. Some students who are aware of the film (women's studies majors) inform me that it is a white film for a white audience, and that a black audience is different, by which they mean less tolerant. They are correct. In the hailstorm that followed the watered-down version of the novel in the film, it is not hard to imagine what would have transpired had the true relationship between Shug and Celie appeared on the screen.

The second part of Walker's title, *Honoring the Difficult*, must be understood within the context of more than just the harsh criticism she received after *The Color Purple* was published as a book and subsequently released as a film. During the filming of the movie, Walker suffered from what she believes was Lyme disease from a tick bite. She also suffered the loss of her beloved mother, whose slow decline from a paralytic stroke was emotionally painful for Walker. The third challenge was also emotional as her partner, Robert Allen, confessed that he had been unfaithful with one of his old girlfriends. The three gifts, or the three challenges, constitute the difficult. Walker chooses to honor the difficult by remembering, accepting responsibility for her choices, forgiving whatever needed to be forgiven, and finally by releasing.

Walker's writing, while therapeutic for her, has produced a book in which some critics judge her to be self-obsessed[6] because it contains, as always with the inclusion of her journal entries, more perhaps than the reader would be interested to know. In a review of *The Same River Twice* David Walton wrote: "Reading the book is like sifting through a drawer, but there are some surprises: Ms. Walker's touching letter to the actor Danny Glover, who portrayed a character based on her grandfather; an account of a dream in which she debated the film with a black angel; a letter from a man whose lover, who was leaving him to enter a lesbian relationship, gave him *The Color Purple* to read."[7] What is also compelling about the book is the section that explicitly honors the difficult.

Regarding the criticism surrounding *The Color Purple*, both the book and the film, Walker acknowledges that neither was perfect. By the time she writes this book, criticism appears to be the least of Walker's worries. Her physical health or the lack thereof is of great concern, and the doctors say they can find nothing wrong with her. She believes the difficulties are "spiritual tests."[8] One test challenged her love and loyalty to her mother and the conflict it presented as she tries to maintain loyalty to herself. Watching her mother's decline caused her grief, but an awareness of her mother's indoctrination by organized religion, especially the Jehovah's Witnesses that her mother joined late in life, caused Walker to become resentful. She believed that her mother became less loving and her thinking more narrow due to her church attendance and adherence to religious dogma. One painful incident concerned a niece that Walker paid to care for her mother. Her mother objected to the once-loved niece because of the latter's lesbianism. Accepting our mothers as human beings with flaws, blind spots, and shadow sides is a difficult task, one that Walker struggled with, and by engaging the difficult she achieved clarity regarding mother/daughter relationships. She concludes that "mothers and daughters are meant to give birth to each other—that is why our challenges to each other are so fierce."[9]

The other difficulty Walker bravely honors is the betrayal of her longtime friend and life partner who confessed to having an affair during the time she was writing *The Color Purple*. The emotional pain of betrayal paled in comparison to the fear and dread she felt because of her undiagnosed illness. She worried that a connection might exist between her illness and her lover's infidelity.[10] Walker's illness caused her to suffer a crisis of faith. Mystics often suffer a dark night of the soul. Walker says, "Pagans (people whose primary spiritual relationship is with Nature and the earth . . . have crises, too."[11] Walker discusses what Evelyn Underhill describes as one of the common features of mysticism, an encounter with the sacred.[12] Walker's encounter, one of many, took place on a day when she began to garden again. Bending upon the earth for Walker serves as a prayer—an act of supplication and worship.[13] In her transcendent moment, she recognizes the earth, nature, and the universe as her own Trinity.

From the beginning pages of *The Same River Twice*, Walker makes clear her spiritual intention. The cover of the first edition features a rendering of the labyrinth at Chartres Cathedral and a long quotation by Jean Shinoda Bolen from *Crossing to Avalon*. Walking the labyrinth, like following the river, can lead to the Goddess—the sacred feminine. Walker announces in the preface that she intends to explore the wounds of the soul. Her crisis of faith leads to an explanation that sounds very much like a Christian characterization of God. She writes that "as a born-again pagan [I] lie on the earth in worship . . . like my pagan African and Native American ancestors, who were sustained by their conscious inseparability from Nature prior to being forced by missionaries to focus all their attention on a God . . . in 'heaven.'"[14] Walker says that because nature has become tired of human abuse, she was bitten by three ticks that cause Lyme disease.

Assigning the earth or nature human qualities, that is, being tired of people or being vindictive, is no different from an anthropomorphic God that suffers from anger and jealousy or gets mad and sends a flood. Perhaps Walker meant that because people have poisoned the environment, and because the law of cause and effect is fully operative, the outcome of a poisoned environment would then be a toxic element in that environment, and the tick that causes Lyme disease might be one of those outcomes.

ENTERING THE TEMPLE

The Temple of My Familiar (1989), Walker's fourth novel, is a pastiche of history according to her. Arranged into six parts or chambers, as it were, the book mimics and satirizes the official history generally accepted as fact.

Critics did not love this book; however, the criticism was not in the same category as that toward *The Color Purple*. Some critics, including Claudia Dreifus, acknowledged the development of themes and ideas introduced in earlier works, but others, Joyce Maynard being one, were harsher in their critique. Maynard called the book "a radical feminist Harlequin romance written under the influence of hallucinogenic mushrooms. . . . There's a little black history here, a little crystal healing there, with a hot tub and some acupressure thrown in for good measure."[15] Walker describes her role as artist in *In Search of Our Mothers' Gardens*, saying the writer must be free to explore and to bring forth what needs to be known. Writers are not called to cheerlead the masses, but to bring them the truth. She admits that the process of writing or creating often leads to loneliness and unique concepts that society might reject.[16] Joseph Campbell supports her idea when he states:

> There's an old romantic idea in German, *das Volk dichtet*, which says that the ideas and poetry of the traditional cultures come out of the folk. They do not. They come out of an elite experience, the experience of people particularly gifted, whose ears are open to the song of the universe. These people speak to the folk, and there is an answer from the folk, which is then received as an interaction. But the first impulse . . . comes from above, not from below.[17]

While Walker's college notebooks do not indicate whether she ever took a class from Joseph Campbell, he was a professor at Sarah Lawrence during the time she was a student there. Her statements on art resonate with his. About *The Temple of My Familiar*, she has said: "What I'm doing is literarily trying to reconnect us to our ancestors. All of us. I'm really trying to do that because I see that ancient past as the future, that the connection that was original is a connection; if we can affirm it in the present, it will make a different future."[18]

Walker is harshly criticized by those who take her writings as New Age gibberish. In the review, "Smiley Face with Dreadlocks," J. O. Tate launches a personal attack on Walker and what he sees as "intimations of personal divinity" and "feminist heresies."[19] The heresy Tate refers to is articulated by Joseph Campbell and only becomes heresies when uttered by a woman. Campbell writes: "The vandalism involved in the destruction of the pagan temples of antiquity is hardly matched in world history."[20] The destruction is carried out by "the organized church." Campbell asks then answers his own query: "And why couldn't Christians live with another religion? What was the matter with them?" His answer, not unlike Walker's, states that "It's power. I think the power impulse is the fundamental impulse in European history. And it got into our religious traditions."[21] Walker's so-called feminist heresies indeed are not derived from thin air, but can be found in uncensored historical records.

The many voices in the novel decenter the text in ways that may be disconcerting. In Walker's first draft of the novel, her editor, John Ferrone, suggested that she eliminate the many chapter titles to establish some continuity, allowing the semblance of one story instead of a collection of many. While she complied by removing titles like "Breath," and breaking the book into six parts, she refused to begin with Suwelo's story, even though the editor thought Suwelo and Fanny were the center of the book. In her correspondence Walker does not say why she refuses to make the changes, but by not doing so, it is clear that the disorganization and fragmentation are deliberate. Bonnie Braendlin describes *The Temple* as "a polyvocal text in a postmodern context, an approach usually reserved for white male authors."[22] The fractured story line supports the postmodernist reading that Braendlin posits. Nevertheless, the novel/romance also continues Walker's message of the mystical unity introduced in Celie's closing letter in *The Color Purple*: "Dear God, Dear stars, dear trees, dear sky, dear peoples. Dear Everything. Dear God."[23] God is Everything. Braendlin acknowledges Walker as mystic when she says: "Undaunted by adverse criticism, perhaps even encouraged by it . . . [she] persists in pursuing her messianic goal."[24] Walker's goal is to produce, as does any good sermonic text, an interrogation of our lifestyle and a questioning of what we truly believe and why. She asks us to interrogate the official version of history that seems irrefutable. What McHale terms the "ontological flicker"[25] destabilizes accepted reality, and "apocryphal history contradicts the official version" of history and blurs the boundaries between the real and the fictional.

The first destabilizing event in *The Temple of My Familiar*, especially so for students, is the sexual intercourse that occurs between Zedé and Arveyda. The occurrence is destabilizing because Zedé is Arveyda's mother-in-law, and Carlotta is his wife and Zedé's daughter. Students in the Alice Walker seminar, the majority of whom are daughters, cannot imagine such a betrayal. Part of their inability stems from the fact that they cannot imagine their mothers as sexual beings. Beyond this unwelcomed surprise comes the question, "What is Walker doing?" Angela Davis has said that Walker "shakes what we most take for granted."[26] Indeed, she does, but further she challenges the reader to think a new thought. In *The Temple of My Familiar*, unlike in the other books she has written, the emphasis is not on the individual—a word that appears to be one but actually contains a divided self, a dueling self that struggles to exist apart from the whole, creating duality (indivi-dual). In this book, Walker moves toward chiasma, erasing the boundaries of the self so that metaphorically Arveyda crosses over, becoming Jesús, Zedé's deceased lover and Carlotta's father. Therefore, on the one hand there is no betrayal because there is no singular self (Carlotta) to betray. On the other hand, Zedé has broken her daughter's heart, for which she begs her forgiveness. Carlotta's suffering, anger, and need to forgive work on one level of the novel. The necessity to forgive the deepest hurt is a requirement for psychic and spiritual wholeness. On another level, Walker insinuates what some might view as a transmigration of the soul or metempsychosis. Zedé's statement that Carlotta had brought her dead father home when she introduced Arveyda[27] offers the clue. Arveyda is used, his body usurped by the soul of Jesús.

Braendlin suggests that Arveyda's desire for Zedé originates in his anger over his own mother's neglect when he was growing up. Perhaps anger produces desire, but it is far more likely that instead of anger, he experiences a longing for the love of his dead mother. He is unable to explain to Carlotta why he has become intimate with her mother. Still, his response offers a clue when he admits to being in love with Zedé and says the Greeks might know what to do.[28] His statement referring to the oedipal complex supports Braendlin's claim that he desires his own mother. Acknowledging that Walker's past works have been critical of and rejected motherhood, Braendlin argues that *The Temple* valorizes motherhood. Walker only honors motherhood, however, as it relates to the great cosmic Mother. Individual mothers continue to fail in too many aspects to be considered valorized. Olivia is not a warm and loving mother to Fanny; Arveyda's mother is insane; Suwelo's mother lacks the courage to leave her abusive husband before he kills her (like Mem and Margaret) and, just as Meridian calls her mother a "willing know nothing" in Walker's second novel, Lissie describes in similar terms her mother as an ignorant person who spoke in a language she had never heard, using words like "taters and rotgut . . . sugar tits." She said she had never in all her lifetimes seen "a more stupid person."[29]

Eventually Lissie and her mother become friends, but only after the mother conforms to the daughter's liking. While "Mothers . . . are given voice and allowed to speak the discourses that have been suppressed through male-authored history,"[30] Lissie's and Zedé's stories do not honor motherhood as much as they valorize womanhood. The fact that they are biological mothers is tangential to their narration of the past. Lissie runs away with the photographer, Henry Laytrum, abandoning her only daughter, and Hal's claim that Lissie was a good mother is not supported by the facts of their lives.[31]

Part 1 of the novel introduces a host of characters: Carlotta and Arveyda, Zedé and Jesús, Lissie and Hal; Fanny and Suwelo. Each person has a spiritual connection to the other, if not in fact *in* the other. When Suwelo has an affair with Carlotta, he sees Fanny's grief in her face. Similarly, when Fanny and Arveyda make love, they share the same vision prompting Fanny to breathe "My . . . spirit" and Arveyda to reply, "My . . . flesh."[32] The plum tree that Arveyda describes represents the tree of life, containing as it does all creatures.

Walker's romance can be compared to a symphony in terms of its organization. Part 1 serves as the introduction, presenting the central characters.

Part 2 is the exposition and depicts other characters that constitute the core philosophy of *The Temple of My Familiar*, including characters from *The Color Purple*: Olivia, Celie's daughter and Fanny's mother; Ola, Fanny's father; Lance, Fanny's stepfather and Olivia's late husband. Part 3, the development, expands the story of Zedé's escape from South America with the infant Carlotta and Mary Ann Haverstock. Modulation takes place in part 4. Suwelo's tempo is adjusted by his conversations with Lissie and Hal. Part 5, the recapitulation, sets forth in no uncertain terms what the text's core message has presented from the beginning, the unity of all things. The recap is contained in "The Gospel According to Shug Avery." The coda, part 6, not only concludes but gives the further development of the characters. Finally, Walker's acknowledgment, "It is a pleasure to have always been present,"[33] might indicate that she is her own narrative device, she is Lissie, and so are we all.

READING THE GOSPEL IN *THE TEMPLE OF MY FAMILIAR*

Nature is visible Spirit; Spirit is invisible Nature.
—Schelling

Toni Wynn describes Walker's *The Temple of My Familiar* as creating a sense of place, which it certainly does. Wynn writes, "The use of the word 'temple' in the novel's title points the reader to Walker's emphasis on place. Although we can consider the body to be a temple, one's most personal vessel for self-care and respect, [Wynn] casts Walker's temple as the physical space that her characters (and their familiars) use and where they reside."[34] Contrarily, I wish to focus on the interior spaces of the soul, the temple not made with hands that Walker's temple represents. I will proceed with the argument based on Corinthians 6:19. While it may seem ironic to quote from the biblical text to explicate the work of one who rejects organized religion, Walker, while recognizing that the institution of Christianity has used the Bible to oppress and exploit women and people of color, understands that the literature of the Bible is rich and symbolic. She has in her archival collection a sheet that contains a list of references to the Bible; thus, it is not illogical to assume that she has read and been influenced by the Bible as literary text. Furthermore, she has stated in interviews that she loves the Gnostic gospels. Of course she would, for as Karen King points out, the Gnostic Gospel of Mary is:

> an intriguing glimpse into a kind of Christianity lost for almost fifteen hundred years.... It presents a radical interpretation of Jesus' teachings as a path to inner spiritual knowledge; it rejects His suffering and death as the path to eternal life; it exposes the erroneous view that Mary of Magdala was a prosti-

tute for what it is—a piece of theological fiction; it presents the most straightforward and convincing argument in any early Christian writing for the legitimacy of women's leadership; it offers a sharp critique of illegitimate power and a utopian vision of spiritual perfection; it challenges our rather romantic views about the harmony and unanimity of the first Christians; and it asks us to rethink the basis for church authority.[35]

Paul's letter to the Corinthians, "do you not know that your body is the *temple* of the Holy Spirit *who is* in you, whom you have from God, and you are not your own?"[36] offers a framework for examining Walker's use of the word *temple* in her title. Lissie's temple, which Walker describes as a literal place, makes it plain to see how one could read the passage as privileging a literal space. Her description is vivid, consisting of lush colors of coral and turquoise. It is a square one-room adobe elaborately decorated with deep blue painted designs.[37] Walker is careful to indicate that it is not stone, but painted mud. These elements and colors described in Lissie's dream-memory are addressed to no one and are sandwiched between Hal's narrative to Suwelo and Arveyda's omniscient narration to Carlotta about her mother and South America. The placement of Lissie's dream destabilizes the reader, moving the text from literal reading to dream vision in which nothing is what it appears to be but stands as symbol for something else. Mud of which the temple is made can be viewed as the image of hue-manity set forth in the second chapter of Genesis: "And the Lord God formed man of the dust of the ground."[38] Mud also signifies "the union of the purely receptive principle (earth) with the power of transition and transformation (water). Mud is regarded as the typical medium for the emergence of matter of all kinds. Plasticity is . . . one of its essential characteristics and it is related, by analogy, with biological processes and nascent states."[39] The prominent colors in Lissie's dream, coral, turquoise, and deep blue, relate to healing and to spirituality. Deep blue or indigo is associated with intuition and the ability to open the third eye and reveal spiritual insight.

Lissie's dream/memory signifies the hue-man-being able to heal itself, possessing spiritual insight and a familiar, spirit/soul, composed of all, birds, reptiles, and fish. The meaning of the dream is situated in the treatment of the familiar. The familiar, as Walker states, "is your own free spirit."[40] The wild, free spirit and symbolic colors, blue being the dominant color, is denied the freedom to express itself. Lissie represents metaphorically the ancient African in the face of the white invaders. White people stood and watched Lissie restrain her lovely familiar.[41] She does this to continue her conversation with whomever she is speaking to, as it is not clear to whom she is telling the dream/memory. Everyone watched as she betrayed the familiar.[42] Self-betrayal is the only kind that exists. Walker's epigraphs indicate as much, from Shug's declaration that "the deliberate invocation of suffering is as much a boomerang as the deliberate invocation of joy"[43] to Ola's reminder that the present we are experiencing can show up as the future.[44] This destabilizing chapter of three pages seems to relate directly to the African professor with the dead-looking eyes, who claimed that African Americans' statements about being sold into slavery by their uncles were cliché.[45] Lissie counters his statement with her own memory of the uncle who sells her and her mother, brother, and sister. Walker interrogates the organization of the African family by demonstrating that the organization of family life that required the uncle to assume responsibility for his deceased brother's wife and children caused many men with more wives and children than they knew what to do with to seek relief by selling away the excess.

Several chapters later, we see the complete destruction of the familiar, indicating the abandonment of the free-spirited self. Attempting to silence the internal voice of our free spirit results from adhering to superimposed customs and traditions, including organized religion that diminishes the voice of woman and devalues her blood. In the Protestant tradition, of which I am most familiar, the blood of Jesus rather than the mother's blood is praised as holy and redemptive, although even Jesus would not have been born without a woman's blood. In patriarchal Christian society, the power of birth is usurped, making another birth necessary. One must be born again, this time not by the labor of woman, and must be rebaptized, not in the water that breaks in the mother.

Myths are public dreams, dreams are private myths.
—Joseph Campbell

That Zedé's story about the priest attempting to become like women should seem farfetched is interesting, considering the stories that exist as official history and what some critics assume to be facts. For instance, in his review of *The Temple of My Familiar*, J. M. Coetzee writes that Walker in her "fabulous stories" that challenge white male mythmaking should understand that "history is not just storytelling. There are certain brute realities that cannot be ignored."[46] Coetzee does not identify what exactly the brute realities are. It is a fact that priests have historically denied their sex by dressing differently from ordinary men, donning long robes symbolic of dresses and by abstaining from intercourse with women. Zedé's comment about the bitter-looking expressions on their faces suggests the outcome of repressing desire and foreshadows Lissie's dream memory.[47] She describes herself as a priest, going to temple in a long white robe.[48] Of course, we know that not all priests were able to successfully repress their natural desires or the unnatural ones, and therefore broke their vows or committed profane acts against children. Zedé's story is no more incredible than the biblical narrative of Adam and Eve, or the Hopi story of Spider Woman, or the Yoruba story of Ife. All creation myths go back to nothing. All come from oral traditions and are based on hearsay. Walker's myth is as valid as any other. The mind fears and sometimes worships what it does not understand, according to Zedé,[49] and according to Walker, when she was still a student at Sarah Lawrence, writing notes on the philosophy of Augustine. Zedé tells Arveyda that she is speaking only of man's mind because, not understanding women, men began to fear them. What Walker does not include here but what Lissie makes known in describing her many lived experiences is that fear often turns to hate. Zedé explains that the mystery surrounding women and their ability to produce life feeds the awe in men, so that in the beginning they worship women. As childbirth becomes less awesome to men, the effort to control the woman's body grows. Not only do men require marriage to be able to identify their progeny, they become physicians delivering the women's babies, they make laws governing what women can and cannot do with their own bodies, and these may be some of the brute realities of history that Coetzee requires of valid history, as opposed to storytelling.

On a metaphysical level, Walker's story about the first women and men plays out in uncanny and perhaps hitherto inexplicable ways. For instance, the entire Christian concept of born-again Christian is obviously skewed, considering Walker's mythmaking. The erasure of woman from the process of salvation is ironic and made so because of the language men use; 1 John 5:6 states, "This is He who came by water and blood," and theologians (women included) have interpreted this to mean the "blood of the cross" instead of the water and the blood of the mother. All men come into the Kingdom of God, which Walker posits as being right here and right now, through the water and the blood of the mother. In some patriarchal traditions, that fact is so undesirable that the myths to replace it state that a child can be produced fully grown from the masculine head or from the mother's side.[50] From Joseph Campbell, Jung, and others, we know that myth represents subconscious fear and the working out of anxieties. Campbell has said that myth, to fulfill its mission, must continually transform, as older myths do not adequately tackle the issues of contemporary society, a fact that Walker recognizes. The changing cosmological reality before the moon walk and after advances in astrophysics produce a new understanding of our cosmology thus require a new mythology. The photograph of the earth from the moon, "Blue Marble," makes visual the unity principle Walker observes. Looking at the earth from outer space, there is no separation, no boundaries, no borders; just one earth and one people. Campbell posited that new myths would arise from the exploration of space and from the photograph of the earth from space. From the perspective of space as new vantage point, it is possible to view the wholeness Walker strives to embrace. Campbell suggests that this unity might be "the symbol [one earth/one people] for the new mythology to come."[51] According to Campbell, the four functions of myth are metaphysical, cosmological, sociological, and psychological. They all function as methods of social control. In this country the biblical tends to rule the metaphysical, tries to dominate the cosmological, and, for some, influences even the psychological and sociological aspects of their being.

Walker's right to make myth is sanctioned by Campbell's statement: "Myth must be kept alive. The people who can keep it alive are artists of one kind or another. The function of the artist is the mythologization of the environment and the world."[52] Zedé says that for the people of the village, the blessings from the priests came not from the men themselves, but from the beauty of the artistic garments they wore. Walker privileges art and artistic creativity over religious dogma or ritual, suggesting that art and prayer are one in the same. Or to state the idea more precisely, the garment—the work of art—is itself a prayer and the artist—the creator of such beauty—is the real priest. Art as therapy, a Jungian concept, appears regularly in Walker's works. Zedé's recounting of the myth of womanhood and motherhood to Arveyda echoes the analysis of Western patriarchal domination of motherhood that Adrienne Rich identified in her groundbreaking book, *Of Woman Born*.[53] The masculine projections of motherhood "are fantasies born of male fears, desires, and needs, featuring the demand for unconditional love, absolute forgiveness, and non-hesitating self-abnegation on the part of all women, even those who are not actually mothers."[54] The most optimistic aspect of Walker's mythmaking is the idea introduced by Lissie's multiple lives and Zedé's explanation to Arveyda that we get to live what we create.

In her narrative to Arveyda, Zedé says, "We are our grandmothers."[55] By this statement she means we are now who they were, just with new experiences added and without the clear memory that Lissie possesses. This idea is just another way to read Ephesians 4:25, "We are members one of another." Once when Walker was asked about her belief in reincarnation, she quipped that if we come here once why is it so hard to believe that we can come here more than once? No one has explained why we come here once, and no one has evidence to prove that we only come once. Lissie embodies Walker's provocative statement regarding memory and the eternality of life. Following a long tradition of spiritual seers and in the spirit of William Wordsworth (1770–1850), who wrote, "Our birth is but a sleep and a forgetting:/ The soul that rises with us, our life's star,/ Hath had elsewhere its setting/And cometh from afar."[56] Walker creates Lissie as one who remembers everything, the meaning of her name. Lissie's section immediately follows Zedé's conversation with Arveyda. Thus, the story Zedé began is continued by Lissie. Lissie has lived many lives and remembers them all. Even though she claims never to have been anything but a black woman, her final self-portrait reveals otherwise. She is ashamed that she has been a white man and responsible for so much suffering and destruction of the world, but she has been white and male and plant and animal. White men live life as black women and men. The outcome is as close to justice as anything one can imagine. Men experience life as women and vice versa, and as human beings mistreat animals and our planet, we get to experience the treatment as animals and plants. We get to experience all that we create.

As scholar Ikenna Dieke clearly articulates, Walker's book angers and frustrates many because it consciously signifies "on a worldview that has become the benchmark of traditional Western metaphysics—dualism."[57] Briefly referred to at the beginning of this book as an aspect of Christianity that Walker rejects, *The Temple of My Familiar* interrogates duality even more than in her previous books. Dieke's definition of dualism is pertinent: "Dualism, essentially, is a theory of knowing that represents reality in terms of an irreconcilable dyad—of two mutually irreducible elements or classes of elements."[58] Duality includes the theory of the Great Chain of Being, which introduced Ruth to racism in Walker's first novel. The Great Chain privileges white males as superior beings in relation to everything and everyone else, including white females. Rationality is accepted as the only reality. Irrationality, identified as feminine, must be avoided at all cost. In *Temple*, Celie's granddaughter Fanny falls in love with spirits and experiences fluid personality boundaries. Along with Lissie, Fanny is the best example of a person capable of embracing the metaphysical. The implication, however, is that all are able, but most are unwilling to fully open to Spirit.

Shug's theology expressed in "The Gospel According to Shug Avery" is systematically enacted in each of the six sections of the book. The first blessings that constitute her gospel begin with "Helped." However, in the drafts Walker used "Blessed" the way it appears in the Bible's Beatitudes. It is unclear why she changed the word to helped. The answer might lie in the difference between the definitions of the two words. A blessing, according to Webster, is to receive God's favor and protection. Helped means to make it easier to do something, which leaves the agency in the person's hands, as opposed to out of her or his control.

The first declaration in Shug's gospel regards racism and further clarifies the need for human agency rather than Divine intervention, though some might beg to differ. "Helped" are those who work to eradicate racism within themselves.[59] Most applicable to Fanny, this statement also applies to Walker who, in one of her student essays, writes that she is "still of the dirt poor, starving, but fighting people in the South who sing out in the midst of their misery."[60] Her lingering resentment makes Walker, like Fanny, an enemy of her own racism as she seeks to eradicate all feelings that are unloving.

Fanny is so determined to alleviate the emotions that prompt her to wish that white people would just slide off the planet[61] that she finds a therapist to help free her from such thoughts and from thoughts of murder: she'd had visions of slicing off the heads of whites.[62] At the core of her anger about the behavior of white people collectively is an unresolved childhood event. Fanny had a white playmate, Tanya, to whom she was close. Tanya had a racist grandmother who one day caught Fanny kissing her granddaughter on the cheek. She slapped Fanny so hard that she knocked her down. This repressed memory is the genesis of Fanny's resentment toward white people. The rest of Shug's gospel states that once racism is conquered, it will be possible to live in harmony in the world and reject the ancestor, in this case the bigoted grandmother, who has passed away. Helped also are those who are considered illegitimate children, for if they have been conceived in love, they will enjoy life despite their suffering.[63] This verse applies to Fanny because her conception, though vague, was the result of the rape of her mother, and her father did not marry her mother, making Fanny what was once called illegitimate. The statement also refers to Carlotta. The sexual encounter between Zedé and Jesús is tantamount to a "father's tenderness and . . . mother's orgasm."[64] Carlotta's life as a bell chemist does lead to dancing and to peace.

Ola, Fanny's father, is too busy living to respond when wrongfully attacked, Shug's gospel maintains. While each verse of the gospel pertains to a character specifically, each character in turn is not one-dimensional. For instance, Ola is especially complicated. To begin with, it appears that he rapes Olivia as punishment for kissing the white man, Ralston Flood. Olivia recalls the event to Lance, her future husband. She had kissed the Englishman that she tutored in Olinka. Ola/Dahvid saw her and became angry. She kissed him, but she says it was not enough.[65] What makes her recounting of the incident sound like rape is that she says he took it upon himself to punish her. Rape is often used as a weapon against women perceived to have made some transgression, and it looms large in all of Walker's works. So Dahvid turned Ola the revolutionary playwright is far from innocent. He is guilty of abandoning Nzingha's (Fanny's half sister) mother, who fought by his side for their country's independence. For all his revolutionary zeal, some of his actions appear retrograde. For example, when he returns from his time in Europe, he brings Nzingha a blonde, blue-eyed doll named Hildegarde. This, coupled with sending his daughter to Catholic school, causes one to wonder if the doll does in fact represent Saint Hildegarde of Bingen, the mystic (circa 1098–1179). Both the doll and a Catholic education would alienate his daughter from her mother and her mother's culture. Describing Ola to Fanny, Nzingha says their father made many mistakes, mainly out of ignorance.[66] Walker's point, apparently, is that all truth is one. Even those who are themselves corrupt can often be revealers of the truth. Ola's plays are provocative revelations of the truth.

Shug's gospel of love is statement for unconditional love and applicable to all the characters. Each one has something to forgive, something to accept about the other, who really is not the other at all but an aspect of the universal self. Fanny must accept Suwelo's limitations, and her mother's limitations and inability to be especially demonstrative toward Fanny. Suwelo must forgive his mother for staying with his father, and his father for his inability to recover from his experience in the war, and for trying to force that experience on him by suggesting that he go to Vietnam. Arveyda has to accept the shortcomings of his mother and her death; Zedé must release the terrible events that happened to her, the gang rape, the murder of her lover, and the shame that she felt as a result of her life in South America. Hal must learn to love Lissie for all the parts of herself, even the aspects that he fears. He must also accept himself as an artist. His artistic vision is the only one that he has, as every time he stops painting, he goes blind. Ultimately Lissie, who some, including John Ferrone, call a narrative device, must accept all of her selves as well, including the parts of which she is ashamed.

Lissie is neither Goddess nor narrative device because her point of view does not encompass the narrative point of view. She is too mortal for the Goddess on the one hand, and on the other, if she were to be taken as Divinity, then what she does and says can be seen as exceptional and beyond our own capacity. I believe Walker is saying that we are all, female and male, Lissie. We can remember. People are like the flock in *Jonathan Livingston Seagull*, too eager to hang on to what is known, afraid to experience the unknown, even though the bird tells the flock that he is not any different from them. This echoes Jesus' statement to his followers: they can do what he does, and even more. Lissie tells Suwelo and, by extension, the reader, that the eye has always seen and the mind is omniscient, capable of recalling all that was ever known.[67] Lissie is a character like the other characters that inhabit the temple. She is Walker's example of the unlimited possibilities of the human experience.

THE ECOLOGY

Marvin Gaye's 1971 release of the album *What's Going On?* did for popular culture in terms of raising environmental awareness, what Rachel Carson's 1962 book *Silent Spring* did to expose the ecological issues. Philosopher Simon P. James poses the question, "Why Conserve Nature?"[68] Walker's answer coincides with that of Chief Seattle, who in 1852 said, "This we know: the earth does not belong to man, man belongs to the earth. All things are connected like the blood that unites us all. Man did not weave the web of life, [sic] he is merely a strand in it. Whatever he does to the web, he does to himself."[69] Therefore, to conserve nature is to save the self.

The final chapters of *The Temple of My Familiar* offer a different perspective for understanding nature, one that is not separate. The inclusion of Frida Kahlo and reference to her deer painting makes plain not only the idea of our oneness with other animals, but also the androgynous nature of being human, to which Walker often refers.[70] In Frida Kahlo's painting she is woman and buck, both feminine and masculine. So, too, is Lissie as lion, not lioness in her final self-portrait. The ultimate image of Lissie as lion, wearing the provocative bright red high-heeled slipper on her back paw, signifies on our limited perspectives and harkens back to Toni Morrison's *Beloved*, in which Paul D tells Sethe that she has two legs and not four, implying that she is above four-legged animals instead of at one with them.

An ecocritical or ecofeminist reading of *The Temple of My Familiar* focuses on the women characters, Zedé, Carlotta, Fanny, and Lissie. These central women characters represent nature, both because as women, they are oppressed, but also because, as Susan Griffin pointed out in her landmark book, *Woman and Nature: The Roaring inside Her*, women are thought to be closer to nature than men.[71] Western civilized man represents himself as rational, and in the novel Suwelo, the Western-educated professor of American history is the prototype. Fanny, his wife, in his mind is irrational. She is emotional whereas he sees himself as unemotional. In patriarchal thought men are objective, detached, and emotionless. These characteristics are the core of Suwelo's problems in his relationship with Fanny. Another male character, although a secondary one, Fanny's father Ola, sees himself as superior to nature as represented by his treatment of his African wife, who epitomizes nature and cultural tradition. He represents intellectual tradition. The women characters as representatives of nature encourage the men to locate nature within themselves. Griffin blames Plato and all Western philosophy and religion for separating Spirit from matter and identifying women with "the earth as sustenance for humanity and as victim of male rage."[72] Walker's vision is hopeful; it suggests that people can change. Instead of utopian, her vision offers an alternative way of seeing.

NOTES

1. Clarissa Pinkola Estes, *Women Who Run with the Wolves: Myths and Stories of the Wild Woman Archetype* (New York: Random House, 1992), 30.
2. From Stephen Henderson's *Understanding the New Black Poetry*, a mascon word contains a massive concentration of black experiential energy and cultural resonance. For example, poplar or live oak refers to types of trees; however, within the context of black experiential memory a hanging or lynching tree is the energy in the word.
3. Donna Seaman, "Alice Walker Banned," *Booklist* (August 1996), 813.
4. Laurens van der Post, *Jung and the Story of Our Time* (New York: Random House, 1975), 66.
5. Walker, *The Same River Twice*, 35.
6. *Kirkus Review* calls the writing self-absorbed (November 1995).
7. David Walton, *New York Times Review of Books*, January 14, 1996.
8. Walker, *The Same River Twice*, 42.
9. Ibid., 172.
10. Ibid., 27.
11. Ibid., 42.

12. Evelyn Underhill, *Mysticism: A Study in the Nature and Development of Spiritual Consciousness* (New York: Dover, 2002).
13. Walker, *The Same River Twice*, 43.
14. Ibid., 25.
15. Joyce Maynard, "The Almost All-American Girls," *Mademoiselle* (July 1989): 72.
16. Walker, *In Search of Our Mothers' Gardens*, 264.
17. Joseph Campbell, *The Power of Myth* (New York: Doubleday, 1988), 85.
18. Walker, "Writing to Save My Life" (interview with Claudia Dreifus), in Rudolph Byrd (ed.), *The World Has Changed* (New York: New Press, 2010), 85.
19. J. O. Tate, "Smiley Face with Dreadlocks," *National Review* 41, no. 12 (1989): 48.
20. Campbell, *The Power of Myth*, 199.
21. Ibid.
22. Bonnie Braendlin, "Alice Walker's *Temple of My Familiar* as Pastiche," *American Literature* 68, no. 1 (March 1996): 49.
23. Walker, *The Color Purple*, 292.
24. Braendlin, "Alice Walker's *Temple of My Familiar*," 48.
25. Brian McHale, *Postmodernist Fiction* (New York: Routledge, 1987), 90.
26. Quoted in *Alice Walker: Beauty in Truth* (film by Pratibha Parmer, 2013).
27. Walker, *The Temple of My Familiar*, 19.
28. Ibid., 26.
29. Ibid., 54.
30. Braendlin, "Alice Walker," 55.
31. Walker, *The Temple of My Familiar*, 114.
32. Ibid., 408.
33. Ibid., "Acknowledgements," n.p.
34. Toni Wynn, "Participant, Witness, Activist: Alice Walker's Novels in Historical Context," in *Alice Walker: Critical Insights*, ed. Nagueyalti Warren (Ipswich, MA: Salem Press, 2013), 207.
35. Karen King, *The Gospel of Mary of Magdala: Jesus and the First Woman Apostle* (Santa Rosa, CA: Polebridge Press, 2003), back cover.
36. 1 Corinthians 6:19.
37. Walker, *The Temple of My Familiar*, 118.
38. Genesis 2:7.
39. *Cirlot Dictionary of Symbols* (New York: Philosophical Library, 1983), 222.
40. Walker, "Interview with John O'Brien," in Byrd (ed.), *The World Has Changed*, 35.
41. Walker, *The Temple of My Familiar*, 119.
42. Ibid., 120.
43. Ibid., 144.
44. Ibid., 236.
45. Ibid., 61.
46. J. M. Coetzee, "Possessing the Secret of Joy," in Gates and Appiah (eds.), *Alice Walker: Critical Perspectives, Past and Present* New York: Amistad, 1993), 26.
47. Walker, *The Temple of My Familiar*, 46.
48. Ibid., 118.
49. Ibid., 49.
50. See the story of Athena's birth in Greek mythology, as well as the story of the birth of the Buddha.
51. Campbell, *The Power of Myth*, 33.
52. Ibid., 85.
53. Adrienne Rich, *Of Woman Born* (New York: Bantam Doubleday, 1977).
54. Judith Arcana, *Every Mother's Son: The Role of Mothers in the Making of Men* (New York: Seal Press, 1986), 197.
55. Walker, *The Temple of My Familiar*, 48.
56. William Wordsworth, *Ode Intimations of Immortality*. www.poetryfoundation.
57. Ikenna Dieke, "Walker's *The Temple of My Familiar*," in Ikenna Dieke (ed.), *Critical Essays on Alice Walker* (Westport, CT: Greenwood Press, 1999), 127.

58. Ibid.
59. Walker, *The Temple of My Familiar*, 287.
60. Alice Walker Archive, Stuart A. Rose Manuscript, Archives, and Rare Book Library, Emory University (1061, 8/3).
61. Walker, *The Temple of My Familiar*, 301.
62. Ibid., 296.
63. Ibid., 297.
64. Ibid.
65. Ibid., 152.
66. Ibid., 262.
67. Ibid., 65.
68. Simon P. James, *In the Presence of Nature* (New York: Palgrave Macmillan, 2009), 90.
69. Quoted in Campbell, *Power of Myth*, 34.
70. Walker, *The Temple of My Familiar*, 323.
71. Susan Griffin, *Woman and Nature: The Roaring inside Her* (New York: Harper, 1978).
72. Ibid., preface (n.p.).

Chapter Seven

Sexual Healing

Sexual healing in Walker's novels *Possessing the Secret of Joy* (1992) and *By the Light of My Father's Smile* (1998) is both physical and spiritual. *Possessing the Secret of Joy* challenges a tradition of controlling female sexuality through genital mutilation or cutting. Female genital mutilation (FGM) is a practice often linked to Islam and purported to be in the Koran by some Muslims; however, there are Muslims who insist that the practice is not supported by the Koran.[1] In *By the Light of My Father's Smile*, sexual healing focuses on remediating Christian beliefs and attitudes toward sex that inhibit women's sexual development. In a worldview that rejects duality, where sacred and secular are one, sexuality is an integral part of spirituality. Walker uses her works not only as a spiritual gateway to enlightenment, but also to support her activism and inspire legal and political changes. The penultimate two novels discussed in this chapter examine sex that many people think is secular at best or sinful at worse.

THE SECRET OF JOY

Unlike reviews of *The Temple of My Familiar*, *Possessing the Secret of Joy* initially received positive reviews. Charles Larson of the *Washington Post Book World* wrote that Walker's novel and its subject were a work whose time had come.[2] Janette Turner Hospital, in the *New York Times Book Review*, recognizes the "mythic strength" of the book and states: "The characters speak as Jason and Medea speak in Greek drama, as Greed and Sloth and Grief speak in the medieval plays,"[3] or as my argument posits, as the bones that come alive and connect in the presentation of a great black sermon.[4] As more people read the book, which made the best-seller list, predictably the negative attacks surged forth, and in some respects for the same reasons that criticism embroiled *The Color Purple*. The book was read by many as sociology instead of fiction. Walker was attacked for making what some called sweeping generalizations about the whole of Africa. In *The Color Purple*, the issue that some men were and are abusive was viewed as an attack on all black men. The tactic is called obfuscation, and turns the conversation from what is to what is not.

Walker assumes a spiritual communal space, one inhabited by both feminine and masculine energies, comprising a universal self, one recognized in Jungian psychology. In the novel, Mzee (Carl Jung) states Walker's case when writing to his niece. Mzee says he is dismayed at what happened to Tashi, but recognizes it as something that is also done to him—affirming a truly universal self.[5] The practice of FGM affects both women and men. In the novel, Tashi's husband Adam's sex life is destroyed because of Tashi's choice to undergo the initiation rite. Adam even tells Tashi that the men do not know what the initiation procedure is. They often hurt themselves when they try to penetrate the women.[6] Pierre, Tashi's stepson, says that blood flows on both sides, meaning from the woman and the man.[7]

The term *female genital mutilation* is deliberately used instead of female circumcision, or genital cutting. Admittedly, FGM is laden with value judgment. One such judgment is that the female body is perfect, whole, and complete without any alteration to its genital parts. Both circumcision and cutting also are value laden. Circumcision is defined as the surgical removal of the foreskin of the penis in a young boy or man. Recently because of objections to the use of FGM, the meaning of circumcision has included the removal of the clitoris in females. But the use of circumcision suggests that what is done to girls is no different than what is done to boys. For boys, at least for those in AIDS-ravaged parts of Africa, the act of circumcision is believed to lower the risk of contracting sexually transmitted diseases and might in fact lower the risk of prostate cancer.[8] There are no health benefits to clitoridectomy. The use of the word *cutting* is thought to be more innocuous than FGM, but gives no indication as to what is cut. Female cutting could just as well refer to the cutting of female hair, which is of no consequence as it can be regrown. Of course, there is objection to the use of mutilation because no one wants to think of herself as maimed or crippled. But the use of euphemisms cannot alter the fact that the word *mutilation* describes exactly what takes place. Taken from the Latin *mutilat*, mutilate means to "lop off." What is lopped off results in maiming the use of a body part, depriving the use of or crippling an essential part of the body. For these reasons I choose to use the term FGM.

Critics have called Walker a cultural imperialist, accused her of imposing Western values and crossing cultural boundaries, and have made other hurtful accusations. Lauret claims that Walker exaggerates when she calls the procedure torture.[9] Fortunately, the World Health Organization (WHO) agrees with Walker and defines torture in the following manner:

> FGM also constitutes torture and cruel, inhuman or degrading treatment ... as affirmed by international jurisprudence, including by many of the UN treaty monitoring bodies ... the Special Procedures of the Human Rights Council ... and the European Court of Human Rights (*Emily Collins and Ashley Akaziebie v. Sweden*).[10]

In 1993, just one year after the publication of Walker's book and creative efforts to raise awareness surrounding the practice of FGM on children and young women with the documentary film Walker made with Pratibha Parmar, the General Assembly of the United Nations, in its Declaration on the Elimination of Violence against Women, stated that indeed FGM is torture. Article 1 states: Violence against women shall be understood to encompass, but not be limited to, the following: Physical, sexual and psychological violence occurring in the family, including battering, sexual abuse of female children in the household, dowry-related violence, marital rape, *female genital mutilation* and other traditional practices harmful to women, non-spousal-violence and violence related to exploitation.[11] In addition, article 4 adds that "States should condemn violence against women and should not invoke any custom, tradition or religious consideration to avoid their obligations with respect to its elimination."[12]

Walker insists that the reason female genital mutilation has taken root [is] because with the rise of patriarchy, men needed to force fidelity on women. Remaining faithful to a man meant the woman would have only his children. It was a way of controlling the patriarchal line and of ensuring that one's material assets were passed only to one's own offspring (sons) after death. In Rome and other places, the chastity belt served the same purpose. The practice itself, like Chinese foot binding, teaches us the extent to which patriarchal power will go to control a woman's body.[13]

Regarding the rhetoric of outsider versus insider, as a person of African descent, Walker is particularly sensitive to the imperialistic, hegemonic, and arrogant encroachment of the so-called West regarding cultures different from white, Anglo-Saxon, protestant, male, and capitalist. Discussing whether Walker should write about the taboo subject of someone else's culture (a culture that might indeed have been her own were it not for slavery and the uncles that decided to sell her ancestors) is beside the point. The question is whether FGM is a problem that needs to be addressed. Can a social problem be fictionalized to reveal a deeper truth? It can and has been. Examples abound: Harriet Beecher Stowe's *Uncle Tom's Cabin* comes to mind. Chinua Achebe's *Things Fall Apart* is an African novel revealing a deeper truth; Margaret Walker's *Jubilee* . . . the list is extensive. Walker did not single-handedly produce change regarding how the world perceives FGM. Her voice joined a chorus of other women and men, black and white, who have taken a stand. Ngugi Wa Thiong'o's 1965 novel, *The River Between*, might have been the first work of fiction to introduce the practice of FGM. Fran Hosken's 1983 publication of *The Hosken Report: Genital and Sexual Mutilation of Females* led to her being accused of "cultural genocide"[14] for daring to broach the subject. In 1975 Hosken established the Women's International Network, and her report, completed in 1979, was instrumental in gaining the support of WHO and the United Nations to view FGM as a human rights violation. Dr. Nahid Toubia, a Sudanese surgeon working since 1985 to enlighten women about the integrity of their bodies, established an organization to eliminate FGM in 1994. Dr. Olayinka Koso-Thomas, a gynecologist, published *The Circumcision of Women: A Strategy for Eradication* the same year as Walker's novel. In 1989 Hanny Lightfoot-Klein published *Prisoners of Ritual: An Odyssey into Female Genital Mutilation in Africa.* Her work focused on the women in Sudan and found that some women who have undergone FGM can retain the ability to experience orgasm.[15] At the end of *Warrior Marks*, the book that accompanies the film of the same name, Walker includes a list of suggested readings as well as organizations.

Walker does not ignore the many Western traditions that result in body alterations. She mentions breast implants and plastic surgery and even vaginoplasty or what some refer to as a facelift for the vulva. The clear distinction is that, while patriarchy is the underlying impetus for women wanting to appear desirable for men, in most cases the choice belongs to the woman. No one forces or tricks her into having what usually is a very expensive procedure, and the procedures are not, as a rule, performed on children for cosmetic purposes.

While I privilege those voices that support Walker in opposing FGM, there are countervailing arguments. In fact, this year, after teaching *Possessing the Secret of Joy* and showing students the film *Warrior Marks*, Dr. Fuambia Ahmadu, an anthropologist from Sierra Leone, spoke on campus in favor of the initiation. My class and I attended her talk. The points she raised were not new, and centered on the insider/outsider issue that Walker herself deals with in the novel. What was interesting about Ahmadu's argument is that it was based on the same premise as the 1960s Black Nationalist argument that some Afrocentric groups espouse today. Clenora Hudson-Weems's *Africana Womanism*[16] is an example. The argument is based on the idea of "complementary," which states that women and men complement each other while maintaining strict gender roles. Complementary and interdependence are the rationales for sexual division of labor. While this custom might have worked in an agrarian society, even Dr. Ahmadu was forced to admit that because of economic changes, women are at a distinct economic disadvantage when they are utterly dependent on men who are free to withdraw their support at any time they choose. Still the questions remain: "Should African women be allowed to engage in the practice sometimes called female circumcision? Are critics of this practice, who call it female genital mutilation, justified in trying to outlaw it, or are they guilty of ignorance and cultural imperialism?" These questions appeared in a *New York Times* article written by John Tierney.[17] The subject is complicated, but the central issue might hinge on informed consent and the age at which one can give consent. Cher once quipped that if she decided to have her breast sewn on to her back she would, and it was nobody's business if she did. But if she did the same thing to her child, we would call it child abuse. The provocative issue in the novel hinges on consent. Why doesn't Walker make Tashi a child, and students often ask why she does not. If, as some critics[18] claim, she is simply advocating her political agenda, then why not use that which will evoke the most support? The novel is more than a political manifesto. Like the works from the beginning of her discourse, choice is the central component. A child is not given a choice. The choice that Tashi has adds to the dramatic tension of the novel.

Possessing the Secret of Joy has been discussed in terms of its social and political implications, to the detriment of its artistic quality; even the narrative elements are often distorted. As with all of Walker's books, this one begins with an epigraph or two. Walker's quotation from *An African Saga* provides the book's title. The quotation for the title, while important, will be discussed later. What is central to the novel is a statement from a bumper sticker, which is humorous because a critic of *The Temple of My Familiar* (J. O. Tate) accused that novel of reading like a series of bumper stickers. Walker writes back to him, saying okay, here's one for you: "When the axe came into the forest, the trees said the handle is one of us. *Bumper sticker*."[19]

The *tsunga* (circumciser) in the novel, M'Lissa, is a woman and the axe handle; the trees are the women and girls on which she performs FGM. The axe blade is patriarchal power that forces women to act as handles to enforce and perpetuate male authority. The novel opens with Tashi, the central character, realizing that she is dead. She then recalls a story about three panthers. Two of the panthers, Baba the male and Lala, were happily married until Lara enters their relationship as co-wife. She is unloved by Baba and resented by Lala. The point of this parable is not to support polygamy, as Lauret claims: "polygamy is not condemned in the novel but condoned, if it is practiced without envy":[20] the focus is on the acceptance of tradition without any critical examination of its purpose. Baba enjoys male privilege without accepting responsibility for it. He tells Lala, the wife he loves, that tradition requires him to have sex with his co-wife. He shirks all responsibility by saying that he did not create the practice.[21] Walker is saying that because they accept without resistance the things that have been handed to them, someone will suffer. In this story it is the co-wife as unloved outsider. Baba and Lala are happy until they comply with tradition; then they are miserable. The word *tradition* derives from the same root word as *traitor*. The mystic Osho writes that "tradition is a betrayal of life. It is treachery."[22] Tradition can prevent people from living in the present moment, as well as from examining with a critical eye why things are the way they are. The panthers' situation mirrors that of Tashi and Adam, who enjoy sex until Tashi conforms to tradition making them both unhappy. Lara, as the outsider, learns to love herself and, as she does, she kisses her reflection into the bottom of the lake, effectively taking her own life, and the life of her unborn child.

If one examines the names that Walker selects for her panther characters, Lara and Lala, it becomes clear that Lala is a variant form of Lara (from Latin, meaning protection). Lala is Slavic in origin, however, and recalls the Russian writer Boris Pasternak, whose 1957 novel *Dr. Zhivago* contains the character Lara. Lara and Lala are aspects of the same self. Distraught because of her choice to follow traditional customs, Lara (in the panther's case, to become the co-wife) is eventually able to recover, as does Tashi, but as with Tashi her recovery ends with her death. Baba, which means father in many African languages, is the father of confusion in this fable. He could have taken a stand against tradition, but he was too busy enjoying making love to two panthers and then blaming it on custom.

The panther threesome also mirrors the relationship between Tashi, Adam, and Lisette, Adam's French mistress. Lala's words regarding polygamy reject tradition, saying that it is painful and cannot be in their best interest.[23] Her statement foreshadows Tashi's courtroom rant, where she asks those present if they know what she has lost.[24] She screams at the judges. In the end, Tashi effectively commits suicide by killing the *tsunga*. She, like Lara is satisfied.[25] Tashi utters the words after she has been killed; indeed, she tells the story after facing the firing squad for killing the *tsunga*.

Walker uses several devices to create a dream-like quality to the novel and to alert the reader that we are not in real time. One such device is the organization or, rather, the disorganization of the book. The story begins with Tashi's tale that foreshadows her life. Then the next chapter is Olivia's, and begins with her pointing to the way Tashi talked.[26] What is the way? To whom is Olivia speaking? Apparently directly to the reader, and assuming that we have heard Tashi's story. Everything that Olivia says is a memory of their childhood and of the first meeting when she observes Tashi crying. Olivia is not developed as a substantial character. She is just a disembodied voice. They are all airy-fairy voices instead of characters. Another device that Walker uses is italics. The chapter following "Olivia," which is Tashi's, begins with the first two paragraphs in italics. It is a memory that Tashi recalls in what some have mistakenly identified as Jung's office. It is not. Tashi says that Olivia has brought her to see this psychiatrist. It is Adam who much later takes her to Jung. The person Tashi describes is "Not the father of psychoanalysis."[27] Therefore, he is not Freud. Her description of dark hair and beard suggests that perhaps it is Wilhelm Stekel, who physically favored Freud, his once-admired mentor. Tashi says the doctor she is seeing favored Freud. His office, across the street from a school, suggests that perhaps they are in London or some other city, not in the Alps.

The memory that Tashi recalls in the doctor's office introduces Dura, Tashi's sister, who has died from the FGM performed by M'Lissa. Tashi recalls a story that her family has kept alive about Dura who as a baby picked up a burning twig and placed it in her mouth. The twig burned her severely enough to leave a scar.[28] The story sets the tone for the callous way children are treated by those in her village. The question, "Did anyone help her?"[29] remains unanswered because Tashi cannot bring herself to remember the rest of the story. One can guess, however, at the outcome because the story is told with laughter that disregards the pain of the crying child. In the film *Warrior Marks*, Walker asks why all the adults are laughing and making merry while the child is in pain. This story, too, is part of the puzzle for understanding Tashi's insanity. Help sometimes is key to having choice. In the previous novel, *The Temple of My Familiar*, the "Gospel According to Shug Avery" says, helped are those who know. One could easily conclude, damned are those that don't! Tashi needs the help of wise and sympathetic adults to make rational and beneficial decisions, just as Dura needed to be rescued from the burning stick. Choice is a matter of consciousness. A crawling baby does not possess the level of consciousness needed to make informed choices. At what age, then, are children capable of making informed choices? Walker's argument raises this question and attempts to unpack the centuries of mythology, religion, and misinformation regarding traditions. Even when we believe that we are making informed choices, there often are missing parts that could better inform our actions. Such is the case with Tashi. To be informed requires discipline and self-reflection. Walker repeatedly says that the answer is within the self, and not in the answer from the priest, the political leader, not even from mothers and grandmothers who may be slaves to tradition. Had Tashi been willing to resist custom and cry out the grief for her sister, she might have avoided her own death.

Instead, Tashi obediently buries the memory of her sister's death. The unresolved conflict of repressed memories and grief, coupled with her own debilitating health condition that results from FGM, is exacerbated by Adam's extramarital affair and drives her mental illness. Adam's first chapter opens with the realization that what he remembers about his wife as a child might not be accurate. Olivia has said that when they first saw Tashi, she was crying. Olivia, Adam, Nettie, Corrine, and Samuel were missionaries to Olinka, Tashi's village in *The Color Purple*. Walker explains that the book is not a sequel, but some of the memories do in fact come from events that take place in *The Color Purple*. Adam does not remember Tashi's tears.

Later in the novel, Lisette tells the son that she has with Adam that "men refuse to remember things that don't happen to them."[30] Olivia's memory is the correct one, because following Adam's chapter is Tashi's, saying how she was told not to cry.[31] She recalls how the people in the village wanted to make a good impression on the new black missionaries. They refused to acknowledge her suffering and demanded her silence. The analogy with the silencing of Celie is clear. She, too, was told that she had better not tell.[32] Silence is an intriguing word, and Walker has used it in several ways. Josie's mother in *The Third Life of Grange Copeland* is silent as her daughter is abused; Grange is silent and turns to stone in the presence of the white land owner; in *Meridian*, because she spoke, Louvinie's tongue is cut out forcing a permanent silence, and Meridian is silent in church when her mother urges her to speak. In *The Temple of My Familiar*, Hal's father harbors resentment because he kept silent when sexually embraced by Heath; Suwelo is silent about his parents' death; Arveyda's mother falls silent, neglecting her son and eventually dying; Zedé is silent about her past. Here, the entire village of Olinka demands Tashi's silent conformity. On the other hand, silence means more than just to refrain from speaking, and can be an act of meditative worship. Since meditation requires a certain level of consciousness, silence appears later in Walker's characters who are most spiritually developed. In *The Temple of My Familiar*, Fanny meditates and masturbates.[33] Spiritual development and sexuality are the central issues in the next novel, *By the Light of My Father's Smile*.

Tashi suffers the loss of autobiographical memories because she kept silent about witnessing her sister's death. She eventually, after undergoing FGM, becomes psychotic. Walker is not suggesting that women who undergo FGM are psychotic afterward. In Tashi's case there are several stressors. The first significant stressor is that Tashi is a witness to what happens to her favorite sister. She slips inside the initiation site at the time that Dura is being mutilated, hears her screams, and sees M'Lissa cast off Dura's vulva by carrying it between her toes so as not to touch it; thus, Walker dedicates the book, "with Tenderness and Respect to the Blameless Vulva." A hen gobbles down the body part,[34] indicating again that it is the female turning in on herself. Research has shown that witnessing trauma is detrimental to children and adults and can result in post-traumatic stress disorder. Even medical trauma and painful, invasive treatment for life-saving reasons can result in acute stress disorder; Tashi is traumatized by her sister's death.[35] The second stressor is only alluded to in this novel. Nettie's letter to Celie in *The Color Purple* is explicit. Colonialism destroys Tashi's village. In the name of progress, the British build a road through the village, knocking down anything in their way; then they charge the people rent for whatever land there is left to live on. Rubber trees are planted where their farms once stood.[36]

Tashi's anger at what has been done to her people explodes in her conversation with Olivia before she runs to the bush to join the freedom fighters and participate in the initiation ceremony, one of the last vestiges of what she views as her dying culture. Colonialism radicalizes her. When Olivia begs her not to go, Tashi, after calling Olivia and her missionary family "the white man's wedge," says: "You want to change us . . . so that we are like you. . . . We look at you and your people with pity. . . . You barely have your own black skin, and it is fading."[37] The loss of property, land, livelihood, this reduction to the status of beggar, is the second trauma that wreaks havoc on Tashi's psyche. She thinks of the starving children, the indigent old people removed from their once thriving farms, and sees her tribe reduced to only their black skin and tribal markings. She wants to recover a symbol of her vanishing culture for herself.[38] A more compelling argument for going to the bush could not have been made.

The third and final stressor that precipitates her psychotic break is the pharaonic FGM M'Lissa performs in the bush. Tashi is unprepared for the physical trauma to her body and totally disillusioned about her role as a warrior. After the procedure, she can hardly move. Her sex life with Adam is destroyed, and for her pain she has gained nothing of value. What begins as dissociation regarding Dura's death by telling stories, which is one way to release traumatic memories, becomes a full-blown psychosis after she marries Adam and moves to the United States.

Tashi goes to several doctors before finding any help. One doctor, not Mzee who represents Carl Jung, but one apparently with little cultural competence, makes the statement about Negro women being difficult to analyze because they can never bring themselves to blame the mother. The psychoanalyst who makes this statement is blind to ethnic differences between Tashi, who is African, and African Americans. His limited view inhibits Tashi's progress because he cannot analyze her if he actually does not see her. Tashi responds that even her psychiatrist could not see her ethnicity. All blacks were Negroes.[39] The issue of blaming the mother brings up a traumatic memory for Tashi and dissociation takes place, indicated by Walker's use of italics. Tashi imagines a story, herself a leopard that leaps for her mother's throat.

When Pierre finishes his studies at Harvard, enrolls at Berkeley, and comes to his father and Tashi's home, she goes berserk and pelts him with stones, drawing blood and sending him away in the taxi in which he arrived. She has refused to discuss his coming with Adam, who finds himself in a predicament because taking in their son is the last request of his dying mistress (she has stomach cancer). On the contrary, his wife responds not just with hurt and anger but with the aggression that characterizes her madness. Pierre does not reside with his father and Tashi. Ironically, not until Adam's son enters their lives does Tashi begin to understand her tormenting dream.

Pierre becomes crucial in helping Tashi unravel the meaning of her *cauchemar*, one that has haunted her throughout adulthood.

> *Who looks outside dreams; who looks inside, awakes.*
> —Carl Jung

The dream that haunts Tashi is embedded in the archetypes of the unconscious. She dreams that she is enclosed in a dark tower, and that her wings have been broken. On one level, Walker calls to mind Langston Hughes's poem, "Dreams." Without dreams, life is like a bird that cannot fly. Certainly, this is the case for Tashi except it is, ironically, reversed. She wants to be free of her dream because it is a nightmare. On still another level Tashi's dream can be interpreted as Pierre does, based on the Dogon myth that is repeated almost verbatim in the novel as it appears on page 18 in *Conversations with Ogotemmêli*[40] by Griaule, the French ethnographer. While it is true that Griaule's work has been challenged by those who cannot believe in anything but material knowledge, what is disputed is the Dogon knowledge of astronomy. No one disputes the myth about why the vulva is excised. The explanation fits well and unravels the mystery within the context of the novel. There is no suggestion that the myth can be generalized to the entire continent of Africa because surely, we know by now that each ethnic group has its own traditions and myths. Walker's Africa, Olinka and its people, is purely imaginary. She says without hesitation that she has made up the names, the language, and the customs. That the events may correspond to one place or another can be likened to an African American axiom: If the shoe fits! Most people know the rest.

Feminists know there is a thread of truth in all attempts to control women's erotic power. Audre Lorde in her now classic essay, "Uses of the Erotic: The Erotic as Power," says women have been warned against their own power by men who "keep women around in order to exercise it [the sexual erotic power] in the service of men" but fear the sexual erotic within themselves.[41] The analogy of the ants emerges in Lorde's essay, and parallels the termites in Walker's novel. Lorde says, "Women are maintained at a distant/inferior position to be psychically milked, much the same way ants maintain colonies of aphids to provide a life-giving substance for their masters."[42]

After suffering through a long list of psychiatrists, Adam takes Tashi to see Mzee, Lisette's uncle who, although retired, agrees to see Adam and Tashi. Lisette and Adam appear to be more confidants than lovers, although she does surprise him by becoming pregnant with his son. Adam talks to her about Tashi, and Lisette is a sympathetic listener. Adam and Tashi travel to Switzerland to see the old man. When Tashi and Adam first arrive at Mzee's place, they tell him that he is their last hope. His reply is that they are their own last hope.[43] Perhaps it is human nature, or the reluctance to accept responsibility, that causes people to look for a savior. Obviously, people need help and healers are helpers, but the savior is inside and ultimately, we must save ourselves. When Tashi recognizes this, she begins the path toward wholeness.

In the sessions with Mzee, Tashi is encouraged to paint, something none of the other doctors had suggested. The painting is therapeutic; in Jungian analysis, "The picture mediates between the patient and his problem."[44] The painting contains the unmanaged chaos of the condition. Tashi paints a humongous rooster. The fowl represents men that demand FGM to consider the women marriageable. Tashi says, "The cock was undeniably overweening, egotistical, puffed up, and it was his diet of submission that made him so."[45] It is not unusual for the oppressed to become the oppressors. The suffering and humiliation of colonialism and submission to it is the diet to which Tashi refers. While she is in therapy with Mzee, Tashi remembers that M'Lissa is the person that has killed (she says murdered) her sister Dura. By repressing the memory, she has created her soul sickness.

Of her sickness, Mzee tells Tashi it is self-inflicted based as it was on her own choices.[46] Because Tashi followed tradition and refused to walk her own path, she in effect bashed her own thumb. Her silence and refusal to acknowledge what she has witnessed make her a prisoner in her tower. She is not unlike Josie in *The Third Life of Grange Copeland*, who suffers from a recurring dream and cannot bring herself to face her demon by naming it. In Science of Mind philosophy, all suffering is the result of one thing: ignorance. This is also a Buddhist belief. Tashi admits her ignorance to Raye, the doctor that Mzee refers her to when she and Adam return to the United States. Tashi says her body was a mystery. This ignorance results in suffering, just as it did for Meridian when she failed to understand the meaning of "be sweet."[47] The ignorance of the body is also an indication of the lack of self-reflection. Looking outward to the message of the leader instead of focusing inward and listening to the still small voice within herself is what maintained Tashi's ignorance. Finally, she does recognize her mistakes. Tashi is amused at the naïve girl she had been.[48]

Tashi's healing takes place but then she commits murder, leading one to wonder if she is not still ill. Has she not defeated the purpose of becoming whole only to, in effect, commit suicide? Is hers an example of revolutionary murder? Love is the path to wholeness and forgiveness, the elixir that heals. Walker has shown this repeatedly in her writings. Even the title of one of her collections, *Anything We Love Can Be Saved*, testifies to her convictions. If Tashi's death ended her life, she would have defeated her own purpose. But Walker has made it clear—with Lissie in *The Temple of My Familiar* and again with Señor Robinson in *By the Light of My Father's Smile*—that death is not the end of life.

One of the most unsatisfying aspects of the book is the ending, the banner that announces, "RESISTANCE IS THE SECRET OF JOY!"[49] Walker's editor, dissatisfied with it, wrote: "I resist resistance, and also 'possessing' in the title. I love the secret of joy. THE SECRET OF JOY. Love it too, that this comes on a banner too, especially how you have prepared this. My resistance is to the word 'resistance.'"[50] Walker did not take the editor's advice. The title comes from *African Saga* by Mirella Ricciardi in which she declares, "Black people are natural, they possess the secret of joy, which is why they can survive the suffering . . . inflicted upon them."[51] The insensitivity of Ricciardi's statement certainly needs to be resisted. My problem with resistance is that, while it can indicate the refusal to comply with FGM or accept the racist idea of a black capacity for suffering, it also carries the meaning "to argue" or "to fight," which may be necessary but certainly is not joyful. On a metaphysical level, resistance gives energy to what one does not desire. The Tao focuses on the path of least resistance for the very reason that one does not want to create more friction. Compliance is not the secret of joy, and compliance might be the opposite of resistance. We do not know how Walker intended for resistance to be joyful because the story ends. "Transcendence is the secret of joy" might have worked better. In the end Tashi does not resist, but goes willingly to meet the firing squad. She rises above the material and is on the level of the transcended when she is "satisfied."[52]

SELF-TRANSCENDENCE

Individual selfhood is expressed in the self's capacity for self-transcendence and not in its rational capacity for conceptual and analytic procedures.
—Reinhold Niebuhr, theologian/author of "Serenity Prayer"

Walker acknowledges the other voices that have been raised in protest against the practice of FGM in the novel's appendix. For doing so, Lauret asserts: "To the reader makes explicit the novel's claim to truth—rather than simply storytelling, and in so doing goes beyond the imperative of imagination to the imperative for education and action."[53] Simply storytelling, which means merely for the purpose of entertainment, has rarely been a viable position for the black writer to assume. The black literary tradition from slave narratives onward and in African literature from the oral tradition forward has tended toward education and the transmission of cultural values as well as a call to action. The tradition of the black sermon, especially in the custom of liberation theology, is a call to action. Walker operates within the well-established tradition of black storytelling.

Possessing the Secret of Joy is a ghost story told by a disembodied Olinka woman produced from the depth of Walker's vivid imagination. Like so much of Walker's work, this book too is a parable, and she is the teacher/

preacher. The opening line of the first chapter, "Tashi," says Tashi did not know she was dead for a long time.[54] The final line in the ending chapter, "Tashi Evelyn Johnson Soul," says the world cracks open with a roar, and Tashi is no more.[55] If we assume that she is alive during the narrative, how can she tell us that she is dead? Given Walker's distaste for chronological order—the only book composed that way being her first—it is not unreasonable to think that in this book, she narrates it from the point of view of a dead woman. Granted, Tashi is dead on several levels, that is, because of the initiation rite enacted upon her body, her sex is dead, and generally this is what students see immediately. However, she is physically dead, having been shot by the firing squad. It takes her a long time to realize that she is dead from the shooting because she still exists, just not in the form of her mutilated body. The other characters, Olivia, Adam, Lisette, Mzee, M'Lissa, Pierre, Benny, all recall the events prior and up to the time of Tashi's execution for killing M'Lissa, the *tsunga* who performed the genital mutilations. Tashi-Evelyn-Mrs. Johnson becomes Tashi Evelyn Mrs. Johnson Soul, whole, no hyphens, connected by the invisible hand of Alice Walker.

WARRIOR MARKS: FEMALE GENITAL MUTILATION AND THE SEXUAL BLINDING OF WOMEN

Walker's claim that her wounded eye is a patriarchal wound makes perfect sense on a number of levels. Her identification with the children who have undergone FGM is uncanny. The eye represents female genitalia. Walker's blind eye was injured by a bullet from a phallic-symbol gun aimed by her brother, and the circumciser's knife that cuts away the vulva causes a sexual blinding. Walker writes: "The fact that I learned to rebalance, to continue, to go on with my life, without the support of my parents' protection and thoughtfulness, means I have by now turned my wound into a warrior mark."[56] Walker recognizes that every woman marked by FGM is not Tashi, is not mentally ill. *Warrior Marks* searches for the truth surrounding the practice of female initiation by going to that territory. If Walker learned anything from the filming of *The Color Purple*, it is that visual media can reach a broad spectrum of people that otherwise would not be affected. The documentary with Pratibha Parmar is Walker's effort to spread information about an issue for which large portions of the Western world is/was ignorant. Her efforts have added to the awareness of what constitutes child abuse.

Tashi is not cast in the role of a young adult only for demonstrating that she exercised choice. One of the troubling ambiguities of choice is: When does choice become no choice? Is it choice if the person is unaware of her options and consequences? Awareness is the beginning of choice. Another reason that Tashi is not cast as a child when she undergoes FGM is because

Walker is not only speaking to societies that practice FGM, she is accusing a world in which women are mutilated daily. Lauret wonders to what audience Walker is writing. Lisette's following statement clarifies who is included: those who wore the chastity belt, even if made of precious jewels should worry and should realize the power of patriarchy. They are the perfect audience.[57] We all are the audience to whom Walker writes.

Walker presents a convincing argument regarding patriarchal violence, yet there is something missing, some ambiguity left unexamined. In other words, the answer is a bit too facile. On coming to the end of *Warrior Marks*, there is a poem dedicated to Bisa Niambi, titled "To a Fallen Warrior."[58] Bisa Niambi was Walker's masseuse. In 1993, Niambi murdered her lesbian lover, Venus Landin, and then committed suicide. Intimate partners, whether male or female, complicate the issues of violence and cause one to question the nirvana-like community of women before the male takeover in *The Temple of My Familiar*. What of matriarchal violence? We do not know because there is no powerful and rich matriarchal society anywhere in the world. But I suspect that patriarchy exists because women allow it, and some women lovers appear to suffer from the same powerful ego impulses as do some men. The will to power, the need to control seems imbedded in the human psyche. Clyde Ford writes that "Warriors march along the razor's edge."[59] Further, he explains that although "some claim the warrior spirit is a bastard of patriarchy, an aberration of masculinity,"[60] the warrior spirit goes beyond the politics of gender. What this might mean is that even with the dismantling of patriarchy—and it does need to be dismantled—feminists/womanists will need to continue to struggle for egalitarian relationships or some other -archy will replace the old patriarchy.

Warrior Marks: Female Genital Mutilation and the Sexual Blinding of Women is not only political in the sense that it represents Walker's activism; her efforts helped Amnesty International modify its definition of torture. It represents the first step in sexual healing that she further develops in her next novel, *By the Light of My Father's Smile.* The book and film lay the groundwork for Walker's interrogation of sex and sexism as they appear in the West.

A LIGHT SOURCE

By the Light of My Father's Smile concerns the healing of the soul and the dis-ease in the mind of the West regarding sex. Many of the reviews of Walker's books following *The Color Purple* are especially mean-spirited. *The Color Purple*, in spite of harsh criticism, was a critical success. The books that follow have not enjoyed the same fate. Richard Bernstein's 1998 *New York Times Book Review* article, "*By the Light of My Father's Smile*:

Limp New-Age Nonsense in Mexico,"[61] trashes Walker's book with such virulence it prompted me to research the reviewer. His angry statements about the book's "spiritual philosophizing" and being "cloying and predictable" led me to wonder if perhaps there was not some motivation here other than his critical opinion. Mr. Bernstein is a journalist and not a fiction writer himself, which may account for his seeming lack of imagination.

The *New York Times* review titled "Sexual Healing" is anything but healing. Francine Prose's 1998 review claims, "Alice Walker Sings a Psalm to the Pleasures of the Flesh" that consists of "new age hocus-pocus" and "goddess religion baloney."[62] I wonder if she thinks of the Jewish/Christian male God as religious baloney. What causes the most irritation, according to Prose, is that the book is poorly written with an implausible plot and cliché sentences. The examples that Prose offers are indeed clichés. But it is possible to go through the pages of any book and find one or more overworn phrases. This certainly seems to be the case in Prose's own works. For instance, her book *Bullyville* is not free of clichéd language; "screamingly funny" is hardly fresh, and "diving into the deep end of the pool and not knowing how to swim"[63] is predictable. Predictability is something else for which she faults Walker. Prose's main character, Bart, is predictably called Fart. Prose also calls Walker's book "soft core porn."[64] Lorde distinguishes between pornography and eroticism as two "diametrically opposed uses of the sexual."[65] She defines pornography as a direct denial of the erotic, a suppression of true feeling that emphasizes sensation without [emotions]. In this book Walker seems to strive for the erotic and to embrace its Greek meaning, which includes all aspects of love and creative power.

All of Walker's novels are contextualized in their preface, whether in the form of an epigraph, long quotation, or, in this case, a poem. The untitled poem is dedicated to the sensual cousins the Bonobo, the black-faced and black-haired chimpanzees of the Congo that exhibit high levels of sexual activity. Their level of sexual expression prepares the reader for Walker's incursions into sex and sexuality in the novel. In a second preface, the quotation by Father Matthew Fox acknowledges the connection between sex and spirituality, "this interpenetration of one another's souls by way of the body . . . human sexuality is a mystical moment in the history of the universe."[66] Walker's own quotation follows, stating that human sexuality is a light source that has been kept in the dark. The second preface ends with the Mundo prayer to help us help our mother (earth). The book divides into three parts: "Angels," "A Kiss between the Dead Is a Breeze," and "Fathers." Within the sections are numerous chapters and chapter titles Walker insisted on retaining.

Originally titled "A Kiss between the Dead Is a Breeze,"[67] part 1 begins with another disembodied narrator. Señor Robinson, the father of Magdalena and Susannah, narrates his view of his daughters and tries to connect with them from beyond. Shockingly, Señor Robinson watches his youngest daughter, Susannah, have sex first with her husband and then with her lesbian lover, Pauline. His reason for doing so is not immediately clear. Chapter 1 is explicit, but not "soft porn" (Prose's designation). It has none of the aspects of exploitation or obscenity that would constitute lewd behavior. It is just that Walker's description leaves nothing to the imagination. As much as she affirms mystery, she destroys it in her love scenes. That the scene is narrated by Susannah's father lends to the awkward quality of the narration. That the father is looking, problematic for so many readers, is appropriate according to Rudolph Byrd, who in his book review reminds the reader that in this age of "terminal sex," referring to the pandemic of AIDS among black women, for fathers to look is imperative.[68] To look away, which is what fathers are inclined to do when it comes to their daughter's sexual activity, may be to invite death. Byrd's argument hardly convinces students who view the father's behavior as voyeuristic.

By chapter 3, "Twigs," it is clear why Señor Robinson is lurking around observing his daughter engage in sex. The older daughter, Magdalena, explains the father's guilt for having physically assaulted her for disobeying him and having sex with her boyfriend before leaving Mexico for good. The Robinsons are African American anthropologists who want to study a black Indian tribe in a remote section of Mexico. Because they are African American, they cannot secure funding, so they concoct a plan that will enable them to travel. The plan is based upon a lie. The tribe they want to study knows that "it takes only one lie to unravel the world."[69] The first and perhaps the biggest lie is that they go to the village pretending to be Christians—a minister, his wife, and two young daughters. The truth is they are atheist;[70] every platitude he rattles off is a lie because he does not believe it. The more he wears the mask, the more fraudulent he becomes, until finally he behaves like a fundamentalist, authoritarian patriarch and beats his daughter with a silver-studded belt given to her by her lover. His attack is severe enough to draw blood. This singular act alienates him from his daughters. Magdalena cannot forgive him.

Langley, Robinson's wife, is useless in that she does nothing to intervene and stop the beating, even though she and her husband have agreed they will never use corporal punishment as a form of discipline for their children. She is angry with her husband but, aside from locking him out of their bedroom—and then only for a spell—she returns to life as normal. Some students cannot or, in the beginning, do not recognize the problem and want to minimize what happens to Magdalena, claiming that their parents used corporal punishment to chastise them. There are, however, several issues imbedded in the punishment that make it unacceptable. To begin with, Magdalena is no longer a child, according to her own father's reckoning. As a child she had been a tomboy and the villagers named her Mad Dog, an admirable quality in Mundo culture. In the tradition of the Mundo (a fictional tribe whose name means "world" in Spanish), mad dogs are wise. Robinson is incensed by the name and changes it to MacDoc. But even that name will not do; when she turns sixteen, he allows her to choose a more appropriate name, one that in his opinion sounds feminine. He says at sixteen she will be a woman and must choose a new name.[71] In her rebellion Magdalena complies with her father's demands, and also does not comply without his knowledge. She names herself June; her father is pleased because he thinks it is soft and feminine. She has chosen a pagan name, a name that marks the summer solstice, the season of the unicorn. To underscore the trick she has played on her father, June hums "a pagan song"[72] not allowed in the church. The changing of her name is her father's recognition of the fact that she is now a young woman. Interestingly, June's given name is provocative. Magdalena suggests Mary of Magda or Mary Magdalene, thought to be a woman of low reputation and misjudged a prostitute. In fact, she was not, and was a favorite of Jesus. The parallels are clear: Robinson misjudges his oldest daughter.

When the family prepares to leave the mountains of Mexico, June is at least fifteen, perhaps sixteen and not fourteen as some critics have reported. She has been sexually active since she was fourteen, but neither she nor Manuelito knew what they were doing. She says later that she might have become pregnant and embarrassed her father, but by then Manuelito had been initiated and knew how not to impregnate her.[73] She is six when they move to Mexico and they spend ten years there.[74] At sixteen, she is too old for the kind of punishment that she received. As a society we are slowly realizing the barbarity of physical violence. Today Señor Robinson could have been arrested for simple battery. At the time that the story takes place, the only protection against fathers for daughters was the mother. The mother is derelict in her duty.

The second issue complicating the punishment is the hypocrisy inherent in the father's morals. He promotes himself to priest, dresses in all black, and professes the forgiveness of other people's sins.[75] The audacity of masquerading as a holy man, then enacting "Godzilla"[76] (June's description) by attacking his daughter instead of talking to her and forgiving her, is despicable. He behaves toward June like sex is a sin, but allows himself to engage in it with abandon. Finally, the father favors Susannah. She is his epitome of femininity, demure and soft. Inherent in his favoring the younger daughter over the older one is something as egregious as the sexism that drives him to privilege what he thinks of as feminine. Colorism inhibits his appreciation of June, not just her willfulness and self-possession. He confesses in the final section that he sees Magdalena as if for the first time: "She was incredibly beautiful; and I was shocked to think I'd never really noticed this. Her skin was very dark, the color . . . of chocolate. Bittersweet."[77] Susannah is not dark but is described as bronze,[78] a shade of brown lighter than dark chocolate. Subtle but insidious color preference seems to have been part of Robinson's judgment of his oldest daughter. Walker has inserted this element into the story, complicating the daughter's disobedience and the father's anger.

Only after he dies does Robinson recognize the enormity of his transgression. He observes his neurotic, morbidly obese daughter as she reunites with her long-lost lover, Manuelito, who has been shattered to pieces (literally) by his service in Vietnam. Observing their devotion, a love that is holy, he is ashamed of himself and says so in a one-page chapter titled "Apology."[79] Under ordinary circumstances, one might assume that it is too late to make amends. However, if life indeed is eternal as so many people profess, then opportunities to become better are endless. They are in Walker's fiction.

SUCKED INTO THE BLACK CLOTH

That the Robinsons are members of a church, even though they are atheists, points to the underlying thesis in most of Walker's works. Religion is a tool of social control. Many believers and nonbelievers attend church for social status and economic opportunity. Walker has shown how the missionaries were sent to Africa to smooth the way for imperialism, colonialism, and social control. Many of the native people who converted to Christianity also did so for reasons other than belief. Some wanted a Western education, others just to know something novel, and still others, like Robinson, saw a way to make a name or assume a title, pastor or priest. The desire to leave a legacy, to be important, to be remembered is one of the causes of destruction, as Susannah knows. She tries to explain to her sister how the quest for fame can corrupt. Susannah is a writer and, upon her death, she instructs her friends to burn all her books. Some readers took this act as a sign that this was Walker's last book. Fortunately, it is not.

Watching her father get sucked into the black cloth of religious dogma, Susannah plans to avoid a similar trap by not taking herself and her work too seriously. Even though she drives a black car and dresses almost entirely in black, she never pontificates like her father does when he wears the black uniform of the priest. Walker explained in *The Temple of My Familiar* why men in particular need to become important. Women, whose bodies hold the development of new life, are by their very nature mysterious and important for the continuation of life on the planet. Men, Manuelito tells Robinson, feel left out and so they had to come up with something—war, crucifixion, any blood and gore to match what they believed to be woman's magic.

To become sucked into the black cloth is to take orders from others, as Manuelito does when he goes to Vietnam. To kill on the say-so of someone else, to become a soldier is to be sucked into the black cloth/uniform. In terms of thinking for oneself, Susannah does not escape the black cloth entirely because she is manipulated by her sister. Her relationship with the father is not the same as June's. She could have taken a different path, one that might have forced her sister and her father to reconcile with each other before they died. But very much like her mother, Susannah does nothing. Robinson succumbs to the black cloth of institutionalized, hierarchal religion by imitating preachers and priests and spewing out to the Mundo a worldview that he neither understands nor fully accepts. He confesses to Manuelito that "once I agreed to 'do what I could' toward your salvation in exchange for the church's help, it was as if I had died to myself."[80] The church supported the Robinson's research in exchange for his proselytizing.

Student readers often lose patience with June because they want her to get over what happened and to move on with her life. More than pointing to a lack of sympathy for June's suffering, the need to move past it quickly might indicate a failure to acknowledge and have compassion for our own suffering. Clearly June is an emotional eater who punishes herself in order to punish her father, but also punishes herself by not forgiving. She knows that holding on to anger and hurt feelings is a toxic elixir. She locks into a cycle of negativity that entraps many adults who can never seem to move past their childhood abuse. Susannah also is a victim, and none of the family members escape that one terrible moment of the father's attack.

NARRATIVE VOICES

Unlike many of Walker's novels, especially *The Temple of My Familiar*, *By the Light of My Father's Smile* contains only eight characters. In a book of many chapters, forty-seven to be exact, eighteen are in the narrative voice of Robinson, eleven are narrated by June, six by Susannah, four by Manuelito, three by Pauline, two by Petros, and three by a third-person omnipotent narrator. Irene and Langley have no narrative voice and their stories are told by the others. For Langley, the impotent mother, the lack of voice makes perfect sense. Irene as a symbol of peace and wisdom instead of a character also works well. A Greek dwarf who travels the world on a yacht, content with her virginity and her years of confinement in a church, can only be representative of the infinite possibilities open for exploration.

Whose story is central to this novel? Who is the main character? The answer is not immediately clear. Some readers have assumed Susannah to be the central character, but she has less than a third of the narrative voice. Her burning of the books along with her own dramatic cremation, which is narrated by June, captures the reader imagination and looms large in one's memory of the novel. However, most of Susannah's story is narrated by others: her father, June, her Greek husband Petros, and her lesbian lover Pauline. In the final chapter where Susannah dies, June has the final word. Certainly, Robinson is central to the narrative and one might read the book as his narrative, his transformation, and his transcendence. But then there is Magdalene/Mad Dog/MacDoc/June. Her story is crucial to the reading of the novel. She, too, is transformed. Next to her father, she has the most to say. The de-centering of the narrative voice is another way Walker attempts to demonstrate the unity of individual experience, to show how what happens to one happens to all. Certainly, what happens to June happens to her sister peeping in at the keyhole, and to the mother and to all who read the book.

METAPHYSICAL READING OF
BY THE LIGHT OF MY FATHER'S SMILE

In 1973 a Christian mystic published a small book titled *Life Never Dies*. The man, Jack Ensign Addington, wrote that "There is only one Life, eternal, indestructible, a life that cannot die."[81] Walker has taken seriously what so many people purport to believe. The Song Celestial, or Bhagavad Gita, proclaims that Spirit was never born and will never cease to be, and that Spirit is birthless and deathless. The African notion of the living dead is still another concept that embraces life as an ongoing principle. Walker's metaphysics in terms of the world/Mundo is healing and enlightening. No part of the body which houses the spirit is cut off. Condemnation is not part of the process that heals. One cannot condemn without herself being condemned. June's condemnation of her father severely censures her own life. The hopeful worldview is that we receive more than one chance to get things right, because life evolves.

Sexuality is a pathway to the Divine. Arthur Versluis maintains that Western sexual mysticism has a secret history, and recognizes erotic mysticism as a spiritual path, tracing its repression in the rise of Christianity and claiming that its roots extend to a period long before organized religion. Despite concerted efforts to control sexual expression, Versluis claims there are periodic eruptions.[82] Sexual mysticism seeks to achieve transcendence of the dichotomy of the self and the other self. Further, he writes: "Sexual union, as the most intimate mingling of two people, represents a potential opening into kinds of consciousness that transcends our ordinary individuality."[83] Sexual mysticism does not occur until each lover becomes an opening for the other, providing a way to move beyond the self into the one self. June and her young lover provide a perfect example as they transcend I and thou, moving beyond the self into the one self, Divine and unified.

Sexual mysticism, gnosis, and the idea of transcendence are circumscribed and closeted because the modern emphasis is on an objectified cosmos and on dualism of subject and object. When it comes to sex, Versluis reminds us that too often we see with literal eyes. A sexual image represents only that which is physical. What we look at "cannot be understood literally at all."[84] Lorde explains why the erotic is feared when she writes that it empowers women, stating: "We have been raised to fear the yes within ourselves, our deepest cravings."[85] Robinson's attempt to squelch the erotic in his daughters is hardly different from those old tribesmen who perpetuate FGM.

Walker is charting the way beyond what we think of as life. She invokes Aido-Hwedo, the African rainbow serpent that, in diasporic translation, is "I do we do." She honors the rainbow serpent of erotic wisdom. Walker's naming of the Mundo points us toward a new worldview, one that examines taboos and calls for a re-evaluation based upon our knowledge of the world today. Walker is not suggesting that we ignore the wisdom traditions of the past. She knows that we should embrace them, and therefore the charge of "new age hocus pocus" is so utterly ridiculous.

NOTES

1. See Walker and Parmar, *Warrior Marks: Female Genital Mutilation and Sexual Blinding of Women* (New York: Harcourt Brace, 1993) as well as the 1994 documentary directed by Pratibha Parmar.
2. Larson, "Possessing the Secret of Joy," in Gates and Appiah (eds.), *Alice Walker : Critical Perspectives, Past and Present* (New York: Amistad, 1993), 27.
3. Jeanette Turner Hospital, "Possessing the Secret of Joy," in Gates and Appiah (eds.), *Alice Walker: Critical Perspectives, Past and Present* (New York: Amistad, 1993), 29.
4. Ezekiel 37.
5. Walker, *Possessing the Secret of Joy*, 84.
6. Ibid., 239.
7. Ibid., 178.
8. See http://www.who.int/hiv/topics/malecircumcision/en/.
9. Maria Lauret, *Alice Walker* (New York: Palgrave Macmillan, 2000), 156–57. See also "African Women Speak Out on FGM," *National NOW Times* (June 1994); "Female Genital Mutilation and Ethical Relativism," in *Second Opinion* (October 1994); and Uma Narayan, "Essence of Culture and a Sense of History: A Feminist Critique of Cultural Essentialism," *Hypatia* 13/2 (1998): 86–106.
10. Statement by Juan E. Méndez, Special Rapporteur on Torture and other cruel, inhuman or degrading treatment or punishment, 1993.
11. UN Declaration on the Elimination of Violence against Women (December 1993). Emphasis added. Retrieved from http://www.un.org/documents/ga/res/48/a48r104.htm.
12. Ibid.
13. Alice Walker Archive, Stuart A. Rose Manuscript, Archives, and Rare Book Library, Emory University (1061, 60/11).
14. *The Hosken Report: Genital and Sexual Mutilation of Females* (Lexington, MA: Women's International Network, [1979] 1993).
15. Hanny Lightfoot-Klein, "Orgasm in Ritually Circumcised African Women," *Proceedings, First International Conference on Orgasm*, 1991.
16. Clenora Hudson-Weems, *Africana Womanism: Reclaiming Ourselves* (New York: Bedford Publishers, 1994).
17. John Tierney, *New York Times*, November 30, 2007.
18. See Lauret, *Alice Walker*. See also Joan Smith, "Book Review/Genitally Does It: *Possessing the Secret of Joy* by Alice Walker," *Independent* (October 18, 1992).

19. Walker, *Possessing the Secret of Joy*, front matter (emphasis in original).
20. Lauret, *Alice Walker*, 175.
21. Walker, *Possessing the Secret of Joy*, 3.
22. Osho, *Journey to the Heart: Discourses on the Sufi Way* (Boston: Shaftesbury, Dorset, 1994), 63.
23. Walker, *Possessing the Secret of Joy*, 4.
24. Ibid., 35.
25. Ibid., 279.
26. Ibid., 6.
27. Ibid., 11.
28. Ibid., 10.
29. Ibid.
30. Ibid., 134.
31. Ibid., 15.
32. Walker, *The Color Purple*, 3.
33. Walker, *The Temple of my Familiar*, 385.
34. Walker, *Possessing the Secret of Joy*, 73.
35. Laura S. Brown, *Cultural Competence in Trauma Therapy: Beyond the Flashback* (Chicago: APA, 2008).
36. Walker, *The Color Purple*, 174–77.
37. Walker, *Possessing the Secret of Joy*, 23.
38. Ibid., 24.
39. Ibid., 18.
40. Marcel Griaule, *Conversations with Ogotemmêli* (New York: Oxford University Press, 1965), 18.
41. Audre Lorde, "Use of the Erotic: The Erotic as Power," in *Sister Outsider: Essays and Speeches* (New York: Crown Press, 1984), 54.
42. Ibid.
43. Walker, *Possessing the Secret of Joy*, 53.
44. Andrew Samuels, *The Alchemical Mercurius: Esoteric Symbol of Jung's Life and Work* (New York: Routledge, 2014), 104.
45. Walker, *Possessing the Secret of Joy*, 78.
46. Ibid., 49.
47. Ibid., 119.
48. Ibid., 121.
49. Ibid., 279.
50. Alice Walker Archive, Stuart A. Rose Manuscript, Archives, and Rare Book Library, Emory University (1061, 59/7).
51. Quoted in Walker, *Possessing the Secret of Joy*, frontmatter (n.p.).
52. Ibid., 279.
53. Lauret, *Alice Walker*, 169.
54. Walker, *Possessing the Secret of Joy*, 3.
55. Ibid., 279.
56. Walker, *Warrior Marks*, 17.
57. Lauret, *Alice Walker*, 157; Walker, *Possessing the Secret of Joy*, 138.
58. Walker, *Warrior Marks*, 359.
59. Clyde Ford, *Hero with an African Face: Mythic Wisdom of Africa* (New York: Bantam, 2000), 68.
60. Ibid.
61. Richard Bernstein, "*By the Light of My Father's Smile*: Limp New-Age Nonsense in Mexico," *New York Times Book Review*, October 7, 1998. www.NYTimes/archive.com.
62. Francine Prose, "Sexual Healing," *New York Times Review*, October 4, 1998.
63. Francine Prose, *Bullyville* (New York: Harper Teen, 2007), 69.
64. Prose, "Sexual Healing."
65. Audre Lorde, "Use of the Erotic," 2–3.
66. Walker, *By the Light of My Father's Smile*, frontmatter.

67. Alice Walker Archive, Stuart A. Rose Manuscript, Archives, and Rare Book Library, Emory University, (61/1).

68. Rudolph Byrd, "Review of *By the Light of My Father's Smile* by Alice Walker," in *African American Review* 33, no. 4 (Winter 1999): 722.

69. Walker, *By the Light of My Father's Smile*, 82.

70. Ibid., 151.

71. Ibid., 20.

72. Ibid., 21.

73. Ibid., 25.

74. Ibid., 15.

75. Ibid., 23.

76. Ibid., 27.

77. Ibid., 207.

78. Ibid., 196.

79. Ibid., 83.

80. Ibid., 154.

81. Jack Ensign Addington, *Life Never Dies* (Camarillo, CA: DeVorss & Co., 1973), 1.

82. Arthur Versluis, *The Secret History of Western Sexual Mysticism* (Rochester, VT: Destiny Books, 2008), 142–43.

83. Ibid., 143.

84. Ibid.

85. Lorde, "Use of the Erotic," 57.

Chapter Eight

Opening to Spirit

The soul wherein God is born must have escaped from time, and time must have dropped away from her.
—Meister Eckhart

This chapter examines *Now Is the Time to Open Your Heart* (2004), Walker's last published novel, and *Absolute Trust in the Goodness of the Earth* (2003), a collection of poems. Her spiritual path is demonstrated in the metaphysics of these books. The novel received mixed reviews. Natasha Walter called the novel a new age sermon filled with "religious epiphanies" but marred by spiritual superiority and smugness.[1] I have argued that all of Walker's novels are sermonic. For many people, a sermon is somehow not artistic. Within the African American homiletic tradition sermons are, in fact, high art forms. Walker's works push the boundaries of what Western-trained critics have been taught to value. *Kirkus Reviews* wrote that *Now Is the Time to Open Your Heart* is "an overwrought pastiche of muddled thinking."[2] In a review titled "Heart Matters," Nicole Moses wrote a positive review, claiming that Walker's "general message—get your mind and body right and your heart will follow—is a universal one that can be understood by people of all ages."[3] Walker neither suffers from ennui, nor is she esoteric. Using the aspects of her own lived experiences, she presents parables for living.

Alton B. Pollard III, a professor of religion, has coined a term to account for the unique aspects of African American thought. He defines the term Endarkenment as "a new épistème or way of knowing—and—being in the world, characterized by belief in the power of wisdom and by transformation of self, community and larger world in the twenty-first century."[4] Endarkenment stands in opposition to the Enlightenment movement of the Western world. While Endarkenment recognizes the value of science and logic, it refuses to discard, diminish, or disrespect intuition or mysticism. A large part of Endarkenment methodology is based on the use of parables. Pollard recognizes parables as a means for expressing sacred truths, and lists Alice Walker among other African American writers who are prominent in their use of the parable in various literary genres. He acknowledges that "African American wisdom literature is filled with many wonderful and provocative parables."[5] The parable is understated and paradigm shifting, and provides new meaning to what one might ordinarily believe. Endarkenment ultimately leads to an encounter with the ancestors, in what Pollard identifies as the "luminous darkness."[6] Discussing her writing process, Walker states: "I gathered up the historical and psychological threads of the life my ancestors lived, and in writing of it I felt joy and strength and my own continuity . . . that wonderful feeling writers get sometimes, not very often, of being with a great many people, ancient spirits, all very happy to see me consulting and acknowledging them, and eager to let me know, through the joy of their presence, that indeed I am not alone."[7]

Walker's last novel brings forth the ancestors and the "luminous darkness." For readers who know all the answers to existential questions, or who believe that the world is currently headed in the right direction, or for those who think that Walker's answers are wrong or impractical, her work will be a waste of their time. For the rest of the world still trying to figure out answers to existential questions, or how to best get along with other people, or how to gain insight into our own souls, Walker's works may have something to offer, and at the very least what she posits provides food for thought.

As with all her novels, meaningful epigraphs introduce *Now Is the Time to Open Your Heart*. Surprisingly, she chose a quotation from Marlo Morgan's *Mutant Message Down Under*, purported to be a hoax and a great insult to the aboriginal people of Australia. No doubt it is the sentiment of the quotation that resonated with Walker, aligning with her own beliefs: "Everything in the universe has a purpose. There are no misfits, there are no freaks, there are no accidents. There are only things we don't understand."[8] The epigraph from Winnie Mandela, "So far, there is no law against dreaming," suggests the luminous darkness—that is, the spirit encountered in dreams, the ancestral images one meets, which no apartheid can prevent.

Kate Talking Tree Nelson, the novel's central character, bears a tremendous resemblance to Walker. In 1994, following the death of her mother the year before, Walker changed her middle name to Tallulah-Kate in honor of her mother and Kate Nelson, the murdered paternal grandmother she never knew. Kate, a well-published author in a relationship with an artist, goes on a journey to the Amazon to meditate and investigate the "Grandmother medicine." Walker, according to a passage in *Absolute Trust in the Goodness of the Earth*, in her "mid-fifties . . . devoted a year to the study of plant allies, seeking to understand their wisdom and to avail [herself] of the aid to insightful living that . . . the earth provides as surely as do meditation centers."[9]

For some readers, Walker's venture to the Amazon and into the secret life of plants may seem new age, but within the context of the African American experience it is rather ancient. There is nothing new about African and other traditional medicines or ancestral traditions. Walker became interested in the secret life of plants, as did Stevie Wonder in 1979 when he produced the album *Journey Through the Secret Life of Plants*, to try to understand the addictive behavior of young people (and perhaps old ones as well). Walker was searching for the Endarkenment. She stated in a 2004 interview with Bill Moyers that she was "looking for the indigenous way of being."[10] As Kate does, Walker too drinks *ayahuasca* or Grandmother medicine and consumes the magic mushrooms. Walker concludes that young people take drugs because of their "desire to have a religious or spiritual or ecstatic and transformative experience, a need hardwired into our being."[11] Another reason we have addicts today is that people earn money from making people addicted to drugs.

The novel opens with Kate in meditation at a Buddhist retreat. In the chapter titled "Cool Revolution," the teacher says, "The only revolution that could possibly succeed ... was the 'cool' one introduced to the world by the Lord Buddha twenty-five hundred years ago."[12] His statement upsets Kate, who suddenly becomes aware of the race and class distinctions of the group. She is the only person of color in attendance, and she knows it is because she is financially advantaged that she can afford to attend. She, however, underestimates the resourcefulness of the poor when she concludes that they have neither the time nor the means to meditate. They have no money to attend a retreat, it may be true; nonetheless, I argue that Kate missed the point. My grandmother, who earned her living by cleaning white people's homes, would sit down in the middle of her own housework and sometimes hum or sometimes fall silent. If I disturbed her she would say, "Shoo, get away; can't you see I'm ruminating!" I did not know it then, but I believe she was in fact meditating. She would rise refreshed and peaceful. The old ones knew that it was not necessary to go anywhere to communicate with Spirit.

The teacher at the retreat might have said that Jesus advocated a cool revolution, or that King did. Therefore it is not what has been said as much as what has been recognized by Kate, based upon her own lived experience, that causes her to balk at the idea. She knows the issues of the poor and the unlikelihood of a cool revolution being successful, at least the way that she understands it at this point in her life. She reaches an impasse with Buddhism for there is something that does not resonate, just as the idea of original sin in Christian theology is unacceptable. Walker cannot abide the idea of being born in sin and shaped by iniquity,[13] choosing instead to believe children are conceived in love.

Chapter 2 of the novel begins with a parable and a dream. Titled "To Kill or to Thaw the Anaconda," Kate dreams she finds an anaconda in her freezer.

Symbolic of change, because it sheds its skin, the anaconda is an aquatic serpent and hides in the deep waters of rivers or the unconscious.[14] According to Jung,[15] the Gnostics saw the snake as representing the spinal cord and the fluid. This image is comparable to the expression of the unconscious, which can appear suddenly. Aido-Hwedo,[16] the rainbow serpent in African (Fon) mythic wisdom, represents vital knowledge. Kate realizes that she will not receive help with the anaconda, that whatever she decides to do with it is up to her. Kate says, "the anaconda was an inside job."[17] Walker has circled right back to her initial pronouncement that choice is the governing factor in life and that we must make our own choices.

The dream of her own snake leads Kate to the memory of a story from the Black Freedom movement. A group of civil rights workers try to convince an elderly black woman to register to vote. She refuses, but tells them a story. This tale comes from the black folk tradition and concerns a man who picks up a frozen snake and warms it in his bosom. When the snake warms up it bites the man, and he dies. Before he dies the snake says, "You knowed I was a snake when you picked me up."[18] Within African American culture the story was often repeated to warn children against trusting white people. The story might end with, all snakes are not poisonous, but do you want to take the chance to find out? In this case the story has an alternative ending: winter will return, and the snake will freeze again. The proverb for this is that a cow needs her tail more than once. But the questions the civil rights workers are left with are: Does [a snake's] true nature ever change? And does ours? These are spiritual questions. Do we kill a shadow or do we acknowledge it, meaning we let it live? The next part of the question is crucial to understanding Walker's concept of unity. Do we ever believe its true nature? The true nature of anything is good, perfect, whole, and complete. Therefore, what we are looking at, snake or otherwise, is what we are looking with. The Sufi mystic points out that "the whole is whole because of all."[19] What we see in others is present in ourselves; otherwise, we would not be able to recognize it.

When questioned about the title of her poetry collection, *Absolute Trust in the Goodness of the Earth*, which is inspired by the "forces of nature and the strength of the human spirit,"[20] Walker defends her celebration of the human spirit by claiming that ignorance and not evil people are responsible for all manner of suffering. She has said that suffering is ignorance,[21] and claims that people have been deliberately kept ignorant. People benefit from the ignorance of others and have little incentive to enlighten them. When asked where God is in the scheme of things, Walker replied, "I think we're it. I think the whole thing is God. Everything is God . . . that it's all God."[22] God knows all, thus people have the capacity and the obligation to comprehend their anaconda.

Walker and Kate have parallel journeys in terms of visiting the Amazon and consuming medicinal plants. They also have mirror experiences in terms of changing their names. The opening chapters reveal Kate dreaming of dry riverbeds. One critic, obviously missing the important symbology represented by the dry riverbed, commented that this was an example of "feminist inanities" in the book, and that Walker was somehow suggesting that "women only dream of dry rivers."[23] For women in the process of change the river refers to menstrual blood, and a dry bed indicates the cessation of menstruation. According to Cirlot, the river is an ambivalent symbol that corresponds to the creative power of both nature and of time. On the one hand, it signifies fertility and the progressive irrigation of the soil; on the other hand, it stands for the irreversible passage of time and, in consequence, for a sense of loss and oblivion.[24] Aging, for women, is symbolized by a dry river. Walker's use of river imagery also calls out to her old friend Langston Hughes, whose poem "The Negro Speaks of Rivers" suggests there is wisdom to be gained from journeys on and across rivers ancient as human blood.[25] By the end of Kate's journey, her soul will have grown deep like the rivers. A woman's menstrual flow is equally ancient. Walker's layering of symbols is anything but inane.

What can be read metaphorically, Walker participated in literally. But for Kate the journey is more for personal growth than for understanding how plants work and why youth are addicted. Kate's first journey takes her on a trip down the Colorado River that is anything but dry. In fact, Kate faces the rapids and becomes violently ill. Her illness comes from old unresolved emotions. Walker gives new meaning to eating your own words. Kate regurgitates "All the words from decades of her life.... Words she had said or had imagined saying or had swallowed before saying to her father,"[26] dead for many years. Kate is an excellent declutterer, Yolo, her lover, reveals. He is the opposite and comes close to being a hoarder. His story parallels Kate's, and although they think that their parting indicates the end of their relationship, it turns out that it does not. But it might well have been the end, had Yolo not decided to grow in a different direction. The novel is written in third person. While Kate's name is significant to Walker, as it represents a member of her family, Yolo, according to students, means you only live once. I do not accept their answer because I doubt that Walker believes we only live once, although she might well be in accord with the idea of *carpe diem*. The name Yolo might come from Yolo County in California, meaning a place abounding in rushes.[27]

On her initial journey down the Colorado, Kate recalls her first marriage and how it ends. The beginning of the end takes place over a serving dish, just as Fanny's and Suwelo's marriage begins its downward slide over a shopping cart in *In the Temple of My Familiar*. While the incidents may appear trivial, they demonstrate how small things can devour relationships.

Also, the small things reveal larger issues. Suwelo's reaction to the shopping cart revealed his dislike, if not hatred, of women. The Valentine gift from Kate's husband, a serving bowl, suggested to her that she is valued only as a servant and not as a lover. When Kate announces her intention to divorce her husband, he rapes her. The marital rape further supports Kate's contention that the husband viewed her as a servant. In the poem "Until I Was Nearly Fifty," Walker describes a relationship that reflects Kate's first marriage in the novel. The poem reveals the fear that the relationship has killed the spirit in the young girl.[28] But the wild-haired girl escapes.

What is most revealing about Kate and the marriage that she recalls are the shadowy children and what happens to them when she leaves. When left on the hiking trail by the husband to whom she announces her decision to leave, she says that she has children that she must get home to. Does she desert the children? If so, she joins a long line of women characters that in one way or another desert their children. Motherhood as it relates to individual women and children is not the focus of *Now Is the Time to Open Your Heart.* Being mothered is, however, central to Kate's development. On the trip down the Colorado River, the first dream that she experiences is of her dead mother. The dream leads her to a story in which she reveals that the mother is dissatisfied with the daughter.[29] Kate also says that she cannot imagine a relationship with a man who cannot mother her.

In Kate's retreat into the Amazon, the Grandmother medicine produces the nausea and vomiting that both symbolically and literally cleanse not just her body, but her soul and her mind so that she can proceed with clear consciousness. Her time in the jungle both literally and symbolically represents a way to integrate all her disparate selves. The stories that are related from the Amazon as well as from Hawaii belong to all of us in terms of our interconnectedness. While Walker rejects the concept of original sin, that is, just by being born one has sinned, there does seem to be a paradox here in that upon entering this plane of existence and becoming part of human beings, we do partake of and suffer from the mistakes that have been made collectively. Perhaps this is where the idea of original sin originated. In any case, it cannot be dissipated by having a priest or preacher intercede, as they are as much a part of the problem as any other human being. They might be able to point one in the right direction, like Armando, but as Walker's character Kate proclaims, the solution is an inside job. And this too may appear paradoxical, turning inward to heal that which appears to be outward.

This novel continues Walker's idea of sexual healing and includes the Hawaiian Mahus to represent the concept of unity expressed in native cultures before the intrusion of Christian missionaries. Information from "Hawaiian Sexuality and the Mahu Tradition" by Kalikiano Kalei is worth quoting:

Transgendered and trans-sexual individuals greatly disturb most God-fearing Christians, who believe that everything other than "conventional" marital sex is a mortal sin. The ancient Hawaiians were not as tightly strung, in their graceful understanding that all human beings possess a complete Tao of male and female qualities within themselves. "Mahu" is a Hawaiian term that describes a man who has chosen to live as a woman and in the ancient (pre-missionary) culture; such individuals were respected and regarded as important members of the community . . . the new expression of Christian chasteness collided head-on with traditional Hawaiian perceptions, as any aspect of social behavior that might be construed as being somehow "sexual" in any way was systematically rooted out. The hula was just the most obvious and prominent cultural heritage that this new and severely proscriptive religious censure came near to stamping out entirely.[30]

The sense of separation that pervades North American culture, the rugged individual, the lone pioneer, and even the idea of a singular God off somewhere by himself, separate from creation and separate from people, is the antithesis of Walker's theology. Cultural relativism works only if one believes in separation, that what might be painfully destructive to one person or group of people will have no bearing on another. Julian Stewart, commenting on the United Nations statement of Human Rights, states: "Either we tolerate everything, and keep hands off, or we fight intolerance and conquest."[31] Cultural relativists would have respected the rights of white southerners to vehemently protect their racist apartheid culture.

With each story that Kate relates, then, Walker seeks to demonstrate how the events reflect parts of the larger collective self. Students often complain that there is a contradiction between the idea of collective identity and the necessity of performing the inside job to which Kate refers. The answer is not either/or, but both/and, with the inside job having a remarkable ability to affect the collective. Kate tells a local shaman, Anunu (a reference, perhaps, to Nunu the spiritual mother in Gerima's movie *Sankofa*), that she believes "all is up to us . . . us humans."[32] Further, Anunu says, "It is all Grandmother . . . *regardless of appearances!* As they say in the Church of Religious Science about God."[33] This concept of oneness regardless of how fragmented things appear to be is what the plant medicine helps Kate to comprehend. The first thing Kate learns is that human beings are creative and have absolute free will, the reason choice is so central to the understanding of life. Then Grandmother tells Kate that there is no way for people to destroy her, they can only destroy their own peace of mind and joy, for She is infinite. Armando's announcement, "A sick person has no history and no nationality,"[34] sets the next phase for Kate's development. If she cannot feel the truth of his statement, she can never hope to become a *curandero*, a shaman or healer.

Kate's problem is hardly different from Fanny's in *The Temple of My Familiar*; she has a resentment of white racists and is angered by the history of oppression in the United States and abroad. She feels that her abused ancestors want her to extract revenge for them. Revenge will not produce healing and, even more profoundly, to take revenge on the so-called other is to enact it on oneself. Some African Americans were irritated with Walker when she announced her Amerindian and European ancestry. They thought it was the same old expression of self-hatred prominent before the cultural revolution of the 1960s, that is, black people were everything and anything but black—Japtalian, Cherokee, anything. But Walker's effort was not to diminish or fail to embrace her blackness. Instead, hers was a spiritual quest to encompass a unitary self, one with Spirit. Perhaps the easiest way to forgive the actions of others is to understand that you are genetically connected to them and have the same capacity for evil. At the time that Walker made her announcement (1970s), not much was known about genetic markers and DNA. Since then many people have been surprised by the identity of their near and distant relatives. The fact is there are probably few African Americans without mixed ancestry. For the fictional Kate, this may enable her ability to forgive.

Kate confronts an ancestor in her dreams. The ancestral demands signified by the appearance of Remus, the enslaved man who had his beautiful teeth sadistically pulled from his mouth, is a trope for Joel Chandler Harris's appropriation of African American folktales and the invention of an Uncle Remus to relate them to white children. Elsewhere,[35] Walker recalls her disappointment upon seeing the stereotype of Uncle Remus in Walt Disney's *Song of the South* and discusses Harris's appropriation of African American culture. Meeting the ancestor is traumatic for Kate because she is trying to heal from historical wounds. The ancestor represents a past that impinges on the present. Anissa Wardi's definition of ancestor fits well with Walker's portrayal in the novel; Wardi claims that "the term ancestor signifies 'a singular entity' created of the family members that merge into one historic body."[36] Jana Hecková's observation that in Walker's later works the ancestor has become problematic is accurate. Remus is a problematic figure for Kate. Noting the importance of ancestral figures in African American literature, Hecková acknowledges each ancestral figure manifests differently in each writer's text.[37]

Unlike Lauret's postulation that Walker is attempting to crack a joke by having Remus ask, "Who's the ancestor here?" which she suggests leads to "Walker's mishandling of—for want of a better word—the novel's tone,"[38] Hecková argues that Walker is humanizing the ancestor for the purpose of "deconstructing the presupposed ancestral superiority."[39] Toni Morrison, who declared the ancestor crucial to African American life and literature, however, does not suggest ancestral superiority; rather she says it is interesting to see what each black writer does with the figure.[40] Morrison makes a profound statement when she says, "When you kill the ancestor you kill yourself."[41] And this speaks to the situation confronting Kate and the ancestor Remus. His question to Kate indicates his realization that in unity, there are no ancestors and others; they in fact are one. Not just one historical body, as Wardi claims, but one spiritual body as well. The joke, if there is one, is in the lesson Kate is to learn. The dream is heavily symbolic, almost heavy-handed. The following passage demonstrates my point: "When Remus looked into [Kate's] eyes, he saw himself, his beaming new smile, his happiness seemed to make him weak. He stumbled and began falling forward, into her. She felt the heaviness of him, his hard head, his broad shoulders, even his scratchy hands, passing into her chest. Though he was inside her, she no longer felt his weight."[42]

When Kate asks whether on a spiritual level there is any difference in terms of age, she might well have asked if there is any difference between herself and the ancestor. The dream and out-of-body experience for Kate has resulted in Remus getting new teeth by biting down on the corn Kate tells him to eat. But the joke on her is when Armando says the ancestor chose her because she is vain.[43] What is inside herself is what draws her to the experiences in the rainforest.

Lalika is another character Kate meets on the rainforest journey. Lalika is weeping at the waterfall. The waterfall stands for the emotions of the subconscious flowing into our emotions, and the permanence of form regardless of changing content. The running water also indicates lack of control of her emotions. She is a murderer, or more precisely she is one who has committed murder. The distinction becomes clear if we refer to the old woman's story about the frozen snake, that is, do we see her *true* nature, which is spiritually sound and intact? Or do her actions obscure the truth? Hugh, another character on the journey, represents the exploitative capitalist, or the inheritor of the exploitative ancestors. But given the genetic connections of North Americans, who is it that can escape the connection of exploitation? The exploited and the exploiter are intimately connected. The Buffalo soldiers certainly played a part in helping to capture Indian lands. Among the other characters are a woman who as a child was sexually abused by her grandfather whom she loves, but needs to forgive; an Italian man who dyes his hair blond and needs to forget his family's role in selling narcotics in African American communities; and the capitalist who owns hundreds of acres of Indian land that includes a lake and underwater burial ground, which he intends to permit contractors to unearth. The message that Kate learns and brings home to Yolo is that forgiveness is for the self and begins within.

Yolo's trip to Hawaii enlightens him about his masculine role. He concludes that men are responsible for the youth, and how men choose to live their lives directly impacts young people. Yolo and the island men with Aunty Pearlua, a Mahu—a man living life as a woman—make a commitment to clean up their lives and give up addictions. Yolo is a smoker and the commitment is difficult for him to keep, but Kate is permissive by allowing Yolo to smoke in the house. Her permissiveness, which works fine for adults, may well have backfired in Kate's role as a parent. Late in the novel we learn that she has two sons. One is in the space program of which she disapproves because it is colonial (space colonies), and the other son is a musician (drug addict). The addicted son, Charles, laughs at his mother's message, and it is no wonder. She says, "I ranted, raved, and cajoled against *overuse* of marijuana."[44] Permissiveness for teenagers is unlikely to produce the same results as it might for adults. Yolo appreciates Kate's kindness and he is seriously attempting to rid himself of the habit of smoking cigarettes.

After their time apart, Kate and Yolo find that they are in love and want to spend their lives together. When he suggests marriage, Kate refuses because of her past experiences. She has no faith in marriage with men or with women. After her divorce, she met and married Lolly. The marriage was not legal, which turned out to be a blessing. The lesbian union encountered problems like a heterosexual relationship when one partner refuses to carry his or her own weight. Lolly was a taker who intended to own Kate's money, house, and jewels. Kate's description of her was contented laziness. The chapter about Lolly and the last of her marriages is titled "Like Elizabeth Taylor" and begins, "Like Elizabeth Taylor, Kate had been married many times."[45] Each chapter, after the first four, begins with the chapter's title for its opening lines. Kate and Yolo represent two aspects of the same self, with each part needing to develop itself to fit with the other. Instead of growing apart, the two grow together.

While she has been involved in several relationships, Walker has never legally remarried. Students often ask if she is against marriage, and we cannot conclude that she is without her explicitly saying so. What is interesting, however, is how mystics conceive of marriage. As one might suspect it has little to do with legal arrangements. Like sex, marriage is a means to salvation. Christian mystic and Franciscan priest Fr. Richard Rohr writes, "Salvation is not as antiseptic, unreal, and sterile as we've made it."[46] He argues that unless we are in the right relationship with at least one person on earth where we can give and receive love, we are not saved. Walker's actions appear to coincide, and she forms loving relationships without much regard for legalities. That is not to say that she fails to understand marriage (the legal right) as a legitimate desire for other people, including gay couples. She recently performed a marriage ceremony for two gay men.[47]

As Melanie Harris points out in *Gifts of Virtue, Alice Walker, and Womanist Ethics*, Walker's ethic is "deconstructive (critique), descriptive, and constructive."[48] Walker's creative body of works exposes the patriarchal system, its imbalance of power, and challenges the "normative ethical codes based in the logic of domination" used to oppress women and people of color.[49] The effort to discredit Walker stems not so much from her role as a writer but as a thinker. Both Katie Cannon and Patricia Hill Collins have critiqued the way in which knowledge is deemed credible. Black women and men and other people of color have not been fully included in the academic production of knowledge. Theories of knowledge that challenge white male conventional thinking are labeled in dismissive terms. Hill Collins has suggested that an epistemology that validates black women's knowledge can be found in "alternative sites such as music, literature, daily conversations, and everyday behavior."[50] Walker has used her literary output for just such a purpose.

ABSOLUTE TRUST IN THE GOODNESS OF THE EARTH: POEMS

> *We should come daily to the Spirit of Goodness for a complete washing away of all mistakes, fears, and troubles.*
> —Ernest Holmes, *The Science of Mind*

Between the writing of *The Way Forward Is with a Broken Heart* and this collection of poems, several events transpired to prompt Walker to pick up her pen again, namely, the violent and tragic events of September 11, 2001, and the resulting war. Her study of plants for healing also left her with information that she needed to share.

In speaking about the events of 9/11, Walker writes something that may equally apply to herself and her critics: "What many North Americans lost on September 11 is a *self-centered innocence that had long grated on the nerves of the rest of the world.*"[51] Walker's autobiographical presence in many of her works stems, it seems, from a self-centered innocence. This is not as apparent when reading one or two of her works as it is when examining the entire corpus.

Walker's study of plants, her participation in healing circles with a shaman and with native people, and her journey to the Amazon infuse her poems with what one might call the wisdom of the earth. The first poem, "I Can Worship You," is the voice of the earth talking to us. The earth can only give what we can receive, thus, if people are unwilling to align with the earth and its water, it cannot produce what people need.[52] The earth says it cannot give us everything. This is a profound spiritual concept: the universe can provide for us all that we are willing and able to accept. Walker demonstrates this in *The Third Life of Grange Copeland* and in her own life as well. Acceptance is a matter of consciousness. Clearly some people can accept more than others, but with the pollution of clear water and the destruction of the body (Earth itself), no one will thrive or survive, which speaks to Walker's reminder that we are all one.

"The Love of Bodies" is Earth again proclaiming to us how we belong to her, how we are part of the earth, and return to Earth at the point of our transition. This poem was written on September 25, 2001, twenty-four days after the tragedy of 9/11. "All the Toys" follows—a poignant poem that points out the trappings of capitalist materialist culture. Walker is both a mystical and a revolutionary poet; however, her poetry is politely ignored, except for the rude remarks from J. O. Tate who claims her poetry is negligible and that "she is probably the worst poet in the history of the English language."[53] Walker's poetry is uneven. Some very rare poets (I am thinking of Natasha Trethewey) can produce a perfect poem every time. Trethewey produces fewer poems, with each one being a jewel. Walker, on the other hand, seems to produce en masse. For example, *Absolute Trust in the Goodness of the Earth* contains eighty-nine poems. *Native Guard*, which won Trethewey the Pulitzer Prize, contains only 29 poems.

In Walker's early poems, form is married to content. In this collection, form and content seem to have come loose at the seams. Walker's characteristic form is free verse. Free verse is propelled by rhythm, and rhythm is enhanced by line breaks. For some reason Walker has chosen to center her poems, and the line breaks appear in the oddest places, destroying any rhythm save perhaps nursery rhyme. For example, "Trapdoors to the Cellar Spring-Grass Green" is choppy personified: 3/3/2/2/2/3/3.[54] Maybe this is deliberate. After 9/11 it could be that we need to return to infancy. Or the form of the poem represents the fractured nature of life after 9/11.

Walker is a present-day mystic, and her revolution and mystical evolution begin within herself. She is seeking a spiritual revolution. Her internal focus has caused some to charge her with a swollen narcissism, but from a spiritual perspective, change must begin from within. Mystical poetry often is based on dreams, visions, and spiritual breakthroughs. About 10 percent of the poems in this collection are about dreams, contain the word *dream* in the title, or otherwise make it clear that they are visions or epiphanies. "Whiter Than Bones" is an example that begins with a dream in a new house.[55] The house dream refers to her sense of herself and reveals her spiritual evolution, thus the new house.[56] She is passing out of the mundane into the spiritual.

"The Same as Gold" recalls a dream of a small child, possibly the poet, who is left with the persona to care for in a house with no roof, indicating openness at the top and the possibility of continued evolution and spiritual growth. Dreams of houses often indicate the condition of the soul and a change in consciousness. One stanza indicates that she is always moving—growing[57] in consciousness. On a literal level, Walker may be using the facts of her life and recounting the numerous times that she moved from shack to shack as a child. On a spiritual level, the poem demonstrates how our soul moves on up a little higher. Walker confesses that childhood poverty has not prepared her for her wealth.[58] But of course, she was prepared. The dreams prepared her.

From the section "Let Change Play God," the poems are less introspective and more political than the dreams and revelations. For instance, "A Native Person Looks up from the Plate" is to the point and chilling; how we of the West have consumed, literally eaten up native people and their possessions. At the end of the poem is spiritual insight; the final lines after the greedy consumption of everything states "the fine meal sours in us."[59] Indeed, we destroy ourselves. Some will say the poem offers no profound insight for we already know it, and some might even call the message banal. My only response is that to know better does not translate into doing better. Prophets and mystics never tell us anything new. They keep repeating the same messages, hoping one day they will be heeded. More than two thousand years ago, someone said it rains on the just and the unjust.[60] But because many Americans consider themselves to be Christians, the idea of being *saved* or *born again* may have led to the belief that they were exempt from the violence experienced by the rest of the world. Walker's poem "The Anonymous Caller" can hopefully bring enlightenment. The caller threatens the person by saying he knows where the person lives.[61] The retort is powerful in its truth. The response is that all of us share the same address. If people know this, that is, if people really believe in the unity of life, would they drop bombs or wage war? Walker's didacticism against war, violence, and murder has been called new age muddled thinking.

"I Was So Puzzled by the Attacks" can be read as Walker's response to 9/11. However, it also addresses her critics regarding *The Color Purple* and the attacks on black women writers in general. The poem's midsection reacts to male critics by saying they believed the women were in a race with them.[62] She reminds us that nothing other than death is the finish line. What folly, then, to be envious. Ishmael Reed's *Reckless Eyeballing*, in which he calls black women writers lackeys for white feminists, is one such vicious attack to which the poem might refer. The "we" in this case would include Walker, Toni Morrison, Michelle Wallace, and Ntozake Shange.

"Dead Men Love War" is a section of the book that condemns our military response to 9/11. Its opening chills and paints a picture of corpses on slaughtered horses, grinning.[63] A favorite poem of students because of its sheer iconoclastic zeal is "They Made Love," in which a bride and groom make love on the church's altar. The poem concludes that it is a good way to marry the church.[64] The spirituality of sex and the holiness of the body is a theme Walker has demonstrated in her novels.

The book ends with the poem "When You Look," which addresses those who still believe in a heaven somewhere in the sky. The poet says it is here and now, and is a matter of recognizing it, and we find our Divinity when we open our hearts,[65] and here is the title of the last novel. There are other sections and poems, some that would irritate readers who have a problem with people hugging trees, but the ones most indicative of Walker's theology I have included.

NOTES

1. Natasha Walter, "Review of *Now Is the Time to Open Your Heart* by Alice Walker," *The Guardian* (November 5, 2004). www.TheGuardian.com.
2. *Kirkus Reviews*, "Review of *Now Is the Time to Open Your Heart*" (May 20, 2010).
3. Nicole Moses, "Heart Matters" (review of *Now Is the Time to Open Your Heart*). *January Magazine*, August 2004. https://januarymagazine.com/fiction/openyourheart.html.
4. "Epilogue: The Endarkenment: A Parable," in *The Black Church Studies Reader*, ed. Alton B. Pollard III and Carol B. Duncan (New York: Palgrave Macmillan, 2016), 319.
5. Ibid.
6. Howard Thurman's phrase. See Thurman, *The Luminous Darkness: A Personal Interpretation of the Anatomy of Segregation and the Ground of Hope* (New York: Harper Colling, 1965).
7. Quoted in Mari Evans, *Black Women Writers (1950–1980): A Critical Evaluation* (New York: Anchor Books, 1984), 453.
8. See *Dumbartung Aboriginal Report* by Robert Eggington.
9. Walker, *Absolute Trust in the Goodness of the Earth*, xii.
10. Bill Moyers, "A Conversation with Alice Walker," June 24, 2004. https://billmoyers.com/content/a-conversation-with-alice-walker/.
11. Walker, *Absolute Trust*, xiii.
12. Walker, *Now Is the Time*, 4.
13. Psalms 51:5.
14. See Harold Bayley, *The Lost Language of Symbolism* (San Diego, CA: Book Tree, 2000).
15. *Symbols of Transformation: The Collected Works of C. G. Jung* (Princeton, NJ: Princeton University Press, 1956).
16. Harold Scheub, *Dictionary of African Mythology* (Oxford: Oxford University Press, 2000).
17. Walker, *Now Is the Time*, 7.
18. Ibid., 9.
19. Osho, *Journey to the Heart: Discourse on the Sufi Way* (Boston: Element Books, 1994), 167.
20. Walker, *Absolute Trust*, back cover.
21. Moyers "A Conversation with Alice Walker."
22. Ibid.
23. Michiko Kakutani, "Books of the Times: If the River Is Dry, Can You Be All Wet?" *New York Times*, April 20, 2004. www.nytimes.com/2004/04/20/books.
24. J. E. Cirlot, *Dictionary of Symbols* (New York: Philosophical Library, 1983), 274.
25. In *The Collected Poems of Langston Hughes*, ed. Arnold Rampersad (New York: Vintage, 1995), 23.
26. Walker, *Now Is the Time*, 23.
27. www.yolocounty.org.
28. Walker, *Absolute Trust* 8, 3.
29. Walker, *Now Is the Time*, 40.
30. Kalikiano Kalei, "Hawaiian Sexuality and the Mahu Tradition." http://www.authorsden.com/visit/author.asp?authorid=77566.
31. Julian Stewart, "Comments on the Statement of Human Rights," *American Anthropologist* 50, no. 2 (1948): 351–52.
32. Walker, *Now Is the Time*, 67.
33. Ibid., 68 (emphasis in original).
34. Ibid., 90.

35. Alice Walker, "Uncle Remus, No Friend of Mine," *Southern Exposure* 21, no. 1–2 (Spring 1993): 37. See also Walker's essay, "The Dummy in the Window: Joel Chandler Harris and the Creation of Uncle Remus," in *Living by the Word*.

36. Anissa Wardi, *Death and the Arc of Mourning in African American Literature* (Gainesville: University Press of Florida, 2003), 40.

37. Jana Hecková, "Timeless People: The Development of the Ancestral Figure in Three Novels by Alice Walker," *Current Objectives of Postgraduate American Studies* 9 (2008).

38. Lauret, *Alice Walker*, 208.

39. Jana Hecková, "Timeless People," 4.

40. Toni Morrison, "Rootedness: The Ancestor's Foundation," in *Black Women Writers*, ed. Mari Evans (New York: Pluto Press, 1987), 343.

41. Ibid., 344.

42. Walker, *Now Is the Time*, 99.

43. Ibid., 94.

44. Ibid., 132 (emphasis added).

45. Ibid., 80.

46. Richard Rohr, *What Mystics Know* (New York: Crossroads Publishing, 2015), 130.

47. Walker, "Marrying Good Men," from *The Cushion in the Road*, 2013. She performed the service for Scott Sanders and his partner Brad.

48. Melanie Harris, *Gifts of Virtue, Alice Walker, and Womanist Ethics* (London: Palgrave Macmillan, 2010), 51.

49. Ibid.

50. Patricia Hill Collins, *Black Feminist Thought* (New York: Routledge, 2000), 202.

51. Walker, *Absolute Trust*, xii (emphasis added).

52. Ibid., 3.

53. J. O. Tate, "Smiley Face with Dreadlocks," *National Review* 41, no. 12 (1989): 48.

54. Walker, *Absolute Trust*, 36.

55. Ibid., 39.

56. Ibid., 40.

57. Ibid., 33.

58. Ibid., 35.

59. Ibid., 55.

60. Matthew 5:45.

61. Walker, *Absolute Trust*, 56–57.

62. Ibid., 58.

63. Ibid., 97.

64. Ibid., 103.

65. Ibid., 128.

Chapter Nine

When the Other Dancer Is the Self

We become the one we gaze upon.
—Meister Eckhart

"WHO DAT SAY WHO DAT WHEN I SAY WHO DAT?"

Walker's mysticism and spiritual views, while controversial, coincide with the beliefs of some physicists in the unity of all things and a connected universe. Mystics have always known that all things are connected. In popular culture the idea of unity expresses in numerous ways. Interestingly, the "who dat" of the New Orleans Saints football team adopted from black folk tradition is one such example. The who dat that says who and the who that answers is the same self and contains the idea of unity, just as Walker's essay and the title of this chapter express a oneness.

Walker's mysticism, characterized as new age nonsense, emanates from the same source as the mystic poet Rumi's, who understood oneness when he declared, "You are not a drop in the ocean, you are the entire ocean in a drop."[1] Walker's profound oneness with nature is equally grounded in the Gnostic scriptures. In the Gospel of Thomas, Jesus says, "It is I who am the all. . . . Split a piece of wood and I am there. Lift up the stone, and you will find me there."[2] As with her fiction, Walker's poetry also illuminates her spiritual worldview. This chapter examines Walker's idea of mystical unity as it is expressed in her poetry, essays, and children's books: *Her Blue Body: Everything We Know*, *Why War Is Never a Good Idea*, *Overcoming Speechlessness*, *There Is a Flower at the Tip of My Nose*, *Finding the Green Stone*, and *The Way Forward Is with a Broken Heart*.

Her Blue Body: Everything We Know: Earthling Poems 1965–1990 Complete (1991) contains the forty-one poems from an earlier poetry collection,

Horses Make the Landscape Look More Beautiful (1984). The poems from *Horses* call to our attention our unity with the landscape. In the introduction to this collection, Walker writes that the poems express her sorrow because of human abuse of the earth.[3] She joins a host of other writers, Erazim Kohák's *The Embers and the Stars* (1984), a significant contribution to environmental literature; Rachel Carson's *Silent Spring* (1962); Thoreau's *Walden* (1854); the writings of Chief Seattle (1854); and the writings of John Muir (1838–1914), who saw nature as the primary source for understanding God. Should we choose to look deeply enough, no doubt we would find so-called primitive peoples concerned for the environment as well.

Walker's own anxieties about the environment seem to intensify after she makes her trek across the Sierra Nevada Mountains to take up residence in northern California. F. Marina Schauffler, in *Turning to Earth: Stories of Ecological Conversion*, identifies the difficulty connected with saving the earth. The belief in duality exacerbates the way people think about environmental issues. Describing what she calls "ecological schizophrenia," Schauffler writes that "a long-standing cultural divide . . . has cleaved Western thought and human identity since the Enlightenment. Most of our historical, literary, and religious texts view humans as distinct from the natural world, living in a 'civilized' realm inherently at odds with the 'wild.'"[4] Walker's effort is to tip the balance of the literary texts by focusing in her poetry and fiction on the spirit in all things. According to Schauffler, a growing number of people are turning away from traditional religion and embracing "Earth-centered belief systems that view the living world as sacred."[5] Walker is among this small but growing group of people who understand the need to respect the planet as a living aspect of what we are as human beings. Since human beings are privileged, Walker identifies everything as a human being.[6]

The title of *Horses Make the Landscape More Beautiful* comes from Lame Deer, a Lakota Indian (mystic) who suggested forgiving the white man for stealing the land because the white man introduced the horse to their tribe. In the collection of forty-one poems, there is not one that deals with horses. There is a poem about "The Diamonds on Liz's Bosom" that argues for the wearing of rocks and feathers instead of precious jewels and gold. Walker's collapsing of the exploitation of Africans, mining, and the wearing of jewelry does not quite work as poem. An essay would have been a better genre. The connection between mining and the destruction of the earth is not made clear in the poem, or in the one that follows, "We Alone," which suggests that people should value what is plentiful. People can bring down the cost of gold by not caring if it rises or falls.[7] One of Walker's unpublished poems warns of dangerous excesses. "You Thought You Could Have It All" begins with "our homes are the bodies of trees/ their lives sacrificed/ for our shelter/ You thought you could have it all/ the house on the hill/ the ocean in your backyard."[8] This poem would have been a nice complement to "The Diamonds on Liz's Bosom," and provided a better context for understanding.

"Torture" directs attention to the primacy of life and healing in the face of inexplicably cruel human acts on each other and on the earth. Walker writes, "when those you love are harmed, plant trees."[9] Here, mother in the poem can be read as mother earth. The poem implores us to always plant even as the trees are tortured and forests cut down; we can plant others. The etymology of the word *torture* is revealing. From Middle French, it means the "infliction of great pain, agony," but the intriguing meaning derives from the Latin torture, which is a "twisting, writhing, torture, torment," that comes from the stem of *torquere*, "to twist, turn, wind, wring, distort."[10] It seems as a matter of course we twist and distort the natural world and the people in it, even turning pain into sexual pleasure, at least according to sadomasochists. The planting of trees refers to ecological restoration, which is the degree to which ecological damage caused by humans is repaired by humans.[11] Scientists, however, perceive the problem to be far more complicated than trying to restore what we destroy.

Her Blue Body also contains never-before-published poems. That section of the book opens with a dedication to Walker's father. The first piece is prose titled "My Heart Has Reopened to You" and subtitled *The Place Where I Was Born* (italics in original). Walker recalls the geography of rural Georgia. In a nostalgic reverie she relates the loss of a favorite tree and her ensuing grief. This piece was published in *Reading the Environment* (1994).[12] Walker writes that she grieved as if the tree had been a person. She recognizes the necessity to grieve in secret because she knew that the members of her family would ridicule her. She also recognized the enormity of her emotional attachment to the tree being greater than for a family member. The prose ends with a poem that begins with the landscape of her birth. This poem illustrates what James seeks to understand philosophically, and that is the human connection to nature and the significance of the natural world.[13] An issue in Western philosophy is whether non-human beings are sentient. In Eastern thought both human and non-humans are sentient beings. African and other native philosophies recognize the natural world as sentient, which means to possess the ability to feel and experience conscious awareness.

The poem titled "Pagan" exposes the conundrum in Western philosophy regarding sentient beings and whether people have a moral obligation to nature. Walker's poem concludes that the dogma of religion is responsible for alienating people from the earth. "Pagan" functions as Walker's credo. The poem rejoices that paganism has survived the proselytization of Islam, Christianity, Judaism, and any other superimposed religion. She is delighted to discover that paganism was black people's religion from the beginning.[14] The nature religion when not stamped out was hidden, covered over with creed, screed, and prevarications.[15] Walker's poem "Pagan," however, says lies.

The concept of unity is a koan or divine paradox, a mystery. Walker has acknowledged that she accepts and is greatly intrigued by mystery. Scientists, on the contrary, would like to validate mathematically what mystics accept based on their personal experiences. A defining difference between religion and mysticism is that the latter encourages people to value their own experiences, whereas religion promotes the belief in the experiences of others. While the mystery of the universe has yet to be solved, it is interesting that some physicists want to reveal the idea of oneness in scientific terms or a unified theory.[16] Their ideas are not accepted by mainstream science, however, which is not surprising given the reluctance of people, even scientists, to change.

In the poem "We Have a Map of the World," dedicated to "The Nevada-Semipalatinsk Anti-Nuclear Movement,"[17] Walker focuses on unity when she says how it is in one country, so it is in another. There is no separation. When nuclear explosions happen, we all choke on clouds of poison fallout.[18] The poem concludes with a powerful image, that of old men whose sperm has turned to plutonium.[19] Unlike in some of her other works, for example, *Finding the Green Stone*, which I discuss later, there is no balancing of the negative with what might be positive when it comes to nuclear experiments. Another poem to note is "Listen." It reiterates Walker's concept of the humanness of everything—tree and rock.[20] Claiming the spirit/life force of both the animate and inanimate harkens to the ancient African animism that Christianity sought to demolish.

"These Days" is the poem that most engages the ethics of ecology and exposes the irony in the ethics of environmentalism. The gist of the poem is the statement that the earth will be saved for people, and Walker adds the name of her friends. Part of the worry over the demise of the earth comes from people's belief that humans are superior to all else.[21] What can save the world, Walker says, is love.[22] Basically, Walker is asking people to just be more thoughtful, but ends the poem with the line about the earth being saved for people.[23] The irony results from the foregrounding of individuals (in the poem, the poet's friends and her daughter) for which the world should be saved. The poem represents, as does much in environmental ethics, a homocentric or human-centered viewpoint. John Cairns Jr. observes that this viewpoint constitutes a major ethical issue, and that it will take more than self-interest to save the earth.[24]

The poem "First They Said" is an indictment of cultural and religious hegemony manifest in missionaries, colonizers, and enslavers who negatively attacked traditional beliefs and replaced them with organized, hierarchal, and patriarchal religions and governments.[25] The poem captures in the first line the psychic assault on native peoples through name calling and designating a people as savages. The following line counters by referring to the behavior of the so-called savages, which is kind and considerate.[26] The order of the poem is accusation followed by defense. The rationalizations end when the "They" in the poem admit that the problem is the very existence of the people they want to destroy, not because they are savages, but just because they exist.[27] If people's right to exist is not challenged, the effort to save the earth indeed is daunting.

"Beast" is a poem that acknowledges the healing power of art. The significance of art and artist is pervasive in Walker's prose fiction as well as in her essays. Creation through art is a gateway to the soul. Walker embraces art as a spiritual practice and, when she fails to create, she confesses she feels like a beast.[28] She defines beast as one who loses its soul. Walker fears that, because of the abuse heaped on the earth, we may have caused the earth to lose its soul and its ability to create. The poem ends with the poet asking earth to rise up and shake off the concrete.[29] She may be inviting an earthquake. The title poem in the *Her Blue Body* collection worships mother earth. The poem speaks of a beautiful mother with a green lap, white stone teeth, blue body.[30] "Once, Again," a haiku, ends the book. The title recalls *Once*, Walker's first published collection of poems. This poem opens into the grass. Walker returns the reader, once again, to that which is natural, like Whitman's *Leaves of Grass*.

SEEK AND YOU WILL FIND

Finding the Green Stone (1991) is both a children's parable and a lesson for adults. Walker dedicates the book to "the eternal child" in herself and in the reader. On the face of it, Walker tells a story of a sister and her brother who own a shiny green stone that they value and play with. The brother loses his and attempts to steal and take by force his sister's stone. Unable to do so, he eventually finds his own, but only after he stops being mean and realizes that he is loved. He understands how much he is valued because the entire community comes out to help him find his missing stone, an effort they know will be fruitless because only he can find it. The takeaway for children is to be nice. Misbehavior diminishes their own value.

Reading the stone as metaphor for Spirit within everyone, the message becomes metaphysical. The story makes clear that no one can steal your spirit. It is also clear that no one can help you find it. The green stone represents enlightenment, and although many may wish to assist—family members, ministers, and friends may want to help find the green stone, the inner light—no one can. The search is internal. In Jungian analysis, the green stone might well have a transcendental function. Certainly, green is meaningful. Taken from nature, green is the universal color of vegetation, of trees specifically, and more abstractly of growth. In some cultures, including the United States, green is indicative of good luck. In the story, Katie and Johnny's father is a pulpwood truck driver who cuts down (green) trees. Johnny has hurt his father's feelings by thoughtlessly saying that he is ashamed of him because he drives "a stupid pulpwood truck."[31] Johnny is forced to apologize when he realizes that his father's job (the father's name is Mr. Oak) provides for the family's food and clothing. The father's name is the unity principle at work. He is the tree that he fells, the who dat, the other dancer. The green stone mediates opposites: "It facilitates a transition from one psychological attitude or condition to another."[32] The stone enables Mr. Oak to maintain his integrity while doing what he hates—harming trees. Mr. Oak's stone is bright and shining, whereas his son's is lost. The transcendent function of the stone enables the father to move beyond the conflict and "avoid one-sidedness,"[33] which traps Johnny.

Another way of understanding Walker's story is to see the stone as integrity. Everyone has it, but in some people it is dull and gray, covered over by negative emotions. In others, depending on their behavior, it is completely lost, as with Johnny. The etymology of integrity is wholeness. The loss of integrity leads to psychic pain. Johnny is unhappy without his green stone. His mother's words remind him that no one can give him the stone, and no one can take it from him.[34] The loss of integrity is always the responsibility of the one who loses it, and for its loss, Johnny must accept responsibility. When he does, he finds his stone.

THE WAY FORWARD IS WITH A BROKEN HEART (2000)

At the turn of the century, with the publication of *The Way Forward Is with a Broken Heart*, Walker pays special attention to the heart as metaphor for love. She insists through the autobiographical stories in this volume that the only way forward is with love at the center of human consciousness. The stories represent a heart fractured from divorce, disillusioned with young love and melancholy memories. It begins with the melding of fact with fiction. There are seven sections in the book, seven being the number of the natural world in Kabbalistic thought represented by seven days, seven notes on the musical scale, and seven directions, north, south, east, west, up, down, center. Seven days in Sukkot represent the world of nature, fitting for Walker but also appropriate for her former Jewish husband to whom the first and last stories are directed. Walker's pilgrimage to the house on Rockdale Drive in Jackson, Mississippi, may connect also with the meaning of Sukkot as a temporary dwelling place.

In "Memoir of a Marriage," Walker (I use Walker because in the preface she introduces the material as her experience) writes to her ex-husband, who is married to someone else (presumably happily so), about a lesbian relationship in which she is involved. Walker takes the woman/lover with her to Mississippi to visit the house where she and her husband once lived. Her motive for sharing in this way remains obscure but reveals threads that appear in *The Temple of My Familiar*. The young husband, like Suwelo in the novel, refuses to read a book written by a black woman, in this case Zora Neale Hurston's *Their Eyes Were Watching God*. Apparently, the husband's refusal marks the beginning of the end for Walker, as it does for Fanny.

The section on "Begging" relates the story of a black woman who came regularly to the house in Jackson to beg for coins, a few pennies. Walker makes the effort to give her more, but the woman refuses, causing Walker to wonder if she is a spy sent by the Klan or if somehow in the woman she saw herself and her fear of poverty. Moving back and forth between memory of past incidents—the beggar woman, the death of Langston Hughes and their invitation to his funeral—she speaks directly to the young husband, sounding every bit like Fanny in *The Temple of My Familiar* when she says, "I miss you. We were good people. And together we were good. Allies and friends. Too good to have those years stolen from us, even by our grief."[35] Apparently, she did not want to be married, but what did she want? After the divorce is final, she wants to have tea and invites the ex-husband, who declines.

She wants the young husband, now middle aged, to remember what she recalls: *The Bridges of Madison County*, a movie reminiscent of their own torrid love affair. Why he would want to do this is not made clear, but the memory is more about her than about him. She says, "When I think of that summer I think of how perfectly my hair was straightened, and how neatly shaped. I think of the tiny, sexy dress I wore."[36] The passage goes on to describe in detail her "seductive" look and her "silky" smoothness. Lauret identifies some of Walker's writing as "narcissistic and vain."[37] "Passion" helps to make the case, centering as it does on the first time she and the young husband made love. She recalls that it was awkward; something the man probably would want to forget. Finally, she reveals the motive for the reminiscences. Walker is preparing to meet the ex-husband again after many years. Rebecca, the "Our Child" in the story, has arranged a meeting with her parents and her therapist. Rebecca reveals in her own book how disruptive the divorce and the shared custody arrangement was for her growing up, living with her father for two years and then living with her mother for two more.

The literal reading of the stories seems superfluous. How else might they be read and understood? Literally, there is something deeply troubling about this writing. To begin with the occasion that has called it forth, Rebecca's need to be in therapy, seeing a psychiatrist, appears not to be the central concern here. Instead, Walker daydreams about the time she and the young husband "snuggle and kiss well into morning."[38] When Our Child speaks and says that her parents appear not to know what happened to them and that for years she has been the go-between and would like to understand, instead of empathizing with the daughter's situation Walker says, "I feel an enormous wave of pity for us, her parents."[39]

A different reading might enable us to see the young husband as bridegroom for something more than the individual man that he was. The dedication may offer a clue. Dedicated to the American race, Walker is possibly setting the individual marriage on a larger spiritual and universal stage. Their marriage was a union that produced and reflected the American race. Walker's emphasis on the political meaning of the marriage may in fact be misunderstood by her daughter, who questioned whether her parents' marriage was just a political statement. In this work, Walker makes it clear that she and Rebecca's father were indeed in love. But their marriage still served as paradigm for the American race. Walker is disillusioned not just by the failure of the marriage but by her experience in the belly of the whale, as it were, in Mississippi during the terminal illness of legal Jim Crow, which did not die without a violent fight.

Perhaps her narrative concerns love, and like the mystic Osho wants to call attention to life as "a constant flux."[40] He writes that life always moves toward the future, but the mind moves toward the past. The mind is closed, as are Walker's memories, Osho says, "closed in the experience that happened already, and life is always open for the experience that has never happened."[41] Fear prevents people from moving forward in life. For Walker, this collection of stories appears to be her journey to the heart. It is easy to get into a marriage; it is difficult to get out. Osho suggests that going backward is a necessary step for advancement. Therefore, Walker's way forward is by and through considering the past.

These stories, in addition to serving as therapy for Walker, who acknowledges that writing saved her life and must continue to do so, provide insight into some elements in her novels. One event related in the memories of living in Jackson, Mississippi, pertains to Harold, a white man from Idaho whose family owned "six thousand acres" of former Indian land. Harold seems like a rough sketch for Hugh in her last novel, *Now Is the Time to Open Your Heart*. Hugh owns thousands of acres of Indian land that includes a sacred burial ground. The story "Kindred Spirits" thinly disguises Walker as the central character Rosa, and her sister Ruth as Barbara. The relationship between sisters also mirrors the relationship between Susannah and her older sister June in *By the Light of My Father's Smile*.

The remaining stories explore betrayal of friends and lovers, and Walker's meditation in section 6 is on her own bisexuality and titled, "This Is How It Happened." It happens because she gets bored with her lover and is attracted to a beautiful lesbian who is a fantastic dancer. "Brotherhood of the Saved," probably a soft veil for the Jehovah's Witnesses whom Walker's mother joined late in her life, includes a mother and daughter discussing the daughter's sinful ways of sleeping with women, which the Brotherhood condemns. This story is humorous. The daughter, who remains nameless except for the nickname Tran that her mother uses, takes the mother and two aging aunts to see a porn film, *Deep Throat*. The elderly women's reaction is comical, although not unexpected. In the second part of the story the daughter invites her father to go to Jamaica, and at Negril Beach she gets him to smoke marijuana. The mother and father are divorced after a lifetime together. The Brotherhood causes the parent's divorce because they tell the mother to cut the sinful daughter out of her life. When the mother continues to attend the church, her husband moves out.

The final section of *The Way Forward Is with a Broken Heart* is written to the husband of Walker's youth. On July 16, 1999, John Kennedy Jr. is killed when his plane crashes into the ocean. Mel's mother has died, and Walker writes to comfort him and uses Kennedy's death as a means for doing so. Calling her ex-husband Stranger, she writes, "I send you my sorrow. And my art."[42] A strange book in terms of the deeply autobiographical nature and because of the unevenness of the writing, *The Way Forward Is with a Broken Heart* nevertheless demonstrates Walker's mystical consciousness. One might wonder why the editors were not more insistent about revisions. They might have been. In some of Walker's archival notes there are suggestions about comma use that she ignores, and there is a warning about the overuse of adjectives. Sometimes Walker makes changes, but often she chooses not to.

The metaphysical aspect of *The Way Forward* is the who dat found in Rumi's "Music Master," which claims, "We are the mirror as well as the face in it."[43] Walker's mysticism may enable her to see beyond all the sorrow and human mistakes of her marriage, divorce, and relationship with her daughter to the core goodness of life, leading to the content of her next book of poems.

GIFTS OF THE SPIRIT

Sometimes writers, especially poets, have the experience of being used by a power greater than they are. The poems in *A Poem Traveled Down My Arm* are a case in point. Feeling fatigued because she was tasked with autographing many copies of her recently published book, *Absolute Trust in the Goodness of the Earth*, the poems came to Walker as gifts. They crystalize her theology. They appear without titles and are illustrated with her playful doodles. Walker declares the omnipresence of God, and that Presence is Love. Love expresses as helpfulness.[44] The book is filled with wisdom, some of which echoes messages from Eastern philosophy, like the poem that suggests we release useless information and stop comparing ourselves to each other.

These poems testify to her belief in immanence, a belief that runs counter to many womanist theologians who conceptualize God as transcendent. The idea of the other dancer as the self continues as a thread throughout her poems. She sees an old woman, suffering the results of war, sitting by a window and asks, how do you know she is not you?[45] This collection of poems ends declaring Walker's belief that love is the future and peace is deserved.

THERE IS A FLOWER AT THE TIP OF MY NOSE SMELLING ME (2006)

Walker's personification of Nature, in this case a flower, the sky, the road, a dog, an ocean, a sunrise, water, a song, a dance, a poem, a pen, and a story, demonstrates for children how to see the world not as a dead thing for them to use, but as something alive with which they can interact. Beautifully illustrated by Stefano Vitale with vibrant colors, this book encourages children who rarely need much prompting to appreciate all things as living. To accept the premise that all is alive might encourage the ethical treatment of the planet. Then again, given the history of how people treat each other, it might well be too much to hope for. Walker is an optimist. Her book, she says, is a thank-you note for her walk among the redwood trees, for the vivid blue skies and the scent of spring. In one transformative moment she felt at one with the universe, which filled her with joy and gratitude.[46]

Her walk in the woods describes a spiritual awakening. I am often intrigued by the spiritual elements voiced in African American vernacular speech. A popular saying nowadays is "stay woke!" While the intent might be focused on the mundane level of staying aware of the danger of hate crimes and other acts of terror, a deeper meaning is for us to wake up and stay awake to the spiritual world in us and around us. Walker's book, for young and old alike, is a meditation in both words and colors of the unity of the world.

WHY WAR IS NEVER A GOOD IDEA (2007)

Walker's message to both children and adults is that what is hurtful to one is hurtful to all. The book points to the so-called collateral damage of war. Personifying war as an old person who is still unwise, Walker, through the vivid illustrations of Stefano Vitale, presents a compelling picture of why war is self-destructive. She writes to children, perhaps because it will take a new generation of humans to internalize the concept of peace.

ALICE WALKER OVERCOMING SPEECHLESSNESS (2010)

As an activist, writer, lecturer, and outspoken critic of injustice anywhere, it is difficult to imagine Alice Walker becoming speechless. The subtitle of the book may offer an explanation: *A Poet Encounters the Horror in Rwanda, Eastern Congo, and Palestine/Israel.* It turns out that Walker is not the one who is speechless. This compact book of seventy-five pages voices the sorrow and outrage of the many destroyed by hatred and genocide.

Howard Zinn, Walker's former professor at Spelman College and lifelong friend, suggests that it takes the talent of a poet to break the silence and speak the truth.[47] The essay is a deep analysis of the situation that brought destruction to Rwanda and the Eastern Congo. Walker traveled to Africa as part of the outreach efforts of Women for Women International. She records what she observed, as well as the stories of some of the survivors. On returning to the United States, Walker realized that she needed *Sangha* a Buddhist support group to assist her in processing the trauma of what she witnessed.

The second part of this book contains writings from Walker's witnessing in the Middle East. When asked to go to Gaza with the women's peace group CODEPINK, Walker agreed. During this time of turmoil, Israeli troops began the twenty-two-day bombing of Gaza, and Walker's sister Ruth died. Walker was grief stricken. Nevertheless, she still witnessed the injustice taking place in Palestine. She draws clear parallels between the genocide of Native Americans for attempting to defend their lands and what is happening in Gaza. All the rationales that the United States used to forcibly move Indians off their land are given by Israel. Walker notes the Golda Meir claim that there is no such thing as a Palestinian. Other familiar myths, for anyone aware of the civil rights movement in the southern United States or the anti-apartheid movement in South Africa, include the claim made by the group in power that the group they seek to oppress is savage, or that the land they desire was uninhabited (the Boers' claim about South Africa). There are many recognizable patterns that Walker never hesitates to identify.

Naturally, she receives the ire of Zionists and other critics. In 2011 when Walker decides to join the Freedom Flotilla to Gaza, British writer Howard Jacobson,[48] in an open letter in the *Guardian*, asks Walker not to sail. He accuses her of self-aggrandizement for putting herself in the company of Dr. King, Gandhi, and other martyrs when in her letter she recalls the actions of the brave for the cause of freedom. Walker sees the Freedom Flotilla as an effort to make change. For her, not going is like not marching across the Edmund Pettis Bridge because it is dangerous or will make things worse. It is impossible for Walker to not be the activist or to rest on her past actions while ignoring the issues of the day. In the concluding essay of *Overcoming Speechlessness*, she says, "I am writing about my refusal, as a woman of color, to be silenced and how black history supports this stance."[49] The book ends with suggested sources to read, including former president Jimmy Carter's *Palestine: Peace Not Apartheid.*

Given the turmoil of Africa and the Middle East, Walker asks: What to do? She says people in America do not want to hear about the horror she witnessed.[50] In answer to her own question she writes, "*Nothing to do, finally, but dance.*"[51] Dance thus becomes an overarching metaphor for her book of poems, *Hard Times Require Furious Dancing* (2010). The Sufi mystics' whirling dervish exemplifies the free spirit of dance. In a spiritual context, dancing unifies the body with the soul. Walker recognizes this when she writes "Learning to Dance" and says that dancing enables one to maintain balance in what often appears to be an off-balance world. In the hard times that this collection of poems covers—the death of her sister, the estrangement of her only child, the death of her beloved black Lab Marley Mu—Walker reminds us to move with the rhythm of life. In the midst of political corruption and the suffering of innocent children, she bemoans the fact that we suffer much but learn nothing as the result.[52] Through dancing, as the poem "Sometimes" says, the body and soul reunite. In those moments it is possible to find joy.

Walker's mysticism coincides with the ideas of many people the world recognizes as great, yet her views, which mirror theirs, are often dismissed as meaningless chatter. I argue that part of the reason for the dismissal is that she is a woman, and a black one. Rarely are women credited with profound spiritual insight, especially when it counters so-called orthodox patriarchal teachings. Given the historical experiences of black women in the United States, there is ample reason to see how spiritual insight has enabled their survival. The following quotation by Rumi concludes this chapter because it answers the question posed in the chapter's opening, "Who dat say who dat when I say who dat?" Rumi writes: I am that cat, this stone, no one . . . / I see and know all times and worlds/ as one, one, always one./ What do I have/ to do to get you to admit/ who is speaking?/ This is your own voice echoing off the walls of God."[53]

NOTES

1. Rumi, *The Essential Rumi* (New York: Harper Collins, 2004), 263.
2. Marvin Meyer (ed.), *The Nag Hammadi Scriptures* (New York: Harper Collins, 2007), Verse 77, 143.
3. Walker, *Horses Make the Landscape Look More Beautiful*, 311.
4. F. Marina Schauffler, *Turning to Earth: Stories of Ecological Conversion* (Charlottesville: University of Virginia Press, 2003), 2.
5. Ibid., 5.
6. Walker, "Everything Is a Human Being," in *Living by the Word*, 139.
7. Walker, "The Diamonds," *Horses Make the Landscape Look More Beautiful*, 328.
8. Alice Walker Archive, Stuart A. Rose Manuscript, Archives, and Rare Book Library, Emory University (44/74).

9. Walker, *Horses Make the Landscape More Beautiful*, 389.
10. *Etymology Dictionary*. https://www.etymonline.com/.
11. John Cairns Jr., "Restoration Ecology: Protecting Our National Global Life Support Systems," in *Rehabilitating Damaged Ecosystems*, ed. John Cairns Jr. (Boca Raton, FL: CRC Press, 1995).
12. Melissa Walker, ed., *Reading the Environment* (New York: Norton, 1994). Also published in Walker, *Her Blue Body: Everything We Know*, 411.
13. Simon P. James, *The Presence of Nature: A Study in Phenomenology and Environmental Philosophy* (New York: Palgrave, 2009).
14. Walker, *Her Blue Body*, 420.
15. Ibid., 421.
16. See, for example, Stephen Hawking and Leonard Mlodinow, *The Grand Design* (New York: Bantam Books, 2010).
17. Ibid., 436.
18. Ibid., 439.
19. Ibid., 441.
20. Ibid., 324.
21. Ibid., 403.
22. Ibid., 406.
23. Ibid.
24. Cairns, "Restoration Ecology."
25. Ibid., 322.
26. Ibid.
27. Ibid., 323.
28. Ibid., 430.
29. Ibid., 431.
30. Ibid., 460.
31. Walker, *Finding the Green Stone*, n.p.
32. Andrew Samuels, Bani Shorter, and Fred Plaut (eds.), *A Critical Dictionary of Jungian Analysis* (New York: Routledge, 2013), 150.
33. Ibid.
34. Walker, *Finding the Green Stone*, n.p.
35. Walker, *The Way Forward*, 13.
36. Ibid., 18.
37. Maria Lauret, *Alice Walker* (New York, Palgrave Macmillan, 2011), 233.
38. Walker, *The Way Forward*, 26.
39. Ibid., 27.
40. Osho, *Journey to the Heart: Discourses on the Sufi Way* (Boston: Shaftesbury, Dorset, 1994), 60.
41. Ibid., 61.
42. Walker, *The Way Forward*, 200.
43. Rumi, *The Essential Rumi*, 106.
44. Walker, *A Poem Traveled Down My Arm*, 7.
45. Ibid., 89.
46. Ibid., backmatter (n.p.).
47. Walker, *Overcoming Speechlessness*, book cover.
48. "Why Alice Walker Shouldn't Sail to Gaza," CNN Opinion, June 24, 2011. www.CNN.com/2011/opinion/6/24.
49. Walker, *Overcoming Speechlessness*, 73.
50. Walker, *Hard Times Require Furious Dancing*, 58.
51. Ibid. (italics in the original).
52. Walker, *Hard Times*, 39.
53. Eryk Hanut and Michele Wetherbee, *The Rumi Card Book* (Tokyo: Turtle Publications Journey Editions, 2000), 15.

Chapter Ten

Mystic Walker

Walker's mysticism runs counter to womanist theology. Her mystical and theological view of life can be found in all her works. One problem, as Melanie Harris points out, is that womanist theological scholarship has given little attention to Walker's own spiritual and ethical voice. Little exploration of Walker's reference to herself as a "womanist woman-loving,"[1] sexually and nonsexually, including her bisexuality—has taken place. Harris also rightly questions why womanist theologians and ethicists have not taken seriously Walker's declaration that she is a pagan, which she defines as a lover of the land, one who respects the divinity of the earth, especially as a descendant of a long line of farmers.[2] She sees the earth as holy.

Walker's expansive and universalist definition of a womanist is worth quoting in full.

> **Womanist** 1. From *womanish*. (Opp. Of "girlish," i.e., frivolous, irresponsible, not serious.) A black feminist or feminist of color. From the black folk expression of mothers to female children, "You acting womanish," i.e., like a woman. Usually referring to outrageous, audacious, courageous or *willful* behavior. Wanting to know more and in greater depth than is considered "good" for one. Interested in grown-up doings. Acting grown up. Being grown up. Interchangeable with another folk expression: "You trying to be grown. Responsible. In charge. *Serious.*
>
> 2. *Also:* A woman who loves other women, sexually and/or nonsexually. Appreciates and prefers women's culture, women's emotional flexibility (values tears as natural counterbalance to laughter), and women's strength. Sometimes loves individual men, sexually and/or nonsexually. Committed to survival and wholeness of entire people, male and female. Not a separatist, except periodically, for health. Traditionally universalist, as in: "Mama, why are we brown, pink, and yellow, and our cousins are white, beige, and black?" Ans.: "Well, you know the colored race is just like a flower garden, with every color

flower represented." Traditionally capable, as in: "Mama, I'm walking to Canada and I'm taking you and a bunch of other slaves with me." Reply: "It wouldn't be the first time."

3. Loves music. Loves dance. Loves the moon. *Loves* the Spirit. Loves love and food and roundness. Loves struggle. *Loves* the Folk. Loves herself. *Regardless.*

4. Womanist is to feminist as purple to lavender.[3]

Katie G. Cannon chose the term womanist to define black feminist theology, but as critics point out, at least in the beginning, Cannon's focus was far removed from Walker's expansive vision. In 1985, Cannon stated that "In essence, the Bible is the highest source of authority for most Black women."[4] Assertions such as this one caused critics to claim that Cannon attempts to Christianize the term *womanist* when it is non-Christian. For many black women the Bible is not the "highest source of authority,"[5] Walker is one such woman. Over the years Cannon's definition has expanded to embrace more than Christian, heterosexual ethics.[6]

Walker's definition is at odds with Christian doctrine. Cheryl J. Sanders, social ethicist, professor, and minister, challenged her colleagues to examine fully Walker's term "Loves the Spirit" in the definition of womanist. In the now famous 1989 "Roundtable Discussion: Christian Ethics and Theology in Womanist Perspective," Sanders objects to Walker's lack of "God-language."[7] She claims the problem in appropriating Walker's term is that it does not fit the experience of "black women whose theology and ethics rest on other foundations."[8] While Sanders poses her argument as terminological, regarding theological and ethical definitions, and states that "to do ethics in womanist perspective presents less of a problem, insofar as the construction of ethical claims can be pursued independently of theological considerations,"[9] her real issue appears to be concerned with Walker's "womanist assertion of sexual freedom."[10] The problem is not that Walker's definition fails to mention the Christian God, but instead, says Spirit, her definition gives too much attention to the sexual, embraces homosexuality, and does not privilege heterosexuality. Sanders adds: "The womanist nomenclature ... conveys a sexual ethics that is ambivalent at best with respect to the value of heterosexual monogamy within the black community."[11] Thus, Walker's stance is too nontraditional for many Christian adherents to embrace fully.

The first theologian and ethicist to appropriate the term *womanist* from Walker's definition and use it to critique black liberation theology, Katie Cannon, responds to Sanders by stating that *womanist* does indeed provide an appropriate term for discussing theology and ethics. She argues: "A womanist liberation theo-ethical framework is an endeavor to identify African American women's moral agency, eliminating, as far as possible, contradictory directives for character and behavior."[12] She further states that the intent of the womanist is to re-appropriate Afro-Christian culture. Cannon points out that Walker's definition enables her to reclaim "Afro-Christian culture" by placing black women at the center of human social relations and ecclesiastical institutions.[13] Furthermore, she claims that the womanist framework lends itself well to questioning various patriarchal paradigms, for example, the linking of black feminism with lesbianism and the issue of "compulsory heterosexuality."[14] While she touches on what probably is the greatest issue embedded in Walker's definition, that of lesbianism and homosexuality, she stops short of interrogating the black Christian position. Paradoxically by using womanist instead of feminist, Cannon avoids the ire the F word often incites. Many black women reject the term *feminist* for a variety of reasons.

Not all black women theologians reject the feminist label. In "Is a Womanist a Black Feminist? Marking the Distinctions and Defying Them: A Black Feminist Perspective," and in "Must I be a Womanist?" Traci C. West, associate professor of ethics, in her Roundtable response to Monica Coleman challenges the idea that feminism belongs solely to white women. While she recognizes the important contributions womanist scholars have made, she maintains the right to chart her "differences with womanist religious thought."[15] Sociologist Patricia Hill Collins's 1996 article, "What's in a Name? Womanism, Black Feminism, and Beyond" states that the issue of naming demonstrates the difficulty of being inclusive. Further, she questions why the name used for "black women's collective standpoint"[16] matters. She concludes that no term currently exists that adequately addresses all the issues black women face. Whether one chooses the term *womanist*, Walker's definition clearly has influenced black women theologians who over the years have grown to embrace much more of Walker's mystical theology than when they first began.

While Cannon's response to Sanders insists: "A Black womanist liberation Christian ethic is a critique of all human domination in light of Black women's experiences, a faith praxis that unmasks whatever threatens the well-being of the poorest woman of color,"[17] she fails to address head-on the topic of female sexual freedom or the challenge of heterosexual, monogamous marriage. Walker's works make clear that neither heterosexuality nor monogamous marriage is the sine qua non for family life. Furthermore, if her fiction fails to exemplify her position regarding religion, her statement in *We Are the Ones We Have Been Waiting For* makes an unequivocal declaration. She writes that most religions, "alpha-male-dominant to the core, have done more harm than good," condemning religions that teach women are inferior to men, white supremacy, or that suffering is inevitable. She rejects religions that sanction war and view people as others to be exterminated.[18]

Feminist bell hooks's response to Sanders is more direct than Cannon's. She says: "If the black church . . . is to survive and sustain its revolutionary theological mission, feminist re-visioning is essential."[19] Other theologians are more direct than Cannon's initial response to the issues that Sanders raises. Emilie M. Townes declares that Sanders "begins with an integral conceptual error that leads her down an unproductive path."[20] Further, she states, and rightly so, Walker is concerned not just with the survival but the flourishing of black people in all their diversity, which Townes names, "age, gender, sexuality, radical activity, accommodationist stance, creative promise."[21] Townes confronts outright Sanders's issue with lesbianism and the privileging of heterosexuality when she insists: "Many Womanist Christian ethicists and theologians extend Walker's challenge to serious questioning of what and who constitutes family structures and healthy models of love and growth.[22] Townes is also correct in stating that Sanders misses the crux of Walker's spirituality by suggesting its marginality, and cites the God-talk within *The Color Purple* to substantiate her position. Delores Williams, in "*The Color Purple*: What Was Missed" sees clearly how traditional ideas about God have victimized women, and argues for a more expansive view.[23]

A central theological question that Sanders raises is how womanist Christian ethicists and theologians can accept Walker's immanent concept of Spirit and their Christian belief in Christology, the belief of many Christians that God became man and that God-made-man is the individual Jesus Christ.[24] Townes answers by pointing to the necessity for inclusivity and the possibility of growth within black religious communities. Philosopher of religion, Mark C. Taylor, describes Christology in literary terms. He compares the literary text to Christ and concludes that analyzing the literary text means dismembering, violating, crucifying it. Taylor points out: "Dismembering is, paradoxically, a condition of remembering, death the genesis of life."[25] Critic Felipe Smith observes as well that Walker's belief in "the redemptive power of writing" can be viewed as "radical Christology."[26]

The other issues of concern for black women theologians are sex and sexuality. In "All the Bearded Irises of Life: Confessions of a Homospiritual,"[27] Walker confronts the silences from her childhood that surrounded homosexuals. In this 1987 essay, Walker declares her bisexuality. The Shakespearian adage "To thine own self be true" (Polonius in *Hamlet*) governs her choice to be whatever she chooses, to be a morally autonomous sexual being. Womanist theologian Emilie Townes argues that the persona in Walker's definition of womanist "does not hold her sexuality as a sign of moral autonomy"[28] but sees herself able to "celebrate herself and her people as agents of a human community."[29] Townes' reading of the voice that asks why are we multicolored certainly is not the only way to understand the question, particularly in light of the conversation in the definition that follows.

Townes claims that the mother in Walker's definition is not resigned to such independent behavior. On the contrary, when the daughter declares: "Mama, I'm walking to Canada and I'm taking you and a bunch of other slaves with me," the mother simply replies with what sounds like resignation when she says: "It wouldn't be the first time." No one "restrains" (Townes' term) the daughter. In any event, Walker herself appears not as interested in her people as agents of a human community as she is in securing freedom for the individual within the community. In "All the Bearded Irises of Life," she claims all people as her people. We must be everyone to ensure freedom for all.[30] Before the National Coalition of Black Gays and Lesbians, Walker declared herself "two-spirited,"[31] a lover (sexually) of both men and women.

Sex and sexuality as well as the sexual freedom of women are problematic for the black Christian church. Anthony B. Pinn, professor of humanities and religion, addresses the problem of religion and sex and sexuality in his introduction to *Loving the Body: Black Religious Studies and the Erotic*. He writes that scholars in religious studies have recognized the value of black literature for describing the culture and history of black people. He suggests, however, that the lessons have either been missed or ignored. He says that "African American literature has given graphic attention to the uneasy presence of sexuality and the erotic within the context of religious life."[32] Walker's novels *Possessing the Secret of Joy* (1992), in which Adam is a minister, and *By the Light of My Father's Smile* (1998), in which the father also is a minister, are examples of her treatment of the erotic discussed earlier.[33] Other examples in black literature include Ann Allen Shockley's *Say Jesus and Come to Me* (1987), in which the central character is a lesbian minister, as well as Gloria Naylor's *The Women of Brewster Place* (1982), in which the traveling minister takes sexual advantage of Etta Mae Johnson. James Baldwin's classic *Go Tell It on the Mountain* (1952) and *Just above My Head* (1978) include examples of the erotic within the context of organized religion, especially in the black church.

Pinn blames African American religiosity on the adherence to the writings of Paul that negate the flesh. He quotes Romans 8:5–8 and Romans 6:12–13. Both passages deny the pleasures of the flesh and describe such pleasure as "carnally minded," and further state "the carnal mind is enmity against God." Paul creates a duality between body and spirit. Walker's short story "The Diary of an African Nun" demonstrates that the dichotomy between Spirit and Eros is Christian, and the nun suffers the dualism imposed by the Catholic Church. Walker's novel *The Color Purple* for many religious scholars brought to the surface the troublesome relationship between the church, sex, and sexuality.

While Pinn is correct in his assertion that African American "religiosity" is responsible for the schizophrenic relationship between the church, sex, and sexuality, another, perhaps more compelling, reason results from the experience of enslavement. In a culture that condoned plantation slave customs, which used men as studs and women as breeders, alienation from the body functioned as a defense mechanism often expressed in the aphorism, they can own my body but not my soul. Rape victims often disassociate from their bodies. Given the historical trauma perpetrated on the black body, it is easy to see how a religion that encouraged a discarding of the flesh would be attractive and meaningful. What is unclear is why the tradition continues. Some explanation can be found in the writings of women theologians.

Long after the 1989 roundtable discussion about ethics and womanist theology, Katie Cannon's essay, "Sexing Black Women: Liberation from the Prisonhouse of Anatomical Authority" discusses "antisensual ambivalence"[34] experienced by black women because of Christian teachings. She quotes Beverly Harrison who, like Audre Lorde, sees the erotic as a source of power and creativity. Her essay uncovers still another reason black women and churchwomen, in particular, have difficulty embracing their whole sexual selves. The problem arises from sexual and racial stereotyping and the politics of respectability.

Cannon refers to Evelyn Brooks Higgenbotham's book, *Righteous Discontent: The Women's Movement in the Black Baptist Church 1880–1920* (1993) as one of the best discussions of the sexual virtues of black churchwomen. Higgenbotham's study demonstrates that the politics of respectability that harken back to the Victorian era and the white middle-class antiquated idea of a cult of true womanhood[35] still is alive today. The reason for its adoption among African Americans was to counteract the negative stereotypes of black women especially and black people generally against the charge of sexual promiscuity, lasciviousness, and animalistic behavior. Cannon argues that the "deferential, Victorian strategy of lady-like, super-morality, result in churchwomen assuming the supplicant-position, renouncing their own erotic pleasures in the name of procreation, and, in turn, engaging in sexual activities as part of one's wifely duty."[36] She concludes that liberating black churchwomen sexually is a "moral imperative"[37] and urges women in the church to engage in dialogues for erotic justice.

In "Erotic Justice: Authority, Resistance, and Transformation," Cannon interrogates the Christian dogma that "taught (and far too many of us continue to teach) that we [black women] must suppress, repress, compress and depress the sexual aspects of our humanity, by reinforcing norms and practices that proclaim pro-creational sex as a gift from God and relational or recreational sex as the devil's handiwork."[38] Critiquing heterosexism, Cannon calls for an end to unjust treatment of lesbians and others based on their sexualities. She concedes that liberation theology demands eliminating injustice in all its forms. This declaration is worthy of Walker's label, womanist theology.

Emilie Townes admits that Walker's immanent concept of God as expressed in *The Color Purple* is not readily found in the African American church tradition. She perceives Walker's understanding of the sacred as an opportunity for growth in the black church. Nonetheless, even as she promotes the womanist perspective to challenge blind spots in the church tradition, when she names those to be included, "Womanist, black feminist, Afro-feminist, or black/Afro-American women,"[39] she stops short of including lesbians, homosexual, bisexual, or transgendered people.

Walker introduced the term *womanist* in her 1979 short story, "Coming Apart by Way of Introduction to Lorde, Teish and Gardner," but she offered no definition other than to say that "a Womanist is a feminist, only more common. Womanist approximates 'black feminist.'"[40] The story's first title was "Fable." In this story/parable Walker presents a womanist stance regarding pornography. Like the novel *By the Light of My Father's Smile*, "Coming Apart" received the label pornographic. Walker responded that being explicit and confronting pornography openly was the way to counteract it and the way writers could contribute to the fight.[41] The sexual conception and context in which womanist is born focuses on women's sexual freedom. Walker's story separates the erotic from the obscene. The wife, whose husband is addicted to porn, reads him part of Audre Lorde's essay, "Uses of the Erotic: The Erotic as Power," which concludes: "And use without consent of the used is abuse,"[42] meaning engaging in sex or anything else without being fully present with and having the permission of the person in the shared experience is exploitative.

Perhaps because of its sexual grounding, some theologians have elected to describe Walker's term *womanist* as secular. Although *womanist* is not Christian, it does not automatically become secular. The term itself appears to reject binary oppositions, and Walker's spirituality does not posit a difference between the sacred and the secular. One could say that everything is sacred, and Walker presents this idea within her works. In the concluding essay in *Living by the Word*, she tells Spelman College women of their "inseparableness from the divine; and everything, *especially* the physical world, is divine."[43] As noted earlier, my effort is to claim for Walker precisely what Shawn Copeland, a professor of systematic theology, asserts for the black woman theologian, and that is to use the "experiences and traditions of black women as a source for theologizing on the black experience."[44] In the essay "No One was Supposed to Survive," Walker theologizes the black experience of members of the MOVE organization who were firebombed in Philadelphia. Much of the essay centers on the antisocial characteristics of MOVE's back-to-nature members. Contained in one line, however, is the crux of the essay: "*Every bomb ever made falls on all of us.*"[45] Walker always points back to wholeness, unity, and oneness.

Black women theologians, arguably the first to embrace Walker's term, did so at their own peril and placed themselves in danger of becoming untenurable, marginalized, and ineffective. They were brave, and they deserve kudos for their efforts. Nevertheless, as second-generation womanist theologian Medusa (Patricia-Ann Johnson) clarifies in her essays "Secular Womynism: A View from the Left" and "Medusa: Secular Womynism Part II: It Is

What It IS,"[46] the forerunners—Jacqueline Grant, Delores Williams, Toinette M. Eugene, Katie Cannon, Kelly Brown Douglas, Marcia Riggs, Emilie Townes, Renita Weems, and others—have concentrated, as perhaps was necessary, on Christian women and their issues. Medusa seeks to break free from the confines of Christian theology and its focus on heterosexual relationships and codified belief systems. To do so, and as a womanist theologian, she has chosen to embrace more fully Walker's definition by calling it secular. Felipe Smith also has written that "Walker secularizes such terms as *redemption* and *salvation* to encompass solutions to social problems such as racial and gender oppression."[47]

Womanist is not secular but is as spiritually grounded as Christian theology. Redemption and salvation are not secularized either, as racial and gender oppression are both spiritual problems. Walker may not concern herself with religious matters per se, but she does consider spiritual ones. A definition of secular states: "not religious or spiritual in nature—not monastic." In an essay titled, "Toward a Monastic Idealism: The Thementics of Alice Walker's *The Temple of My Familiar*," Ikenna Dieke makes a compelling argument for recognizing Walker's spirituality. He defines idealism as metaphysical, that which regards reality as spiritual.[48] *The Temple of My Familiar*, Dieke claims, "creates a salutary vision, which points toward a monistic idealism in which humans, animals and the whole ecological order coexist in a unique dynamic of pancosmic symbiosis."[49] *Secular* carries the connotation of moral corruption by intemperance or sensuality and includes that which is unholy. Further, some synonyms for *secular* are profane, worldly, materialistic, and tellurian, none of which describes Walker's work.

At the same time, Walker's works can appear blasphemous; several of the novels employ profanity and descriptions of explicit sex acts or rape. If blasphemous is the grossly irreverent toward the sacred, then the problem clearly centers on what is sacred versus what is not, again leading to duality. A mystical standpoint allows the darkness, which some might consider the profane. Richard Rohr, Christian mystic, believes: "Any allowing of the hidden side of things, the dark side of things—while also holding onto the attractive and knowable side—usually marks the beginning of nondual consciousness."[50] He admits most people cannot easily embrace such mystery and paradox. Walker embraces both mystery and paradox in ways that womanist theologians appear not to. My argument is not against the term *womanist* being employed within a theological context. Clearly Walker introduced the term for its utility in the articulation of black women's issues. Walker has a theology, however, that is unacknowledged or outright denied when attempts are made to secularize her beliefs.

Smith claims in "Alice Walker's Redemptive Art" that Walker is committed to saving lives, stating that it is central to her work. Indeed, Walker has written that her purpose as a writer is to save lives.[51] The reason Walker gives in 1976 is consistently articulated throughout her literary corpus: the life saved is one's own. The ancestral presence that Smith observes in Walker's works constitutes the saving grace in her art. Walker has called Spirit the Ultimate Ancestor.[52] Her focus on ancestors is more African than Afro-Christian, and in this way too Walker diverges from Christian theological practices. According to archeologist Umberto Sansoni, ancient African art and artifacts suggest that Africans in all their continental diversity "venerated their ancestors."[53]

Walker identifies sexuality as having descended into a morass in the essay "When Life descends into the Pit" included in the *We Are the Ones We Have Been Waiting For* collection. She declares that the loss of human sexual integrity results in rigidity in terms of sexual identity; fluidity and the spiritual aspect of sex and sexuality have been corrupted through commercializing sex and the body in the free markets of capitalist societies or through the dichotomy of religious fanaticism that perpetuates the idea of virgin or whore with regard to women's sexual freedom. Still another point of departure in Walker's works and that of womanist theology is the issue of rape of African American women and girls. According to journalist Kellee Terrell,[54] the African American community refuses to address sexual violence. If there is a code of silence in the African American community surrounding sexual assault, and there is, the silence is deeper within the church. Delores Williams's *Sisters in the Wilderness: The Challenge of Womanist God-Talk* (1993) never mentioned sexual violence and tended to focus on enslavement and biblical figures. Her discussion of *The Color Purple* focuses on motherhood and God, but ignores Celie's rape and sexual abuse.

The third-generation womanist theologians have broken the taboo and called for saying "RAPE" in the sanctuary. Monica Coleman's *The Dinah Project: A Handbook for Congregational Response to Sexual Violence* (2004) is a step in the right direction. Other womanist theologians forcing the issue into discussion include Eboni Marshall Truman[55] and Kelly Brown Douglas, whose 1994 essay, "Black and Blues: God-Talk/Body-Talk for the Black Church"[56] declares that something is wrong when people are having sex, but it is rarely discussed in the Black church.

ECOTHEOLOGY

Walker has an ecotheology that is quite apparent in her works but not articulated in her definition of womanist. African American theologians have been slow to take up the banner of ecology; however, they are no strangers to environmental racism. The environmental justice movement and Walker's activism and writings have helped to inspire womanist theologians and ethicists to examine their positions regarding the ecological crisis and the role of the church in it. Ecology and religion as a movement may date back to 1963 in North America when the Faith-Man-Nature Group was organized by Philip Joranson and supported by the National Council of Churches. Joseph Sittler's 1961 speech to the World Council of Churches called for an "earthy Christology and greater emphasis on cosmic redemption."[57] By 1971, Marvin Gaye's album *What's Going On* and the cut "Ecology" had entered the cultural consciousness of African Americans resulting in a greater awareness of environmental issues and how they affected black communities.

The protest against toxic waste being dumped in the rural and mostly black town of Afton in Warren County, North Carolina, in 1982, prompted the support of African American clergy. Rev. Ben Chavis and Rev. Joseph Lowery, the Southern Christian Leadership Conference (SCLC), and Rev. Leon White of the United Church of Christ's Commission for Racial Justice brought national attention to the movement.[58] In 1987, Chavis published *Toxic Wastes and Race in the United States*.[59] This publication became the catalyst for the environmental racism movement, as it documented how African Americans and other people of color and low income had become targets for the placement of hazardous waste sites and chemical plants in their neighborhoods. By the turn of the century, the religious position on the environment was clear. C. W. Mills's 2001 essay, "Black Trash" and James Cone's "Whose Earth Is It Anyway?"[60] further extended the conversation. Even earlier than Cone's statement was the 1993 article by critic Shamara Shuntu Riley: "Ecology Is a Sistah's Issue Too: The Politics of Emergent Afrocentric Ecowomanism."[61] She calls womanist theologians to task for their failure to embrace ecological issues. She examines issues that may inhibit African American women from embracing nature.[62] One inhibiting factor is similar to the problems surrounding sex and sexuality. Black women have been compared to nature and abused in similar ways. Often described as feral, said to resemble wild animals, called negress, bitch, mule, heifer, and even referring to nature itself as irrational then generalizing irrationality to the entire female sex, black women were not quick to embrace what the politics of respectability had warned against.

Walker offered a solution in her 1982 essay, "Only Justice Can Stop a Curse." She reprints Zora Neale Hurston's "curse prayer" that calls for the destruction of the oppressors, the killers of the earth to which Walker adds her own prayer/poem that called or the destruction of those who destroy.[63] While the destruction of white men might be a just revenge, she knows the idea of extinction would bring little satisfaction. Walker concludes that only justice for every living thing will save humankind. A single savior will not be the redeemer.

By 2016, womanist theologian Melanie L. Harris's article, "Ecowomanism: Black Women, Religion, and the Environment," and her 2017 book

Ecowomanism: Religion and Ecology Earth Honoring Faiths, both demonstrate how effective Walker's theology and mysticism have been in influencing African American women's theology. Using *The Color Purple* as a starting point, Harris claims black women's connections with the earth. Whereas Walker made this connection in the twentieth century, her path-breaking pagan stance has yielded twenty-first-century results in the growing recognition among womanist theologians of the significance of the earth. Harris pays homage to Walker when she acknowledges that the conversation between Shug and Celie and Walker's essay, "The Only Reason You Want to Go to Heaven Is That You've Been Driven Out of Your Mind, Off Your Land and Out of Your Lover's Arms,"[64] are literary examples from which to glean ethical values that can help shape earth-honoring ethics, earth-honoring faiths, and eco-theologies. She acknowledges Walker's work as ecoliterature, and she is right. Walker early on developed a mystical understanding of the earth and developed a spiritual relationship with it.

WHAT MIGHT BE THE END OF THE ROAD FOR WALKER'S PUBLISHED WORKS

Even though Walker announced her retirement in 2007 with the publication of *We Are the Ones We Have Been Waiting For,* several books followed, including *The Chicken Chronicles, The World Will Follow Joy,* and *The Cushion in the Road.*

The Chicken Chronicles (2011) saw publication without much fanfare. *Kirkus Reviews* called it "Life affirmative and eccentrically inspirational."[65] The chronicles are a trope for the biblical First and Second Chronicles that record the history of the return from exile of the Hebrew people. Chicken, while literally referring to Walker's flock, also is symbolic of spiritualization. According to Jung, any winged animal represents spirits or angels or supernatural aid. The conundrum of the chicken and the egg also comes into play. For Walker, the mystery of the Bali chicken is also relevant. In her essay, "Why Did the Balinese Chicken Cross the Road?" Walker appeared to be unusually concerned with the chicken. Years later she understands why the chicken made such an impression on her. The chicken spoke to her subconscious. Walker thus claims that in sitting with and caring for her brood, she comes to terms with suppressed childhood memories. In other words, her chronicles record her return from the exile from her painful memories.

The Chicken Chronicles reveals several levels of pain and memory unrelated to her childhood. Walker writes that when small children are injured, they leave their bodies.[66] Based on her childhood wounding, not just the blinding of her eye but also her memory of having wrung a chicken's neck, caused what in psychology is known as disassociation. Tashi's story of pain and suppressed memory illustrates disassociation. The collective black church may also disassociate when confronting issues of sexuality and the black body. Walker recognizes that because of the pain she encountered in her own childhood, she was absent: "And not being there, she could not appreciate how they [her family] suffered, too, along with her."[67]

What is left unsaid is revealed in the language that Walker chooses. Written in third person as a way of providing distance, she refers to herself as Mommy to the chickens. Recalling the Balinese chicken, she says to the chickens: "It was your beauty ... your grace and capable behavior as mother hen to many small chicks, but more terrifyingly perhaps Mommy was on her way to recalling a chicken's severed head, the impression of which lived in her palm."[68] Walker makes a connection between the suppressed memory and her need to remember the trauma of killing the chicken ... a trauma that had happened to her.[69] The connection also may have involved her own baby chick, Rebecca, and not just the memory of childhood. Walker recalls the lost years with her family of origin, but Rebecca also recalls the lost years with her mother, revealed in her own memoir, *Black, White, and Jewish*.[70]

The chickens, one named Gertrude Stein (acknowledging Stein for her sensitive portrayal of Melanctha in *Three Lives*); four named Gladys because Walker is so glad to have their eggs; Hortensia (famed for oratorical skills); Agnes of God (chickens can represent a virgin birth because they lay eggs regardless of whether a rooster is present); Rufus (biblical name meaning red) not named for its looks because it is black and white and not he but a she; and Glorious, for her beauty, are her pets. Walker thought that Rufus acted like a rooster and did not discover her hen-ness until she laid an egg. The chronicles, aside from demonstrating Walker's dilemma with her own childhood and her daughter's, presents a way of seeing deeply into human behavior.

The pecking order of chickens is not too unlike hierarchical behavior seen in people. Walker wonders if being a *"guardian turn[s] them into tyrants."*[71] Rufus, the chicken with the "masculine" tendencies, is at the top of the pecking order. She bosses the other chickens around, but Walker reflects on the good that she does, like keeping the chickens safe by watching out for danger, standing guard, and keeping order. Rufus and her partner were good guardians, just as some men are. Walker's question about tyrants does not just apply to chickens. Apparently, chickens, as well as some men, believe they pay the cost to be the boss. Furthermore, some women, just as some chickens, sacrifice their freedom for safety.

The final chapter of Walker's chronicles is humorous, endearing, and sad. The title, "HA HA, HA HA, HA HA" is the sound of "Mommy being wrong."[72] Walker admits to misjudgment about her chicken—that sending the bully Rufus away did not cure or punish her because Rufus had a great time during her punishment. The central point in this final chapter appears to be a shifting of maternal responsibility. Walker concludes: "Mommies can be mistaken. Mommies, especially human Mommies, can be wrong. And there's a very good reason for this. It is because human Mommies, like all Mommies on the planet, whether fish or fowl, insect or reptile, are only surrogates. In fact, all creatures on the planet have the same parent."[73] Lauret and Rebecca both comment on what they believe to be Walker's willingness to "mother the world's daughters."[74] Rebecca has said that her mother's offering herself up as a mother figure seemed out of character based on her experience as Walker's daughter.[75] Lauret admits that Walker's "willingness to mother the world's daughters, [is] . . . less an individual idiosyncrasy marked by hyperbole and narcissistic overreach than a rhetorical style and spiritual conviction."[76] Walker's statement is a spiritual conviction that emanates from a long line of African American women activists from Sojourner Truth and Harriet Tubman to Fannie Lou Hamer.

Those critics who attempt to read Walker in a strictly literary context harshly criticize her. While Walker fits squarely within the African American spiritual tradition in which her homiletic style certainly does belong, she is also a bona fide member of the literary realm. Walker is not the only mystical writer to be harshly criticized. For his spiritualism, William Butler Yeats was roundly critiqued, and yet he received the Nobel Prize for Literature. W. H. Auden was denounced as a "deplorable spectacle of a grown man occupied with mumbo jumbo of magic and the nonsense of India."[77] The mystic William Blake believed that he was visited by the prophet Elijah and received visits from his deceased brother and, like Walker, he criticized organized religion. Critics called him a pervert because he believed in sexualized spirituality. As Joseph Campbell observed: "We are not well acquainted with the literature of the spirit,"[78] nor do we seem to appreciate literary works that focus on the inner life or challenge our preconceived notions.

The Cushion in the Road (2013) repeats many of Walker's spiritual themes including the unity of all, as well as that of choice. She begins with an essay in the form of an open letter to African American women. She says that she offered the word womanism years ago for use in a time like the present.[79] These times, Walker insists, require an acknowledgement of "our singular path as women of color in the United States."[80] She cautions not to follow a black person who is unworthy simply to uphold racial solidarity. Furthermore, in reference to the presidential election, she urges to not be distracted by race or sex but to look for and align with truth.[81]

The final section of the book voices a way of seeing that leads directly to recognizing the significance of choice. Exhausted from international travel, Walker and her companion reluctantly go on a tour of Brasilia. Initially, she sees the place with tired and somewhat jaded eyes; she has seen most of the world. Brasilia appears ugly and uninviting. She complains of the lack of gardens, animals, and describes it as a place bereft of birds. Spiritual lessons so often appear in ironic ways. On the evening prior to the tour, Walker made a presentation, and someone complained because she did not lecture. Her response to the complainer was to "talk about the gracefulness of accepting what is offered rather than what is desired."[82] Her words apply perfectly to her own response the following day on the tour. Eventually the scales fall from her eyes and she sees beauty. What enables her to see the beauty of a place, "Even Brasilia,"[83] is to see the self of the other reflected in you and to accept what is offered with grace.

Walker's collection of poems, *The World Will Follow Joy: Turning Madness into Flowers* (2013) preaches against war, praises the Dalai Lama, defines an immaculate heart as one that hates no one and no thing, and calls for democratic womanism. Calling for a complete regime change, democratic womanism would enlist feminine wisdom and honor the dark mother. This form of governing would not eliminate man. Walker points out that he is there in the middle of the word *womanism*, but he is surrounded. The collection fittingly ends with the image of a garden. "Going Out to the Garden" demonstrates that Walker, who began her search by looking for her mother's garden, has successfully found her own.

Alice Malsenior Tallulah-Kate Walker's contributions to the spiritual and literary world consists of writings in almost every genre. Her mystical focus on peace and love earned her the Humanist of the Year Award in 1997. In 2006, she was inducted into the Hall of Fame in the California Museum for History, Women and the Arts, and in 2007, she received the Domestic Human Rights Award. Despite the harsh criticism she has sometimes received for taking unpopular positions on controversial and taboo subjects, Walker never wavers in her quest for truth.

NOTES

1. Melanie L. Harris, *Gifts of Virtue, Alice Walker, and Womanist Ethics* (New York: Palgrave MacMillan, 2010), 85.
2. Walker, "The Only Reason You Want to Go to Heaven Is That You Have Been Driven Out of Your Mind (Off Your Land and Out of Your Lover's Arms)," in *Anything We Love Can Be Saved*, 25.
3. Walker, "Womanist," from *In Search of Our Mothers' Gardens: Womanist Prose*, xi.
4. Katie Cannon, *Katie's Canon: Womanism and the Soul of the Black Community* (New York: Bloomsbury, 1998), 56.
5. Ibid.
6. See Katie Cannon, "Sexing Black Women: Liberation from the Prisonhouse of Anatomical Authority," in *Loving the Body: Black Religious Studies and the Erotic,* ed. Anthony B. Pinn and Dwight N. Hopkins (New York: Palgrave Macmillan, 2004), 11–30.
7. Cheryl Sanders, Cheryl Townsend Gilkes, Katie G. Cannon, Emilie M. Townes, M. Shawn Copeland, and bell hooks "Roundtable Discussion: Christian Ethics and Theology in Womanist Perspective," *Journal of Feminist Studies in Religion* 5, no. 2 (Fall 1989): 87.

8. Ibid., 87.
9. Ibid.
10. Ibid., 88.
11. Ibid., 90.
12. Quoted in Sanders et al., "Roundtable Discussion," 92.
13. Ibid., 93.
14. Ibid.
15. Traci C. West, response to Monica Coleman's "Must I Be a Womanist?" *Journal of Feminist Studies in Religion* 22, no. 1 (2006): 125.
16. Patricia Hill Collins, "What's in a Name? Womanism, Black Feminism, and Beyond," *The Black Scholar* 26, no. 1 (Winter/Spring 1996): 9–10.
17. Cannon, in Sanders et al., "Roundtable Discussion," 94.
18. Walker, *We Are the Ones*, 117.
19. Quoted in Layli Phillips, *The Womanist Reader: The First Quarter Century of Womanist Thought* (New York: Routledge, 2006), 22.
20. Townes, in Sanders et al., "Roundtable Discussion," 94.
21. Ibid.
22. Ibid., 95.
23. Delores Williams, "*The Color Purple*: What Was Missed," *Christianity and Crisis* 46 (1986), 230–32.
24. *Encyclopedia of Theology: A Concise Sacramentum Mundi*, ed. Karl Rahner (New York: Seabury Press, 1975).
25. Mark C. Taylor, "Text as Victim," in *Deconstruction and Theology*, ed. Thomas Altizer (New York: Crossroads, 1982), 67.
26. Felipe Smith, "Alice Walker's Redemptive Art," in *Critical Essays on Alice Walker*, ed. Ikenna Dieke (Westport, CT: Greenwood Press, 1999), 438.
27. Walker. "All the Bearded Irises of Love," in *Living by the Word*, 163.
28. Emilie Townes, in Sanders et al., "Roundtable Discussion," 95.
29. Ibid.
30. Walker, "All the Bearded Irises," 166.
31. Quoted in Evelyn White, *Alice Walker: A Life* (New York: Norton, 2004), 443.
32. Anthony Pinn, "Introduction," in *Loving the Body: Black Religious Studies and the Erotic,* ed. Anthony Pinn and Dwight Hopkins (New York: Palgrave Macmillan, 2004), 1.
33. See chapter 7 in this book.
34. In Pinn, "Introduction," 12.
35. Also known as the "cult of domesticity," which proclaimed that true women should possess four cardinal virtues: piety, purity, domesticity, and submissiveness.
36. Cannon, "Sexing Black Women," 12.
37. Ibid., 25.
38. Katie G. Cannon. "Erotic Justice: Authority, Resistance, Transformation," *Journal of Feminist Studies in Religion* 23, no. 1 (2007): 23.
39. Townes, in Sanders et al., "Roundtable Discussion," 96–97.
40. Walker, *You Can't Keep a Good Woman Down*, 48.
41. Ibid., 42.
42. Audre Lorde, *Sister Outsider: Essays and Speeches* (New York: Ten Speed Press, 1984), 46.
43. Walker, *Living by the Word*, 192.
44. Copeland, in Sanders et al., "Roundtable Discussion," 101.
45. Walker, *Living by the Word*, 160 (emphasis in original).
46. Both articles are in Johnson, *Feminist Theology* 16, no. 2 (2008): 238–74.
47. Felipe Smith, "Alice Walker's Redemptive Art," 109 (emphasis in original).
48. Dieke, *Critical Essays on Alice Walker*, 127–41.
49. Ibid., 129.
50. Richard Rohr, *What Mystics Know* (New York: Crossroads Publishing, 2015), 60.
51. Walker, *In Search of Our Mothers' Gardens*, 14.
52. Walker, *The Color Purple*, preface.

53. Quoted in Walker, *We Are the Ones We Have Been Waiting For*, 122.

54. Kellee Terrell, "Without Consent: Confronting the Rape of Black Women and Girls," *Ebony* (April/May 2016): 112–17.

55. Eboni Marshall Truman, *Towards a Womanist Ethic of Incarnation: Black Bodies, the Black Church and the Council of Chalcedon* (London: Palgrave Macmillan, 2013).

56. Kelly Brown Douglas, "Black and Blues: God-Talk/Body-Talk for the Black Church," in *Sexuality and the Sacred: Sources for Theological Reflection*, ed. Marvin M. Ellison and Kelly Brown Douglas (Louisville, KY: Westminster John Knox Press, 2010), 54–57.

57. Quoted in the Forum on Religion and Ecology at Yale, Center for the Study of World Religions. www.fore.yale.edu/religion/christanity.

58. Renee Skelton and Vernice Miller, "The Environmental Justice Movement," Natural Resources Defense Council, March 17, 2016. https://www.nrdc.org.

59. Benjamin Chavis Jr., ed., *Toxic Waste and Race in the United States* (United Church of Christ, 1987).

60. C. W. Mills, "Black Trash," in *Faces of Environmental Racism*, ed. L. Westra and B. E. Lawson (Lanham, MD: Rowman & Littlefield, 2001), 73–91; James H. Cone, "Whose Earth Is It Anyway?" in *Earth Habitat: Eco-Injustice and the Church's Response*, ed. Dieter Hessel and Larry Rasmussen (Minneapolis: Fortress Press, 2001), 23.

61. Shamara Shuntu Riley, "Ecology Is a Sistah's Issue Too," in *Ecofeminism and the Sacred*, ed. Carol Adams (New York: Continuum, 1993), 193.

62. Ibid.

63. Walker, *In Search of Our Mothers' Gardens*, 341.

64. Walker, *Anything We Love Can Be Saved*, 3–27.

65. *Kirkus Reviews*, April 4, 2011. www.kirkusreviews.com/book-reviews/alice-walker/chicken-chronicles.

66. Walker, *The Chicken Chronicles*, 152.

67. Ibid., 153.

68. Ibid., 152.

69. Ibid., 101–2.

70. Rebecca Walker, *Black, White, and Jewish: Autobiography of a Shifting Self* (New York: Riverhead Books, 2001).

71. Walker, *The Chicken Chronicles*, 181 (emphasis in original).

72. Ibid., 183.

73. Ibid., 185.

74. Maria Lauret, *Alice Walker* (New York, Palgrave Macmillan, 2011), 233.

75. Rebecca Walker, "How My Mother's Fanatical Feminist Views Tore Us Apart," *Daily Mail*, 23 May 23, 2008. https://www.dailymail.co.uk/femail/article-1021293/How-mothers-fanatical-feminist-views-tore-apart-daughter-The-Color-Purple-author.html.

76. Lauret, *Alice Walker*, 233.

77. Edward Mendelson, *Early Auden, Later Auden: A Critical Biography* (Princeton, NJ: Princeton University Press, 1981), 352.

78. Joseph Campbell, *The Power of Myth* (New York: Doubleday, 1988), 1.

79. Walker, *The Cushion in the Road*, 11.

80. Ibid.

81. Ibid.

82. Ibid., 160.

83. Ibid., 162.

Selected References

Angelou, Maya. *I Know Why the Caged Bird Sings.* New York: Random House, 1969.
Armstrong, Karen. *The History of God.* New York: Ballantine Books, 1994.
Baker, Houston, and Charlotte Pierce Baker. "Patches: Quilts and Community in Everyday Use." *Southern Review* 21, no. 3 (July 1, 1985): 706–20.
Barthes, Roland. "The Death of the Author." In *Image Music Text.* Trans. Stephen Heath, 142–48. New York: Hill and Wang, 1977.
Bates, Gerri. *Alice Walker: A Critical Companion.* Westport, CT: Greenwood Press, 2005.
Bauer, Margaret, "Alice Walker: Another Southern Writer Criticizing Codes Not Put to Everyday Use." *Studies in Short Fiction* 29, no. 2 (1992): 143–51.
Bell, Bernard. *The Afro-American Novel and Its Tradition.* Amherst: University of Massachusetts Press, 1989.
Ben-Bassat, Hedda. *Prophets without Vision: Subjectivity and the Sacred in Contemporary American Writing.* Lewisburg: Bucknell University Press, 2000.
Bennett, Lerone. "Roots of Black Love." *Ebony* (August 1981): 31–36.
Bentham, Jeremy. *Introduction to the Principles of Morals and Legislation.* 11 March 1748. 1823 reprint. Library of Economics and Liberty, March 2010. https://socialsciences.mcmaster.ca/econ/ugcm/3ll3/bentham/morals.pdf.
Bernstein, Richard. "*By the Light of My Father's Smile:* Limp New-Age Nonsense in Mexico." *New York Times Book Review* (October 7, 1998). https://archive.nytimes.com/www.nytimes.com/books/98/10/04/daily/walker-book-review.html.
Blanton, Smiley. *Love or Perish.* New York: Simon and Schuster, 1956.
Byrd, Rudolph P. (ed.), *The World Has Changed.* New York: New Press, 2010.
Camus, Albert. *The Rebel.* New York: Vintage, [1951] 1992.
Christian, Barbara, ed. *Everyday Use: Alice Walker.* New Brunswick, NJ: Rutgers University Press, 1994.
Clements, Jennifer. "Organic Inquiry: Toward Research in Partnership with Spirit." *Journal of Transpersonal Psychology* 36, no. 1 (2004): 26–49. http://www.atpweb.org/jtparchive/trps-36-04-01-026.pdf.
Curtis, Donald. *Your Thoughts Can Change Your Life.* New York: Hachette Books, 2009.
Davies, Paul, and Niels Henrik Gregersen, eds. *Information and the Nature of Reality: From Physics to Metaphysics.* Cambridge: Cambridge University Press, 2010.
Dieke, Ikenna, ed. *Critical Essays on Alice Walker.* Westport, CT: Greenwood Press, 1999.
Ferguson, John. *Encyclopedia of Mysticism and Religions.* New York: Crossroads, 1982.
Fillmore, Charles. *Metaphysical Bible Dictionary.* New York: Dover, 2007.
Fudge, Erica. *Perceiving Animals.* New York: St. Martin's, 2000.

Gates, Henry Louis, Jr., and Anthony Appiah (eds). *Alice Walker: Critical Perspectives, Past and Present.* New York: Amistad, 1993.
Gibbs, Nancy, et al. "When Is It Rape?" *Time* (June 3, 1991): 1–8.
Gillespie, Carmen. *Critical Companion to Alice Walker.* New York: Facts on File, 2011.
Goldsmith, Joel. *The Foundations of Mysticism.* Santa Barbara, CA: Acropolis Books, 1998.
Griaule, Marcel. *Conversations with Ogotemmeli: An Introduction to Dogon Religious Ideas.* New York: Oxford University Press, 1975.
Harris, Melanie, L. *Ecowomanism: African American Women and Earth-Honoring Faiths.* New York: Orbis Books, 2017.
Harris, Trudier. "Folklore in the Fiction of Alice Walker: A Perpetuation of Historical and Literary Traditions." *Black American Literature Forum* 11, no. 1 (1977): 3–8.
———. "On *The Color Purple*: Stereotypes, and Silences." *Black American Literature Forum* 18, no. 4 (Winter 1984): 155–61.
———. *Saints, Sinners, Saviors: Strong Black Women in African American Literature.* New York: Palgrave, 2001.
Holmes, Ernest. *The Science of Mind.* New York: Tarcher, 1999.
Lindbergh, Anne Morrow. *Dearly Beloved: A Theme and Variations.* New York: Harcourt Brace & World, [1962] 1990.
Manis, Andrew M. *A Fire You Can't Put Out: The Civil Rights Life of Birmingham's Reverend Fred Shuttlesworth.* Tuscaloosa: University of Alabama Press, 1999.
Meisler, Stanley. "Afro Hairdo Riles Africa's Blacks." *Milwaukee Journal* (September 22, 1970).
Nin, Anais. *Memorable Quotations of French Writers of the Past.* Ed. Carol A. Dingle. Lincoln, NE: iuniverse, 2000.
Petry, Alice Hall. "Alice Walker: The Achievement in Short Fiction," *Modern Language Studies* 19, no. 1 (Winter 1989): 12–20.
Rilke, Rainer Maria. *Letter to a Young Poet.* New York: W.W. Norton, 1993.
Sanders, Cheryl J., Cheryl Townsend Gilkes, Katie G. Cannon, Emilie M. Townes, M. Shawn Copeland, and bell hooks. "Roundtable Discussion: Christian Ethics and Theology in Womanist Perspective." *Journal of Feminist Studies in Religion* 5, no. 2 (1989): 83–112. http://www.jstor.org/stable/25002114.
Simcikova, Karla. *To Live Fully, Here and Now: The Healing Vision in the Works of Alice Walker.* Lanham, MD: Rowman & Littlefield, 2007.
Singer, Peter. *Animal Liberation.* New York: HarperCollins, 2009.
Thielman, Pia. *Hotbeds Black-White Love and Its Representation in Selected Contemporary Novels from the U.S., Africa, and the Caribbean.* Malawi University: Kachere Series, no. 19, 2000.
Warren, Nagueyalti. *Critical Insights: Alice Walker.* Ipswich, MA: Salem Press, 2013.
Whisitt, Sam. "In Spite of It All: A Reading of Alice Walker's *Everyday Use*," *African American Review* 34, no. 3 (2000): 443–59.
White, Evelyn. *Alice Walker: A Life.* New York: Norton, 2004.
Wilson, August. *Fences.* New York: Plume, 1986.
Winchell, Donna Haisty. *Alice Walker.* New York: Twayne, 1992.
Wright, Richard. *The Long Dream.* New York: Doubleday, 1958.
———. *Native Son.* New York: HarperCollins, 1940.

WORKS BY ALICE WALKER (IN ORDER OF PUBLICATION)

Once. Orlando, FL: Harcourt Brace & Co., 1968.
The Third Life of Grange Copeland. Orlando, FL: Harcourt Brace & Co., 1970.
Revolutionary Petunias. New York: Harvest Books, 1973.
In Love & Trouble. New York: Harvest Books, [1973] 2004.
Meridian. New York: Harvest Books, [1979] 2003.
Good Night Willie Lee, I'll See You in the Morning. San Diego: Harcourt, [1979] 1984.
You Can't Keep a Good Woman Down. New York: Harcourt Brace Jovanovich, 1981.

The Color Purple. New York: Harcourt Brace Jovanovich, 1982.
In Search of Our Mother's Gardens: Womanist Prose. New York: Harcourt Brace Jovanovich, 1983.
Horses Make the Landscape Look More Beautiful. San Diego: Harcourt Brace Jovanovich, 1984.
Living by the Word: Selected Writings, 1973–1987. San Diego: Harcourt Brace Jovanovich, 1988.
To Hell with Dying. San Diego: Harcourt Brace Jovanovich, 1988.
The Temple of My Familiar. San Diego: Harcourt Brace Jovanovich, 1989.
Her Blue Body: Everything We Know: Earthling Poems, 1965–1990 Complete. San Diego: Harcourt Brace Jovanovich, 1991.
Finding the Green Stone. San Diego: Harcourt Brace Jovanovich, 1991.
Possessing the Secret of Joy. New York: Harcourt Brace Jovanovich, 1992.
Warrior Marks: Female Genital Mutilation and Sexual Blinding of Women (coauthored by Pratibha Parmar). New York: Harcourt Brace, 1993.
Alice Walker Banned. San Francisco: Aunt Lute Books, 1996.
The Same River Twice: Honoring the Difficult—A Meditation on Life, Spirit, Art, and the Making of the Film, The Color Purple, *Ten Years Later.* New York: Scribner, 1996.
Anything We Love Can Be Saved: A Writer's Activism. New York: Random House, 1997.
By the Light of My Father's Smile. New York: Random House, 1998.
The Way Forward Is with a Broken Heart. New York: Random House, 2000.
Sent by Earth: A Message from the Grandmother Spirit after the Attacks on the World Trade Center and Pentagon. New York: Seven Stories, 2001.
A Poem Traveled Down My Arm: Poems and Drawings. New York: Random House, 2003.
Absolute Trust in the Goodness of the Earth: New Poems. New York: Random House, 2003.
Now Is the Time to Open Your Heart. New York: Random House, 2004.
We Are the Ones We Have Been Waiting For: Inner Light in a Time of Darkness. New York: New Press, 2006.
Overcoming Speechlessness: A Poet Encounters the Horror in Rwanda, Eastern Congo, and Palestine/Israel. New York: Seven Stories Press, 2010.
The Chicken Chronicles. New York: New Press, 2011.
The Cushion in the Road. New York: New Press, 2013.
The World Will Follow Joy. New York: New Press, 2013.
"Convergence: A Short Story Response to O'Connor." *Flannery O'Connor Review*, 12 (August 2014). http://libguides.gcsu.edu/c.php?g=392325&p=2665105.

Index

Absolute Trust in the Goodness of the Earth: New Poems (Walker), 145, 146, 148, 155–157, 169
abuse, 89–91. *See also* domestic violence; rape
acquaintance rape, 73. *See also* rape
African American culture and heritage: Black Arts movement, 3, 7; black beauty, 91–92; the black body, 179–180, 183; black love, 44; Black Power movement, 3, 30, 31, 47, 65–66; civil rights movement, 3, 58, 64–66, 69; and environmental justice, 183–185; folk medicine tradition, 52–55, 146–147, 149; homiletic tradition, 9, 76, 145, 187; knowledge and expression of, 155; liberation theology, 75–77, 132, 175–178, 180; literary tradition, 179; and sexuality, 176–179; storytelling in, 132, 148; and Uncle Remus, 152. *See also* racial injustice and oppression
Africana Womanism (Hudson-Weem), 124
African culture and heritage: ancestral veneration in, 22, 23, 105, 183; animism in, 163, 164; expression of, 48–52, 123
"African Images: Glimpses from a Tiger's Back" (Walker), 4–5
African Methodist Episcopal Church, Walker's speech to, 2–3

African Saga (Ricciardi), 132
Against Our Will (Brownmiller), 74
agency, xii, 114, 176. *See also* choice, as theme; self-determination
Ahmadu, Fuambia, 124
Albert (character), 83–86
"Alice Walker's Redemptive Art" (Smith), 182–183
"Alice Walker: Telling the Black Woman's Story" (Bradley), 92
Allen, Robert, 104, 105
"All the Bearded Irises of Life" (Walker), 178–179
"All the Toys" (Walker), 156
"Am I Blue?" (Walker), 10, 11–12
Amin, Idi, 25
Amnesty International, 134
Animal Liberation (Singer), 10
animal suffering and meat-eating, 10–13. *See also* vegetarianism
animism, 155–156, 163, 164. *See also* paganism
Anne-Marion (character), 63, 70
"The Anonymous Caller" (Walker), 157
Anything We Love Can Be Saved: A Writer's Activism (Walker), 41, 131
apartheid, 1, 146, 151
Armah, Ayi Kwei, 17
Arveyda (character), 107–108
assassinations, 63, 66
Auden, W. H., 187

authenticity, 14–15, 48–52
awards, 58, 77, 82, 188

Baker, Houston, 50
Baldwin, James, 179
"Ballad of the Brown Girl" (Walker), 4
"Baptism" (Walker), 59
Baraka, Amiri, 30
Barthes, Roland, 9
Bates, Gerri, 23, 24, 81, 94
"Beast" (Walker), 165
beauty, 91–92
Beloved (Morrison), 117
Ben-Bassat, Hedda, 55–56
Bennett, Lerone, 44
"Be Nobody's Darling" (Walker), 5
Bentham, Jeremy, 10–11
Bernstein, Richard, 15, 134–135
betrayal, 104, 105, 107–108
Bhagavad Gita, 140
bisexuality, 168, 175, 178–179. *See also* sexuality
Black Arts movement, 3, 7. *See also* Black Power movement
black beauty, 91–92. *See also* African culture and heritage, expression of
the black body, 179–180, 183. *See also* rape
Black Elk, 15, 63
black homiletic tradition, 9, 76, 145, 187
black liberation theology, 75–77, 132, 175–178, 180. *See also* ecotheology; womanism, defining
black love, 44. *See also* love
Black Power movement, 3, 30, 31, 47, 65–66. *See also* civil rights movement
Black, White, and Jewish (Rebecca Walker), 186
Blake, William, 187
Blanton, Smiley, 15
blasphemy, 182. *See also* heresy
blindness, xi, 1–2, 133
"The Blue Meridian" (Walker), 64
The Bluest Eye (Morrison), 88, 91
Bolen, Jean Shinoda, 105
Bonetti, Gay, 17
Braendlin, Bonnie, 107, 108
Brasilia, Brazil, 187–188
"Brotherhood of the Saved" (Walker), 168

Brownfield (character), 21–24, 27, 33–35
Buddhism, 131, 147, 171
"Burial" (Walker), 59
Buscaglia, Leo, 15
Butler-Evans, Elliott, 35
Byrd, Rudolph, 64, 136
By the Light of My Father's Smile (Walker), 121, 128, 134–141

Cairns, John, Jr., 164
California Museum for History, Women and the Arts, 188
California State Board of Education, 12
Campbell, Joseph, 106, 111, 112–113, 187
Camus, Albert: on death and suicide, 30; on poverty, 4; *The Rebel*, 59, 64, 71; on suicide, 45; Walker's thesis on, 95
Cannon, Katie, 155, 176–177, 180
capitalist materialism, 22
Carlotta (character), 107–109, 110, 115
Carson, Rachel, 116
Catholicism, 7, 11, 115, 179
Celie (character), 71, 81, 82–83, 87–89, 91
censorship, 10, 12, 93
Chavis, Ben, 184
Cheatwood, K. T. H., 14
The Chicken Chronicles: A Memoir (Walker), 185–187
Chief Seattle, 116, 162
childhood, xi, 1–2, 167, 185–186
The Children of Sanchez (Lewis), 21
choice, as theme: in *The Cushion in the Road*, 187–188; in "Elethia", 57–58; in "Everyday Use", 48–49; in Gnostic Gospels, 7–8; in *Possessing the Secret of Joy* and female genital mutilation, 125, 127, 133; in *The Third Life of Grange Copeland*, 22–24, 27–28. *See also* agency
"Choosing to Stay Home" (Walker), 7–8
Christian, Barbara, 27, 65
Christian tradition: on animals, 11, 12; black homiletic style, 9, 76, 145, 187; and black liberation theology, 176–178; in *The Color Purple*, 87–89, 94–96; on environmental justice, 183–184; and eroticism, 180; on Hawaiian sexual identities, 150–151; martyrdom and salvation in, 74; music in, 3–4; on

sexuality, 179; on suffering, 76–77; in *The Temple of My Familiar*, 109–110, 112; as a tool for social control, 138–139; unity in, 161; Walker's speech on education and, 2–3. *See also* patriarchy
circle/community, 93
circumcision, 122. *See also* female genital mutilation
The Circumcision of Women (Koso-Thomas), 124
civil rights movement: novels on, 64–66; poems on, 3; Student Nonviolent Coordinating Committee, 58, 69. *See also* African American culture and heritage
Clements, Jennifer, 42
Clinton, Bill, 9
clitoridectomy. *See* female genital mutilation
CODEPINK, 171
Coetzee, J. M., 111
colonialism, 128–129, 138
colorism, 137–138. *See also* racial injustice and oppression
The Color Purple (Walker): author's reading of, xi; awards for, 77, 82; censorship of, 12, 93; character connection with *Possessing the Secret of Joy*, 127; film based on, xi, 101–105; masculinity in, 83–87; metaphysical reading of, 94–98; reception of, 14, 82–83, 92–93; transformation theology in, 81–82, 178
comedy vs. tragedy, xii
"Coming Apart by Way of Introduction to Lorde, Teish and Gardner" (Walker), 181
The Concubine (Amadi), 44
Cone, James, 184
consent, 125. *See also* choice, as theme
Conversations with Ogotemmêli (Griaule), 130
Cooke, Michael, 49
Copeland, Shawn, 181
Cowart, David, 48
Crawford, Elaine, 76
creativity, 7, 8, 93, 165
Cuba, 9

cult of domesticity, 180, 189n35
Curtis, Donald, 38
The Cushion in the Road: Meditation and Wandering as the Whole World Awakens to Being in Harm's Way (Walker), 185, 187–188
cutting. *See* female genital mutilation

dancing, 172, 176
date rape, 73. *See also* rape
Davies, Paul, 2
Davis, Angela, 107
Davis, Thadious, 59
"Dead Men Love War" (Walker), 157
Dearly Beloved (Lindbergh), 42–43
deCille, Ann, 44
Declaration on the Elimination of Violence against Women, 91, 123
Dee/Wangero (character), 48–52
"The Diamonds on Liz's Bosom" (Walker), 162, 163
"The Diary of an African Nun" (Walker), 55–57, 179
Dieke, Ikenna, 114, 182
The Dinah Project (Coleman), 183
disassociation, 179–180, 186
"The Divided Life of Jean Toomer" (Walker), 45–46
divorce, 150, 154, 166, 167, 168. *See also* marriage
Domestic Human Rights Award, 188
domestic violence, 89–91, 136–137. *See also* abuse; rape
Douglas, Kelley Brown, 183
"Dreams" (Hughes), 130
Dreifus, Claudia, 106
drugs, 147
dualism, xii, 24, 55, 65, 114, 140
Dura (character), 127, 128

earth-based belief systems. *See* paganism
Eastern Congo, 171
Ecocriticism (Garrard), 13
ecotheology, 183–185. *See also* nature and environment
"Ecowomanism: Black Women, Religion, and the Environment" (Harris), 184
Ecowomanism: Religion and Ecology Earth Honoring Faiths (Harris),

184–185
education, 2–3, 4, 24. *See also* ignorance
"Elethia" (Walker), 57
The Embers and the Stars (Kohák), 162
Emerson, Ralph Waldo, 96
Emory University, xi
Endarkenment, 145–146
environment. *See* nature and environment
eroticism, 130, 135, 140–141, 179, 180. *See also* sexuality
Estes, Clarissa Pinkola, 24, 101
Ettling, Dorothy, 42
"Everyday Use" (Walker), 48–52
"Everything Is a Human Being" (Walker), 15
evil, 24–25, 26, 57
eye injury, xi, 1–2, 133

Faith-Man-Nature Group, 184
"Family Of" (Walker), 14
Fanny (character), 16, 114–116
Farrell, Susan, 48
fear, 15
femininity. *See* sacred feminine
feminism, 86, 176, 177. *See also* womanism, defining
Fences (Wilson), 32
Ferrone, John, 107
female genital mutilation (FGM), 121, 122–132
Fike, Matthew, 15
Finding the Green Stone (Walker), 164, 165–166
"First They Said" (Walker), 164–165
Fisk University, xi
folk medicine, 52–55, 146–147, 149
Ford, Clyde, 134
forgiveness, 8, 17, 71
"For My Sister Molly Who in the Fifties" (Walker), 50
Fox, Matthew, 135
Frazier, Celeste, 71
Freedom Flotilla, 171–172
Fudge, Erica, 13
Furse, Margaret, xiii

Garrard, Greg, 10, 13
Gates, Henry Louis, Jr., 31–32
Gaye, Marvin, 116, 184

Gaza, 171–172
gender roles, 86, 124–125, 172
A General Theory of Love (Lewis), 41
Gifts of Virtue, Alice Walker, and Womanist Ethics (Harris), 154
Giovanni, Nikki, 30
Gnostic Gospels, 7, 55, 109, 148, 161. *See also* Christian tradition
God's Trombones (Johnson), 8
Goldsmith, Joel, 41
Good Night Willie Lee, I'll See You in the Morning (Walker), 58
"Good Night Willie Lee, I'll See You in the Morning" (Walker), 58
"The Gospel According to Shug Avery", 109, 114–116, 127
Go Tell It on the Mountain (Baldwin), 179
Graham, Maryemma, 93
Grange (character), 6–7, 22–24, 28–35
Grant, Jacquelyn, 75, 76
gray rape, 73. *See also* rape
Green, Donna, 92–93
Greenfield, Sidney, 68
green stone, as metaphor, 165–166
Griaule, Marcel, 130
grief: over environmental abuse, 5–6, 10, 162–163; in *Meridian*, 63. *See also* suffering
Guardian, 171

Haramein, Nassim, 164
Hard Times Require Furious Dancing (Walker), 172
Harpo (character), 86–87
Harris, Joel Chandler, 152
Harris, Melanie, 175, 184–185
Harris, Trudier, 53, 82, 87–88
Harrison, Beverly, 180
Hawaiian sexual identities, 150–151
The Healing Wisdom of Africa: Finding Life Purpose through Nature, Ritual, and Community (Somè), 13
health, 2, 4, 104–105
heart, as metaphor, 166
Hecková, Jana, 152
hell, defined, 6
Her Blue Body: Everything We Know: Earthling Poems 1965–1990 Complete (Walker), 3, 161–165

Index

heresy, 106. *See also* blasphemy
"Her Sweet Jerome" (Walker), 46–47
Hill Collins, Patricia, 155, 177
Holmes, Ernest, 2, 24, 76
Holt, Patricia, 12
homosexuality, 9, 104, 168, 177. *See also* sexuality
Hooker, Deborah Anne, 53
hooks, bell, 177
Hoover, Mary, 92
Horses Make the Landscape Look More Beautiful (Walker), 14, 161–162
The Hosken Report: Genital and Sexual Mutilation of Females, 124
Hospital, Janette Turner, 121
Hughes, Langston, 130, 149
Humanist of the Year Award, 188
Hurston, Zora Neale, 45, 166, 184
"Hymn" (Walker), 3–4

"I Can Worship You" (Walker), 155
ignorance, 24–25, 131, 148. *See also* education
incest, 88
In Love & Trouble (Walker), 42, 43–57
"In Search of Our Mother's Gardens" (Walker), 8, 15
In Search of Our Mothers' Gardens: Womanist Prose (Walker), 7–9, 106
intersectionality, 92
"In the Closet of the Soul" (Walker), 14
"In These Dissenting Times" (Walker), 58
Invisible Man (Ellison), 88
Islam, 31, 121
Israel, 171–172
"I Was So Puzzled by the Attacks" (Walker), 157

Jackson, Rebecca Cox, 18n5
Jacobson, Howard, 171
James, Simon, 5–6, 116
James, William, 96
Jampolsky, Gerald, 15
Jehovah's Witnesses, 104, 168
Jenett, Dianne, 42
Jerome (character), 46–47
Johnson, Patrica-Ann, 181–182
Jones, Quincy, 103
Joranson, Philip, 184

Josie (character), 36–37
Jubilee (Margaret Walker), 123
Jung, Carl, 24, 130
Just above My Head (Baldwin), 179

Kalei, Kalikiano, 150–151
Kate (character), 146–154
killing vs. murder, 29–30, 70–71
"Kindred Spirits" (Walker), 168
King, Karen, 109–110
King, Martin Luther, Jr., 8, 63
Kirkus Reviews, 145, 185
Koran, 121
Koss, Mary, 73

Lame Deer, 162
Larsen, Nella, 45
Larson, Charles, 121
Lauret, Maria, 8–9, 21, 38, 122, 125, 132; on Walker's mothering statement, 187; on Walker's narcissism, 167
"Learning to Dance" (Walker), 172
Leaves of Grass (Whitman), 165
Lerner, Gerda, xiii, 26
lesbianism. *See* bisexuality; homosexuality
"Let Change Play God" (Walker), 157
Letters of Love and Hope: The Story of the Cuban Five (Walker), 41
Letters to a Young Poet (Rilke), 44
Leventhal, Mel, 4
Lewis, Oscar, 21
Life Never Dies (Addington), 140
Lindbergh, Anne Morrow, 42–43
Lissie Lyles (character), xii, 108–109, 110–117
"Listen" (Walker), 164
Living by the Word: Selected Writings, 1973–1987 (Walker), xii–xiii, 10–11, 17, 181
The Long Dream (Wright), 29
Lorde, Audre, 130, 135, 141
love, 15, 41–45, 85
"The Love of Bodies" (Walker), 155–156
Love or Perish (Blanton), 15
Loving the Body (Pinn), 179
Lowery, Joseph, 184
Lyme disease, 2, 104, 105

Mademoiselle magazine, 73

Magdalena/June (character), 136–138, 139, 140
Mahu, 150–151
Malcolm X, 63, 66
Mandela, Winnie, 146
Marcus, Greil, 64
Margaret (character), 35–36, 71–72
marital rape, 150. *See also* rape
marriage, 4, 42–43, 154, 166–168. *See also* divorce; weddings
martyrdom, 74–75
mascon words, 101, 117n2
masculinity: in *The Color Purple*, 83–87; and evil, 26–27; in *Meridian*, 67–68; in *Now Is the Time to Open Your Heart*, 153; in *The Third Life*, 34; and violence, 22
materialism, 22
maternalism, 36, 65, 67, 68. *See also* mother/child relationships
Maynard, Joyce, 106
McDowell, Deborah, 75
meat-eating, 10–13
medicine, 52–55, 146–147, 149
meditation, 25, 71, 128, 147
Medusa (Patricia-Ann Johnson), 181–182
Meir, Golda, 171
Mem (character), 27, 37
"Memoir of a Marriage" (Walker), 166
Meridian (Walker): black men's responses to, 14; character naming in, 64, 65; civil rights and Black Power movements in, 64–66, 69; killing vs. murder in, 30; liberation theology in, 75–77; martyrdom in, 74–75; masculinity in, 67–68; motherhood in, 66–67, 68, 69–70; Native American themes in, 13, 63; rape in, 72–74; silence in, 128; title of, 63–64
Meridian Hill (character), 64, 66–68
Merton, Robert K., 96
Metaphysical Bible Dictionary, 6
Meyjes, Menno, 103
Middle East, 171–172
Mills, C. W., 184
mining, 162
Mister (character), 6, 14, 83
M'Lissa (character), 125, 127, 128, 129, 131, 133

"More Love in His Life" (Walker), 58
Morrison, Toni, 88, 91, 117, 152–153
Moses, Nicole, 145
mother/child relationships: in *Meridian*, 66–67, 68, 69–70; in *Now Is the Time to Open Your Heart*, 150; in *The Temple of My Familiar*, 108; of Walker, 104, 104–105, 167, 168, 186, 187. *See also* maternalism
MOVE organization, 181
Moyers, Bill, 25, 147
Mr. Sweet (character), 6–7
Ms. magazine, 12, 73
Muir, John, 162
murder. *See* killing vs. murder
music, 3–4, 53, 70, 176
Mutant Message Down Under (Morgan), 146
"My Father's Country Is the Poor" (Walker), 9
"My Heart Has Reopened to You" (Walker), 163
mystics and mysticism: defined, 2, 41; on love, 41; Osho, 126, 168; poetic expression of, 156; sexual mysticism, 140–141; societal criticism of, 187; in Sufism, 172; trauma of, 18n5, 105; unity in, 2–3, 5, 56, 161; Walker's early expression of, 2–3, 38, 41. *See also* religion and spirituality
Mzee (character), 122, 129, 130–131

namaste, 102
names, 23, 48–49, 51
National Book Award, 58, 77, 82
National Coalition of Black Gays and Lesbians, 179
Nation of Islam, 31, 121
Native American ancestry, 13, 14, 16, 105, 152
Native American belief systems, 13, 15, 17, 163. *See also* paganism
Nature (Emerson), 96
nature and environment: earth-based belief systems, 17, 155–156, 162–164, 183–185; expressed grief over abuse of, 5–6, 10, 162–163; medicine from, 52–55, 146–147, 149; popular culture and wisdom on, 116; river, as symbol,

101, 117n2, 149; salvation of, 164–165; snakes, as symbol, 147–148; in *The Temple of My Familiar*, 116–117; Walker's illness from, 104, 105. *See also* animal suffering and meat-eating
"The Negro Speaks of River" (Hughes), 149
Neibuhr, Reinhold, 132
Nelson, Jill, 10
Nettie (character), 50, 91–92
"Never Offer Your Heart to Someone Who Eats Hearts" (Walker), 58
New Age movement, 96, 106
New Thought movement, 13, 96
New York Times, 92, 125, 135
New York Times Book Review, 121, 134–135
Niambi, Bisa, 134
Nietzsche, Friedrich, 45
Nin, Anais, 32
9/11 tragedy, 155, 157
nonviolence, 3, 7, 31
"No One Was Supposed to Survive" (Walker), 181
"Not Only Will Your Teachers Appear, They Will Cook New Foods for You" (Walker), 10
Now Is the Time to Open Your Heart (Walker), 7, 145, 146–155, 168

O'Brien, John, 4, 17
Ola (character), 115
O'Leary, Stephen, xii
Olivia (character), 126
Once (Walker), 3, 4–5, 53, 165
"Once Again" (Walker), 165
"One Day in Georgia" (Walker), 3
"Only Justice Can Stop a Curse" (Walker), 184
oral tradition. *See* storytelling
Organic Inquiry, 42
Osho, 126, 168
Overcoming Speechlessness: A Poet Encounters the Horror in Rwanda, Eastern Congo, and Palestine/Israel (Walker), 171–172

"Pagan" (Walker), 163–164

paganism: about, 163–164; animist beliefs in, 155–156, 163, 164; ecotheology, 183–185; of Walker, xiii, 5–6, 155–156, 162, 163; of Walker's characters, 56. *See also* Native American belief systems; nature and environment
Palestine, 171–172
Palestine: Peace Not Apartheid (Carter), 172
panther fable, 125–126
Parmar, Pratibha. *See Warrior Marks: Female Genital Mutilation and Sexual Blinding of Women* (Walker and Parmar)
"The Part Education Plays in the AME Church" (Walker), 2–3
paternalism, 26
patriarchy: eye injury as wound of, xi, 1–2, 133; and female genital mutilation, 123, 133–134; in *The Third Life*, 26. *See also* Christian tradition
Peck, M. Scott, 24–25
People of the Lie (Peck), 24
Perceiving Animals (Fudge), 13
Petry, Alice Hall, 42
"Phallus(ies) of Interpretation: Toward R=Engendering the Black Critical 'I'" (duCille), 44
Pierce-Baker, Charlotte, 50
Piercy, Marge, 74
Pinn, Anthony B., 179
Pius IX (pope), 11
plants. *See* medicine; nature and environment
"Poems of a Childhood Poetress" (Walker), 2
A Poem Traveled Down My Arm: Poems and Drawings (Walker), 169–170
Pollard, Alton B., III, 145–146
polygamy, 125–126
pornography, 135, 136, 168, 181
Possessing the Secret of Joy (Walker), 121, 121–132
poverty, responses to, 4, 21–22, 156
preach vs. preachy, 98
pregnancy and abortion: in *The Third Life*, 27; of Walker, 2, 4
The Presence of Nature (Walker), 5–6

Prisoners of Ritual (Lightfoot-Klein), 124
Prose, Francine, 135
Pulitzer Prize, 77, 82
purple (color), 81–82

racial injustice and oppression: black liberation theology on, 181–182; colorism, 137–138; in Cuba, 9; and environmental abuse, 10; environmental racism movement, 183–185; in Georgia, 1; in Middle East, 171–172; poems on, 3, 5; in South Africa, 146, 171; in *The Third Life*, 25–26. *See also* slavery
Rannie (character), 52–55
rape, 67, 72–74, 115, 150, 179–180, 183. *See also* abuse; domestic violence
"Reading Alice Walker" (course), xi
Reading the Environment (Melissa Walker), 163
"Really, Doesn't Crime Pay?" (Walker), 45–46
The Rebel (Camus), 59, 64, 71
Reckless Eyeballing (Reed), 157
"Recording the Seasons" (Walker), 7
religion and spirituality: Buddhism, 131, 147, 171; Catholicism, 7, 11, 115, 179; Islam, 31, 121; in Native American traditions, 13, 15, 17, 163; New Age, 96, 106; New Thought, 13, 96; overview of Walker's, xii; paganism, xiii, 5–6, 17, 56, 155–156, 163–164; as a tool of social control, 138–139. *See also* Christian tradition; mystics and mysticism
Remus (character), 152–153
resistance, 132. *See also* nonviolence
Revolutionary Petunias (Walker), 58–60
"Revolutionary Petunias" (Walker), 59–60
Righteous Discontent (Higginbotham), 180
Riley, Shamara Shuntu, 184
Rilke, Rainer Maria, 44
river, as metaphor, 101, 117n2, 149
The River Between (Wa Thiong'o), 124
Robinson (character), 135–138
Rohr, Richard, 154, 182
rose, as symbol, 6–7
"Roselily" (Walker), 12, 42–43

Rumi, 161, 169, 172
Ruth (character), 37
Rwanda, 171

sacred feminine, 86, 97, 105. *See also* mystics and mysticism; religion and spirituality
sacrifice, xii, 46, 68–69, 186
Saints, Sinners, Saviors (Harris), 88
salvation, 74
"The Same as Gold" (Walker), 156
The Same River Twice: Honoring the Difficult—A Meditation on Life, Spirit, Art, and the Making of the Film, The Color Purple, *Ten Years Later* (Walker), 101–105
Sanders, Cheryl J., 176–178
San Francisco Chronicle Book Review, 12
Sansoni, Umberto, 183
Say Jesus and Come to Me (Shockley), 179
Schopenhauer, Arthur, 95
Science of Mind philosophy, 2, 13, 24, 76, 131
Seaman, Donna, 101
secularism, 181–182
self-determination, 48–49. *See also* choice, as theme
sermons as art, 9, 76, 145, 187
sexuality, 134–138, 140–141. *See also* bisexuality; eroticism; homosexuality
sexual violence. *See* FGM (female genital mutilation); rape
Shields, Lisa, 42
Shug (character), 6, 71, 103–104, 114
silence, 128
Silent Spring (Carson), 116, 162
Simcikova, Karla, 10, 13, 16
Singer, Peter, 10, 11
Sisters in the Wilderness (Williams), 183
Sittler, Joseph, 184
slavery: and the black body, 179–180; motherhood in, 67; names and identity in, 23; and parallels with animal treatment, 10, 11–12. *See also* racial injustice and oppression
Smith, Amanda Berry, 18n5
Smith, Dinitia, 98
Smith, Felipe, 81, 178, 182
Smith, Huston, 17

snakes, as symbol, 147–148
solitude, 93–94
"Sometimes" (Walker), 172
Song of Lawino: A Lament (p'Bitek), 22
"Song of Myself" (Whitman), 13
South Africa, 146, 171
Southern Christian Leadership Conference (SCLC), 184
"South: The Name of Home" (Walker), 3, 5, 53
Spielberg, Steven, xi, 87, 103
Spillers, Hortense, 38
spirituality. *See* religion and spirituality
Stein, Karen, 65
Sternberg, Robert, 43–44
Stewart, Julian, 151
storytelling, 111–112, 132, 148
strong black woman stereotype, 43, 88
"Strong Horse Tea" (Walker), 52–55
Student Nonviolent Coordinating Committee (SNCC), 58, 69
submission of women, 94–95, 97
suffering, 10–11, 21–22; *Science of Mind* on, 76, 131; in *The Third Life*, 24. *See also* grief
Sufi mystics, 172
suicide: Camus and Nietzsche on, 30, 45; in *In Love & Trouble*, 46, 51; in *Meridian*, 69, 76; in "My Father's Country Is the Poor", 9; in *Possessing the Secret of Joy*, 126, 131; in *The Third Life of Grange Copeland*, 22, 32, 35–36; in *Warrior Marks*, 134
"Suicide" (poem by Walker), 4, 5
sun, as symbol, 4–5, 6
"Sunday School, Circa 1950" (Walker), 59
Susannah (character), 135–139

Tashi (character), 122, 125–133, 186
Tate, J. O., 106, 156
Taylor, Mark C., 178
The Temple of My Familiar (Walker): Christian tradition in, 109–110, 112; dualism in, 114; masculine identity in, 138; nature and animals in, 116–117; reception of, 105–107; relationships of characters in, 107–109; silence in, 128; spiritual readings of, 109–116, 127; unity in, 16

Terrell, Kellee, 183
There Is a Flower at the Tip of My Nose Smelling Me (Walker), 170
"These Days" (Walker), 164
"They Made Love" (Walker), 157
"They Who Feel Death" (Walker), 5
Things Fall Apart (Achebe), 90, 123
The Third Life of Grange Copeland (Walker), 6–7; black men's response to, 14; choice as theme in, 22–24, 27–28; female characters in, 35–38; masculinity in, 26–27, 34; murder incident in, 28–30; poverty as theme in, 21–22; silence in, 128
"This Is How It Happened" (Walker), 168
Tierney, John, 125
"To a Fallen Warrior" (Walker), 134
To Hell with Dying (Walker), 6–7
Toomer, Jean, 45, 53, 64, 81
"Torture" (Walker), 163
torture, definition of, 123, 134, 163
Toubia, Nahid, 124
Townes, Emilie M., 178–179, 180–181
Toxic Wastes and Race in the United States (Chavis), 184
tragedy vs. comedy, xii
Transcendentalist movement, 96
transgender, 150–151
"Trapdoors to the Cellar Spring-Grass Green" (Walker), 156
Trethewey, Natasha, 156
Truman, Eboni Marshall, 183
truth, xii, 7, 13
Truth, Sojourner, xiii, 18n5
Tucker, Lindsey, 94
Turning to Earth (Schauffler), 162
Two Thousand Seasons (Armah), 17

"Uncles" (Walker), 59
Uncle Tom's Cabin (Stowe), 123
Underhill, Evelyn, 105
United Nations, 91, 124, 151. *See also* Declaration on the Elimination of Violence against Women
unity, xii–xiii, 14–15, 161, 164
"Until I Was Nearly Fifty" (Walker), 150
"Uses of the Erotic: The Erotic as Power" (Lorde), 130

vegetarianism, 10. *See also* animal suffering and meat-eating
Versluis, Arthur, 140
"View from Rosehill Cemetery: Vicksburg" (Walker), 59
violence against women. *See* domestic violence; female genital mutilation; rape
Violence against Women Act (1994), 91
Virgin Mary, 7
Vitale, Stefano, 170, 171
Vivekananda, Swami, 11

Walden (Thoreau), 162
Walker, Curtis, xi, 1
Walker, Rebecca, 167, 168, 186, 187
Walter, Natasha, 145
Walton, David, 104
war, 170–171
Wardi, Anissa, 152
Warrior Marks: Female Genital Mutilation and Sexual Blinding of Women (Walker and Parmar), 124, 127, 133–134
Washington Post Book World, 121
The Way Forward Is with a Broken Heart (Walker), 166–169
"We Alone" (Walker), 162
We Are the Ones We Have Been Waiting For: Inner Light in a Time of Darkness (Walker), 177, 183, 185
weddings, 43, 154, 159n47. *See also* marriage
"We Have a Map of the World" (Walker), 164
West, Traci C., 177
What's Going On (Gaye), 116, 184
"When Life Descends into the Pit" (Walker), 183
"When You Look" (Walker), 157
whirling dervishes, 172
White, Leon, 184
"Whiter Than Bones" (Walker), 156
Whitsitt, Sam, 51

who dat, 161, 166, 169, 172
"Why Did the Balinese Chicken Cross the Road?" (Walker), 12–13, 185
Why War Is Never a Good Idea (Walker), 170–171
wife-beating, 89–91. *See also* domestic violence
Williams, Delores, 178
Williamson, Marianne, 86
Wilson, August, 32, 33
Winchell, Donna Haisty, 13, 16–17, 22, 47, 49–50, 51, 66, 70
"Winking at a Funeral" (Walker), 58–59
Woman and Nature (Griffin), 117
womanism, defining, 16, 175–176, 180–182. *See also* black liberation theology; feminism
Women for Women International, 171
The Women of Brewster Place (Naylor), 179
women's movement, 64–65. *See also* feminism
Women Who Run with the Wolves (Estes), 24
Wonder, Stevie, 146
World Health Organization (WHO), 123, 124
The World Will Follow Joy: Turning Madness into Flowers (Walker), 185, 188
Wright, Richard, 22–23, 29
Wynn, Toni, 109

Yeats, William Butler, 187
Yolo (character), 149, 153–154
You Can't Keep a Good Woman Down (Walker), 42, 57
"You Had to Go to Funerals" (Walker), 59
"You Thought You Could Have It All" (Walker), 162–163

Zedé (character), 107–108, 111–113, 116
Zinn, Howard, 171

About the Author

Nagueyalti Warren is a professor in the Department of African American Studies at Emory University, where she has taught literature and a seminar on the works of Alice Walker for thirty years. Also a poet, her poetry publications include *Temba Tupu! (Walking Naked): Africana Women's Poetic Self-Portrait*, and *Margaret, A Persona Poem*, which won the Naomi Long Madgett Poetry Award. *Braided Memory* received the Violet Reed Haas Award for Poetry. Her other books include *Grandfather of Black Studies: W.E.B. Du Bois*; and *Critical Insights: Alice Walker*. Warren is a Cave Canem graduate fellow and holds an MFA from Goddard College and a PhD from the University of Mississippi.

www.ingramcontent.com/pod-product-compliance
Lightning Source LLC
Chambersburg PA
CBHW020119010526
44115CB00008B/887